Beneficial Economics: A Red State Citizens Guide to Crafting A Better Constitution When the Government Fails the Citizens.

Laurie Thomas Vass

Printed in the United States of America.

ISBN 979-8-218-81735-0
ISBN 979-8-218-81735-0
9 798218 817350

The Great American Business & Economics Press
GABBY PRESS

Table of Contents

Introduction: Beneficial Economics: A Red State Citizens Guide to Crafting A Better Constitution When the Government Fails the Citizens. 6

Executive Summary: How Red State Citizens Can Craft A Better Economic Constitution. Draft of Proposed Constitution. 13

Chapter 1. Constitutional Solutions to The Great American Betrayal of U. S. Citizens. 42

Chapter 2. Visualizing The U. S. Economy As Complex Adaptive Systems. 67

Chapter 3. How A Person's Brain Naturally Creates Social Order Through Their Everyday Market Choices. 94

Chapter 4. Replacing Madison's Constitution of 1787 With A Better Economic Constitution. 128

Chapter 5. The American Economic Transition to Predatory State Capitalism 179

Chapter 6. How Modern American Crony Capitalism Prevents the Emergence of A Beneficial Social Order. 230

Chapter 7. The Emergence of American Beneficial Social Order Under Buchanan's Fair Constitutional Rules and Kant's Moral Values. 248

Chapter 8. The Imperative of Economic Growth For The Emergence of A Beneficial Social Order. 263

Chapter 9. The Beneficial Economics of Tacit Knowledge Creation and Diffusion In The Metro Regional Ecosystem of Trust. 295

Chapter 10. Self Managed Regional Securities MarketsWhere Citizens Manage Their Own Regional Economic Growth. 325

Schedule of Diagrams and Images.

Chapter 1. Diagram 1. U. S. Household Net Worth, 1990 – 2025.

Chapter 1. Diagram 2. Retail Consumption by the American Rich.

Chapter 1. Diagram 3. Generation Z Erosion of Attaining Benefits of Original American Social Contract.

Chapter 1. Diagram 5. Evolution of Global Corporate Average Markups Over Marginal Costs of Production.

Chapter 2. Diagram 1. From Prigogine Order Out of Chaos, p. 296.

Chapter 2. Diagram 2. Regional Economy Breaking Away From Equilibrium. From Theory of Technology Evolution, 2019.

Chapter 2. Diagram 3. Regional Economy Economic Decline. From Theory of Technology Evolution, 2019.

Chapter 3. Diagram 1. Neural Circuits, From Faisal Mohammed.

Chapter 3. Diagram 2. Location of Area 39 and Area 40 in Middle Part of Brain.

Chapter 5. Diagram 1. St. Louis Federal Reserve Bank GDP-Based Recession Indicator Index. 1967 – 2020.

Chapter 8. Diagram 1. Economy Breaking Away From Equilibrium.

Chapter 8. Diagram 2. Regional Economy Breaking Away From Equilibrium in Time Period 1 to Distant Future Attractor Point of Economic Decline in Time Period 2.

Chapter 8. Diagram 3. Nearly Neutral Economic Drift of Nash Equilibrium.

Chapter 8. Diagram 4. Chronology of Events Leading to A New Future Regional Market.

Chapter 8. Diagram 5. Chronology of If-Then Statements.

Chapter 8. Diagram 6. The Dual Flow Of Knowledge and Price Transactions In A Regional Market.

Chapter 8. Diagram 7. The Tacit Knowledge Regional Deal Flow Pipeline.

Chapter 8. Diagram 8. The Tacit Knowledge Regional Economic Growth Model, Leading to the Emergence of Beneficial Economic Growth.

Chapter 9. Diagram 1. The Creation of Knowledge from Kreutz.

Chapter 9. Diagram 2. Organizational Management of Tacit Knowledge Creation Within Proctor & Gamble.

Chapter 9. Diagram 3. Theoretical Chronology of Regional Tacit Knowledge.

Chapter 10. Diagram 1. U. S. Metro Regions Based upon Commuting Patterns, by Garrett Nelson and Alasdair Rae.

Chapter 10. Diagram 2. Managing the Regional Securities Market Deal Flow Pipeline.

Chapter 10. Diagram 3. List of Regional Professional Deal Flow Managers.

Chapter 10. Diagram 4. The Regional Citizen Self-Management Tools and Methods For Managing the Regional Securities Market.

Chapter 10. Diagram 5. Regional Administration and Management of the Deal Flow Pipeline

Chapter 10. Diagram 6. The Chronology of Bootstrapping Regional Capital Market Investments.

Chapter 10. Diagram 7. Regional Securities Market Blockchain Deal Creation Internet Application.

Introduction: Beneficial Economics: A Red State Citizens Guide to Crafting A Better Constitution When the Government Fails the Citizens.

The starting premise of this book is that the political polarization between citizens in red states and citizens in blue states has reached a threshold level.

At this point in American history, middle and working class citizens in red states are confronted with two paths.

Red state citizens could do nothing, and accept the path of blue state Democrat Marxism, that increases the power of the central government over the lives of citizens.

That path leads to a global police state of citizen surveillance and a social credit system controlled by central banks, private corporations, and tech companies.

Alternatively, citizens in red states could restore the original 1776 principles of liberty that animated the first American Revolution, by implementing a decentralized political system, based upon a metro-decentralized entrepreneurial capitalist economic system.

We wrote about the irreconcilable cultural and moral differences between citizens in red and blues states, leading up to a political civil dissolution, at this point in history. (Laurie Thomas Vass, A Civil Dissolution: The Best Solution to America's Irreconcilable Ideological Conflict, 2023).

In this book, we extend our analysis, that after a political civil dissolution, what comes next for citizens in the red states is creating a new, better constitution.

Our book explores how red state citizens might craft a more fair constitution that puts political power back in the hands of ordinary people, at the state and local levels of government.

We combine a political dissolution with a constitutional dissolution that aims at creating fair economic rules.

- Political geographical dissolution - the cultural/geographic separation along red/blue state lines that is inevitable.
- Constitutional dissolution - the fundamental redesign of economic rules and institutional structures, moving away from Madison's system that enabled the original ruling class aristocracy, that eventually turned into a global predatory state capitalism.

In this book, we do not advocate destruction of the entire U. S. constitutional framework because two parts of the original government framework continue to work well for red state citizens.

In our earlier book, George Mason's America: The State Sovereignty Alternative to Madison's Centralized American Ruling Class Aristocracy, (2023), we explained that existing state and local governments (the political institutions) can remain as organizational structures, but that states need a new constitution to return to the initial relationship advocated by George Mason between state and the national central government.

In George Mason's America, we advocated a return to founding-era decentralized state sovereignty principles that were available in the Articles of Confederation, 1781, but were not adopted, by Madison, in 1787.

As we argued in George Mason's America, the state sovereignty framework advocated by Mason and other Anti-Federalists would have provided a better constitutional foundation for preventing ruling class capture and protecting individual liberty.

Returning to Mason's and the anti-federalist economic constitutional redesign (preventing ruling class domination) can happen through existing political institutions (state/local governments) once they're operating under beneficial economic principles rather than the current global predatory capitalist framework.

In our proposed constitutional solution, state and local governments become the building blocks for a new national power-sharing structure.

The very first step for red state citizens to take is to have a representative in their state legislature introduce a resolution for a study commission to study "The Constitutional Relationship Between the States and the National Government."

This first step places the management and administration of a new constitutional relationship under the jurisdiction of elected representatives.

The study commission would be staffed by legislative staffers who have legal and constitutional training, and who can manage the citizen participatory elements in the pre-constitutional rule setting era.

We combine both political and economic strategies, and we cite Adam Smith's "Invisible Hand" as the original accurate description of how competitive free markets lead to beneficial social order.

Adam Smith explained this concept in the Wealth of Nations, in 1776.

Smith wrote,

"It is not from the benevolence of the butcher, the brewer, or the baker that we expect our dinner, but from their regard to their own self-interest. We address ourselves not to their humanity but to their self-love, and never talk to them of our own necessities, but of their advantages"

Our book builds upon Smith's insight about the social benefits of a competitive market society.

What is new about our theory of beneficial economics is that Adam Smith's original insight about the emergence of a fair stable social order is now supported by modern scientific theories of quantum physics of how dynamic complex systems attain order in the natural world of physics and chemistry.

Many other conservative writers have analyzed the current dysfunction in the American political system.

Many other writers have also suggested that a solution to the dysfunction in government is a national divorce, as we have, in our book, A Civil Dissolution.

We go a step beyond the current analysis to present our ideas on what Red State Citizens must do to reclaim liberty.

Most of our book, after the Executive Summary, presents the logic of why this new system of decentralizded government and economic power will work better than the existing system.

The Executive Summary at the top of our book is the abbreviated Cliff Notes version of the longer book.

Our citizen's guide to crafting a new constitution includes:

- crafting fair constitutional rules,
- supporting decentralized knowledge networks, and
- demanding national constitutional protections against concentrated power and corporate controlled deployment of artificial intelligence.

James Buchanan called these new political national constitutional functions the "protective state," and the new set of fair economic rules the "productive state."

Buchanan called the existing global order the "Predatory State," which we describe in Chapter 10.

Our beneficial economic rules are based upon the idea that Buchanan's fair constitutional rules lead all citizens to the voluntary allegiance to obey the rule of law because all citizens understand that obeying fair rules benefits all citizens, when the law is applied equally.

By understanding the constitutional principles outlined in this book, ordinary red state citizens can start reclaiming their heritage of liberty, in order to shape the future economic outcomes that affect their daily lives.

Our book is organized into four integrated sections:

At the very beginning, we provide an executive summary, plus a draft of the proposed constitution, that in most books would be at the end of the book, as the conclusion.

We invert the normal chronology of the book because we realize that:

- A busy small business owner in rural Texas isn't going to work through complex economic adaptive systems theory.
- A working parent juggling multiple jobs needs clear, actionable steps on what a new constitution would look like.
- College and university conservative political activists want practical organizing tools, which help them defeat the university communist ideology of individual subjugation to the power of the communist state.

These types of ordinary middle and working class citizens are the intended audience for our book.

We see them as the latent leaders of the political movement to restore individual liberty, and our book is intended to provide a roadmap on how to get that job done.

Executive Summary and Proposed Draft of New Constitution.
How Red State Citizens Can Craft A Better Economic Constitution.
Draft of proposed constitution.

The fiirst chapter of the book presents the solution to the U. S. economic transition to the global corporate predatory state. The chapter explains why the existing Madison constitution of 1787 cannot be amended, but must be abolished.

- Chapter 1. Constitutional Solutions to The Great American Betrayal of U. S. Citizens.

Section Two: Theoretical Foundations of Beneficial Economic Order (Chapters 2-3) Chapters 2-3 establish the theoretical foundation of markets as complex adaptive systems and explain how the human brain naturally creates social order through everyday market choices. This section introduces the core principle that stable social order emerges spontaneously from decentralized market interactions guided by fair constitutional rules.

- Chapter 2. Visualizing The U. S. Economy As Complex Adaptive Systems.
- Chapter 3. How A Person's Brain Naturally Creates Social Order Through Their Everyday Market Choices.

Section Three: Constitutional Challenges and Threats (Chapters 4-6) Chapters 4-6 identify the critical problems with our current constitutional system and examine the specific threats to liberty posed by artificial intelligence, robotics, and corporate globalism.

This section explains why Madison's constitution is defective beyond repair, and why a new, better constitution is needed to restore liberty.

This section explains how these forces have transformed the American government into what we call the "predatory state" and outlines the constitutional barriers needed to restore individual liberty.

- Chapter 4: Drafting A Better Economic Constitution Than Madison's Constitution of 1787.
- Chapter 5. The American Economic Transition to Predatory State Capitalism.
- Chapter 6. How Modern American Crony Capitalism Prevents the Emergence of A Beneficial Social Order.

Section Four: The Economic Theory of Beneficial Economics. (Chapters 7-10). Chapters 7-10 present the practical considerations for crafting a new economic constitution, within a regional geographical framework.

This section focuses on metro regional economic decentralization, knowledge creation, knowledge diffusion, and building a knowledge economy that delivers both sustained economic growth and fair income distribution.

- Chapter 7. The Emergence of American Beneficial Social Order Under Buchanan's Fair Constitutional Rules and Kant's Moral Values.
- Chapter 8. The Imperative of Economic Growth For The Emergence of A Beneficial Social Order.
- Chapter 9. The Beneficial Economics of Tacit Knowledge Creation and Diffusion In The Metro Regional Ecosystem of Trust.
- Chapter 10. Self Managed Regional Securities Markets Where Citizens Manage Their Own Regional Economic Growth

Executive Summary: How Red State Citizens Can Craft A Better Economic Constitution.

George Mason, and the Anti-Federalists, accurately saw the flaws in Madison's centralized constitutional design.

Madison insulated the government from the influence of common citizens, and the old constitution does not have rules that allow citizens to reclaim their authority.

The first, most important goal for red state citizens is to re-create a constitution of limited national government powers.

This first step can be taken by creating a new Preamble that establishes the goal of future prosperity and happiness of citizens as the purpose of government.

For example, the proposed Preamble of the new constitution states,

Preamble:

We, the citizens of the Democratic Republic of American States, establish this constitutional contract between our respective states and the National Government of the Democratic Republic of American States.

We solemnly swear and affirm that we establish this contract to preserve and protect the natural and civil rights of citizens in each state, and to protect and defend the sovereignty of each state and the nation, from foreign and domestic threats.

By freely and voluntarily joining our state government into the union of Democratic Republic of American States, we affirm that the National Government and the National Supreme Court will be guided by the following principles of a National Government of expressly limited powers:

"...that all legitimate government authority is derived from the consent of the citizens governed..."
"...that those citizens governed by the laws and whose individual freedom is restricted by the laws should have the greatest say and consent in making of the laws..."
"...that those who make the laws and give consent to the laws, acting as representatives of the citizens, bind themselves and their constituents to following the laws..."
"...that individual citizens who freely give their consent to form a national government through constitutional conventions are bound by the original contract until the operation of the government becomes destructive to the original intent of obtaining individual freedom and the pursuit of happiness..."
"...that the parties to the constitutional contract are individual citizens acting through their elected representatives at the states and the institutional agencies of the National Government..."
"...that the citizens of each state have mechanisms in place in the constitutional contract to modify or abolish the national government, including the right of each state to vote on remaining a member of the national government in a binding referendum to be held every 20 years from the date of admittance..."
"...that as the consequence of the sovereign authority of citizens, citizens have an inalienable natural right to remove an elected representative in the National Congress from office upon a referendum of 60% of registered voters in a state..."

Our toolkit for red state citizens has two components that address the need for political and economic decentralization.

Political Decentralization

In the implementation of political decentralization, the constitutional constraints on the power of the National government are written into the new constitution, at the very top of the introductory text.

The limitations on the power of government would prevent the kind of top-down centralized power that enabled the recent transisiton of the U. S. society to the destructive aspects of predatory capitalism.

For example, in our proposed text to limit the power of the National government, we state:

"This Constitution creates a National Government of limited powers. Powers not expressly delegated to the National Government by this Constitution are reserved exclusively to the citizens, in their respective states.
The purpose of this constitutional contract is the creation and enforcement of fair rules to govern the lives of citizens, including…"

We remove the ambiguous text of Amendment 10 in Madison's constitution,

"The powers not delegated to the United States by the Constitution, nor prohibited by it to the States, are reserved to the States respectively, or to the people."

We replace the old Amendment 10 at the top of the new constitution, and make the intent of the text more clear by inserting the word "expressly," which was left out of Madison's final text.

We clarify the term "the people," in Madison's text by inserting the term "citizens."

Madison's term "the people" does not legally define the welfare of citizens as the intended beneficiaries of the new constitution.

"People" could mean anything, including illegal immigrants or anti-American terrorists.

The text of the new constitution refers explicitly to the rights of individual citizens, not racial groups, the rights of corporations, or other collectivist group rights.

For example, Section 9 of the proposed text, reads in part,

"Section 9. National Budget and Regulation of Money and Banking.

The National Congress will operate the Democratic Republic of American States according to a balanced budget, during a budget cycle of two years, where the projected expenditures of the Government do not exceed the tax revenues set to meet those expenditures…

…The National Congress shall have the power to issue government bonds, and to borrow money on the credit of the Democratic Republic of American States. All proposals to borrow money or issue debt shall occur once in the two year budget cycle, and all proposals to issue debt must be approved by 50% of the State legislatures of the Democratic Republic of American States, no later than January 21 of the year of issuance…

…The term of debt and interest on any issuance of debt shall not exceed 10 years, and must be paid in full by the end of the 10th year…

The National Congress shall have the power to increase or decrease the supply of money, benchmarked to the rate of national economic growth, in the prior two-year budget cycle, coin money, regulate the value of physical and synthetic coin, thereof, regulate the circulation and creation of money and money instruments, regulate the national banking system and establish the currency value of foreign coin, and fix the Standard of Weights and Measures."

The new national government requires a relationship with a private commercial depository bank, that the National Congress appoints for a 10 year term."

In terms of creating fair rules for protecting the interests of citizens from abuse by artificial intelligence and human-like robots, we place the National Government's power at the very top of the text.

We state:

"The National Government shall Protect Citizen Liberties and Individual Welfare in the Deployment of Artificial Intelligence and the Use of Human-Like Robots. Citizens have a right of privacy and right of protection against the deployment of artificial intelligence and human-like robots to protect and preserve their lives, wealth, and happiness."

The goal of National government restrictions on the deployment of AI is to restrict unelected, unaccountable corporate power concentration rather than technology prohibitions on an individual's use of AI.

As we stated in the Introduction, a proposed state legislative study commission would manage and administer the blockchain algorithm for maximum citizen input in the design of the new constitutional rules.

The blockchain algorithm is an important tool that can be used for citizen networking at both the macro and micro level of Buchanan's constitutional two-step process.

At the macro level of creating fair rules, in the pre-constitutional era, blockchain offers a transparent proposal framework that enables citizens to submit constitutional provisions.

It is the responsibility of state legislatures in red states to establish and fund the operation of state-level citizen blockchain networking and communication system.

And, it is the responsibility of red state citizens in each state to provide the political action that forces the elected representatives to establish the legislative study commission.

The great benefit of using blockchain at both the macro and micro levels of rule-making is that it provides a tamper-resistant communication network for transparent authorship of ideas.

The blockchain algorithm creates an immutable record of all suggested changes, and tracks citizen responses to proposals, as the constitutional proposals wind their way to citizen ratification.

Economic decentralization in a metro regional entrepreneurial society.

The macro constitutional rules of the game, in the pre-constitutional rule making era, create the level playing field of micro economic rules for citizens to play the game, after the constitution has been ratified.

For example, at the very top of the text of our proposed constitution, under the Purposes of the National Government, we propose:

"Decentralized Economic and Political Decision-Making
Economic and political power shall be dispersed among states and regional communities rather than concentrated in the national government. Citizens have the right to form local economic institutions that reflect their community's economy and moral values..

Protection Against Economic Coercion
No entity, whether governmental or private, shall use economic power to coerce citizens into actions against their will or their best interests. Citizens have the right to be secure their livelihood without surrendering their fundamental liberties."

In the section on the powers of the National Government, we state:

"…that a citizen's private property obtained through legal contract and title transfer, have a right to appropriate income and profits from the use of their private property, and their rights to dispose and transfer their private property are inviolate and derived from natural rights granted to them by God, and that no National Government or constitutional contract may ever abrogate or subordinate these natural property rights of citizens...."

We make this distinction clear by dismantling the artificial legal symmetry between the civil contractual rights of corporations to sue and be sued, and the natural rights of citizens.

For example, the text of the 14th article of the Citizen Bill of Rights states,

“14. That the natural rights of citizens contemplated in this Bill of Rights inure, exclusively, to the benefit of natural citizens, and do not extend to artificial or synthetic entities created by legislation to conduct economic or business transactions.

We place an additional protection for citizens to engage in entrepreneurial ventures right at the top of the text by stating,

“Equal Economic Opportunity.”

All citizens possess an equal right to participate in economic activities without discrimination or artificial barriers. No law shall grant special economic privileges to specific individuals, corporations, or industries that are not available to all citizens under the same terms. Government shall neither create monopolies nor protect existing ones, ensuring that markets remain competitive and open to new competitors.”

The proposed text limits the ability of the National Government to tax and spend, and restricts the future national bank from engaging in interest rate manipulation.

In summary, we propose that each individual red state citizen does not need to be an expert, or understand all the rules which govern society, but each citizen follows their natural instinct of fair rules because a citizen believes that all other citizens are following the same fair rules, which leads to the emergence of a beneficial social order.

The goal of fair rules is voluntary compliance with the rule of law because citizens agree to follow the rules that they make for themselves.

The Future of Individual Liberty Depends On The Path Taken by Red State Citizens.

Our book describes the very fragile and tenuous condition of individual liberty and economic freedom in the United States, today.

At this stage of citizen polarization, red state citizens can continue down the Democrat Marxist path of continued centralization, leading to economic stagnation and erosion of liberty.

The current predatory global capitalist model is a new version of a corporate-government alliance that ends in an irreversible global totalitarianism, which deploys the tools of AI and human-like robots to subjugate free citizens.

The better path is the emergence of Beneficial Economics, through state-sovereignty decentralization and constitutional renewal of the original American social contract.

A better constitution to defeat the Predatory Capitalist State would add moral values of trust, reciprocity and a promise of mutual honesty among citizens in a new social compact.

When the Government fails the citizens, it is the moral responsibility of red citizens to abolish the old regime, and begin, again, the task of creating a better constitution.

Full Draft of Proposed Constitution For the Democratic Republic of American States.

The Constitution of the Democratic Republic of American States

Preamble:

We, the citizens of the Democratic Republic of American States, establish this constitutional contract between our respective states and the National Government of the Democratic Republic of American States.

We solemnly swear and affirm that we establish this contract to preserve and protect the natural and civil rights of citizens in each state, and to protect and defend the sovereignty of each state and the nation, from foreign and domestic threats.

By freely and voluntarily joining our state government into the union of Democratic Republic of American States, we affirm that the National Government and the National Supreme Court will be guided by the following principles of a National Government of expressly limited powers:

"…that all legitimate government authority is derived from the consent of the citizens governed…"
"…that those citizens governed by the laws and whose individual freedom is restricted by the laws should have the greatest say and consent in making of the laws..."
"…that those who make the laws and give consent to the laws, acting as representatives of the citizens, bind themselves and their constituents to following the laws..."
"…that individual citizens who freely give their consent to form a national government through constitutional conventions are bound by the original contract until the operation of the government becomes destructive to the original intent of obtaining individual freedom and the pursuit of happiness..."

"…that the parties to the constitutional contract are individual citizens acting through their elected representatives at the states and the National Government…"
"…that the citizens of each state have mechanisms in place in the constitutional contract to modify or abolish the national government, including the right of each state to vote on remaining a member of the national government in a binding referendum to be held every 20 years from the date of admittance..."
"…that as the consequence of the sovereign authority of citizens, citizens have an inalienable natural right to remove an elected representative in the National Congress from office upon a referendum of 60% of registered voters in a state…"

The Purpose of this Constitution.

This Constitution creates a National Government of limited powers. Powers not expressly delegated to the National Government by this Constitution are reserved exclusively to the citizens, in their respective states.

The purpose of this constitutional contract is the creation and enforcement of fair rules to govern the lives of citizens, including:

Equal Economic Opportunity
All citizens possess an equal right to participate in economic activities without discrimination or artificial barriers. No law shall grant special economic privileges to specific individuals, corporations, or industries that are not available to all citizens under the same terms. Government shall neither create monopolies nor protect existing ones, ensuring that markets remain competitive and open to new competitors.

Decentralized Economic and Political Decision-Making
Economic and political power shall be dispersed among states and regional communities rather than concentrated in the national government. Citizens have the right to form local economic institutions that reflect their community's economy and moral values..

Transparency in Economic and Political Governance.
All citizens have the right to complete information about the legal rules under which they live and work. Laws affecting economic activity must be written in plain language accessible to ordinary citizens. No economic regulation shall be implemented without public disclosure of its full costs, benefits, and effects on different segments of society.

Protection Against Economic Coercion.
No entity, whether governmental or private, shall use economic power to coerce citizens into actions against their will or best interests. Citizens have the right to be secure their livelihood without surrendering their fundamental liberties.
Citizen Bill of Rights of the Democratic Republic of American States.

We affirm and swear that all citizens in each of the respective states of the Democratic Republic of American States are guaranteed equal rights for all, and special privileges for none. Among them are:

1. That all citizens are due the equal application of justice and that no citizen is entitled to special or unequal treatment of the application of the law.
2. That all citizens have a natural right to worship and exercise their own religion and that the National Government is prohibited from making and enforcing any law respecting the establishment of an official national religion and compelling citizens to worship a national religion.
3. That all citizens have a natural right to truthful and honest statements from government agents and from elected representatives, and that it is the duty of the free press to report the truth.
4. That the most certain form of protecting civil liberties and natural rights is guaranteeing that all citizens in the respective states have a natural right to own and use weapons, and a right to organize themselves into citizens militias to protect their rights, and that the National Government shall make no laws which abridge the right of

law-abiding citizens from owning, keeping and bearing weapons to defend themselves from tyranny.

6. That all citizens are judged innocent until proven guilty in a trial of due process by a jury of their peers.

7. No warrants or judicial orders in any criminal investigation shall be issued by a national court, except upon probable cause, determined in a judicial hearing, supported by an oath or affirmation of the government agent describing the specific items or locations to be searched and a judicial description of the crime being investigated.

8. No citizen shall be subject for prosecution for the same offence, previously tried by jury, to be twice put in jeopardy of life or limb for an offense previously tried by jury.

9. No citizen in a National Government criminal proceeding shall be compelled in any criminal case to be a witness against himself.

10. In all National Government criminal prosecutions, the accused shall enjoy the right to a speedy and public trial, by an impartial jury of the State and judicial district wherein the alleged crime shall have been committed, which judicial district shall have been previously ascertained by law, and to be informed of the nature and cause of the accusation; to be confronted with the witnesses against him; to have compulsory process for obtaining witnesses in his favor, and to have the assistance of counsel for his defense.

11. The right of trial by jury shall be preserved, and no criminal prosecution previously tried by a jury, shall be otherwise re-examined in any Court of the Democratic Republic of American States.

12. Excessive bail shall not be required, nor excessive fines imposed, nor cruel and unusual punishments inflicted, nor imprisonment for longer than 5 days, in the absence of specific charges and allegation of a National crime.

13. The right of citizens of the Democratic Republic of American States America to vote, hold elected office, or deliberate in public debates, shall not be denied or abridged by the National Government, or by any State, on account of race, color of skin, biological sex, or religious beliefs.

14. That the natural rights of citizens contemplated in this Bill of Rights inure, exclusively, to the benefit of natural citizens, and do not extend to artificial or synthetic entities created by legislation to conduct economic or business transactions.

Article 1. The Powers of the National Government.

The National Government is instituted to allow individual citizens to pursue individual happiness and to limit the arbitrary application of government power over the lives of citizens..."

The National Government that is created by this union of states shall never usurp the sovereign power or authority of the individual states or the sovereignty of the citizens in each state and that states have an inalienable right to call a convention of the states, without Congressional approval, to modify, amend, or abolish this Constitutional Contract."

"…that a citizen's private property obtained through legal contract and title transfer, have a right to appropriate income and profits from the use of their private property, and their rights to dispose and transfer their private property are inviolate and derived from natural rights granted to them by God, and that no National Government or constitutional contract may ever abrogate or subordinate these natural property rights of citizens...."

Article 1. Section 1.

The National Government shall Protect Citizen Liberties and Individual Welfare in the Deployment of Artificial Intelligence and the Use of Human-Like Robots.

Citizens have a right of privacy and right of protection against the deployment of artificial intelligence and human-like robots to protect and preserve their lives, wealth, and happiness.

Article 1. Section 2.

Citizen Grand Juries Created.

"…that a citizens Grand Jury of 18 citizens is impaneled, in the National Judiciary, for a term of 12 months, to protect and preserve the rights of citizens against the arbitrary application of government power against citizens…"

"…that a citizens Grand Jury of 18 citizens must inspect all national penal facilities within its district every 6 months, and report their findings to the Chief District Judge, who shall act to remedy the deficiencies found by the Grand Jury…"

"…That citizens have a civil right of action against elected representatives or agents of the National Government, for violation of the natural rights of citizens, upon a presentation of a motion of grievance to a Grand Jury of 18 citizens, who shall hear the case and determine the outcome and set the penalties for the violation by a majority vote.

"…No citizen in any state shall be seized or imprisoned, or stripped of his rights or possessions, or outlawed or exiled, or deprived of his standing in any other way, nor shall agents of the government proceed with force against him, or send others to do so, except by the lawful judgment of a true bill of indictment by a majority vote of a grand jury of 18 citizens, or in times of invasion by a foreign force, by the rules of judicial civil procedure of the Judiciary of the National Government.

"…No citizen shall be held to answer for a capital, or otherwise infamous crime, unless on a presentment or indictment of a majority vote of a Grand Jury of 18 citizens who conduct an inquiry into the legitimacy of the government's allegation of a national crime.

"…that the Citizens Grand Jury in any State retains the right of initiating a citizen initiative on legislative proposals by a petition to the U. S. Citizens House of Representatives, which must respond to the petition within 30 days of receipt.

"…No citizen shall be deprived of life, liberty, or property, without due process of law; nor shall private property be taken for public use, without just compensation, determined by a majority vote of a Grand Jury of 18 citizens.

Article 2. The National Congress.

Article 2. Section 1.

All legitimate authority of the National Government and the expression of the consent of the governed, is vested in the National Congress of the Democratic Republic of American States.

The National Congress shall have two chambers:

- The Citizens House of Representatives.

- The Senate of State Legislature Representatives.

Legislation proposed in one chamber of the National Government must be voted upon, and ratified by a majority vote of the other Chamber, and delivered to the President for his signature before a law is effective.
Neither Chamber of the National Congress shall, without the consent of the other Chamber, adjourn for more than three days.
A session of Congress begins on January 21, of each year, adjourns for the month of August, and resumes the first Tuesday in September, and is in session until December 20, of each year.

Article 2. Section 2. Term Limits.
No elected representative of the National Congress may serve more than two consecutive terms, in the same office, nor more than 10 years in the same office, in a lifetime.
No law varying the compensation for the services of the Senators and Representatives shall take effect during an interval of 10 years.
All elected representatives of the National Congress and all senior civil servants and agents are subject to the same laws and welfare benefits as common citizens who are bound by the laws made by the National Government.

Article 2. Section 3. National Congressional Elections.
The times, places and manner of holding elections for Senators and Representatives, shall be prescribed in each state by the legislature thereof, according to the results of the enumeration of verified citizens in each state, every five years, conducted by the House of Representatives.
No person shall vote in a Congressional election who is not a citizen.
The state legislature has authority to determine the verification of the qualification of a citizen to vote.

Article 2. Section 4. Certification of Elections.
The members of the House and Senate shall be the judge of the legitimacy of elections, returns and qualifications of its own members, and of the Office of President.

Upon a petition from any member, or upon a petition from a citizens Grand Jury, the members of the House and Senate shall punish and remove a member for disorderly conduct upon a conviction vote of 60% of the members of the respective House or Senate.
The deliberations of both houses are open public records and procedures, to be broadcast or transmitted to the public on a frequent, periodic basis.

Article 2. Section 5. Compensation.
The Senators and Representatives shall receive compensation for their services, to be ascertained every 10 years, and confirmed by a majority vote of a Grand Jury of 18 citizens, impaneled in the election district of the representative.
No Senator or Representative shall, during the time for which he was elected, be appointed to any civil office of the Democratic Republic of American States, nor be entitled to any civil emoluments, and no person holding any civil office in the Democratic Republic of American States, shall be an elected member of either House during his term of civil service, nor shall he be a candidate for any office, during his term of civil service.
No Senator or Representative may be appointed to serve as an employee of the National Government for a period of 3 years, after the term of office ends.

Article 2. Section 6. National Budget and Regulation of Money and Banking.
The National Congress will operate the Democratic Republic of American States according to a balanced budget, during a budget cycle of two years, where the projected expenditures of the Government do not exceed the tax revenues set to meet those expenditures.
The National Government budget, and all bills for raising revenue, shall originate in the Senate, to be completed no later than the day before the August adjournment in the year prior to the start of the 2-year budget cycle.
Every budget bill which shall have passed the Senate shall be transmitted to the House. The House must vote on the proposed

budget of the Senate by November 30, of each year, or the national budget will revert to the same budget as the previous 2 years.
A budget passed by the House, and the proposed rate of taxes to meet the budget, must be presented to the President of the Democratic Republic of American States on December 1, to approve or reject, by December 20 of each year.
Upon a rejection by the President, the budget reverts to the same budget as the previous 2 years.
The National Congress shall have power to lay and collect taxes, duties, imposts and excises, to meet the expenditures of the 2 year balanced budget. All duties, imposts and excises shall be uniform throughout the Democratic Republic of American States.
Tariffs on the import of foreign goods, or the export of domestic goods, are proposed and enforced by the President upon the advice and consent of a majority of the Senate, within 7 days of the President's proposal.
The National Congress shall have the power to issue government bonds, and to borrow money on the credit of the Democratic Republic of American States. All proposals to borrow money or issue debt shall occur once in the two year budget cycle, and all proposals to issue debt must be approved by 50% of the State legislatures of the Democratic Republic of American States, no later than January 21 of the year of issuance.
The term of debt and interest on any issuance of debt shall not exceed 10 years, and must be paid in full by the end of the 10th year.
No tax, tariff, or duty shall be laid on articles, goods, or services, exported from any state to another state.
No State shall enter into any trade treaty, or trade alliance with a foreign nation.

Article 2. Section 7. Other Powers of the National Congress.
The National Congress shall have the power to increase or decrease the supply of money, benchmarked to the rate of national economic growth, in the prior two-year budget cycle, coin money, regulate the value thereof, regulate the circulation and creation of money and money instruments, regulate the national banking system and establish the currency value of foreign coin, and fix the Standard of Weights and Measures.

The National Congress shall have the power to appoint a central bank to conduct the transactions of the National Government, as a depository institution, every 10 years.
The National Congress shall have the power to provide for the punishment for the national criminal felony of counterfeiting the securities and money of the Democratic Republic of American States.
The National Congress shall have the power to establish a national Post Office and a national system of roads and transportation routes.
The National Congress shall have the power to authorize regional capital securities markets, and to establish regulatory guidelines for the operation of regional private and public security exchanges designed to promote maximum national and regional economic growth rates.
The National Congress shall have the power to establish and maintain a national patent office to promote the progress of science and useful arts, by securing for limited times to authors and inventors the exclusive right to their respective writings and discoveries.
The National Congress shall have the power to protect the patents of citizens from foreign and domestic criminal usurpation of the right of citizens to enjoy the benefits of their invention.
The National Congress shall have the power to define and punish intellectual property piracies and criminal patent felonies committed against citizens of the Democratic Republic of American States by foreign and domestic criminals.
The National Congress shall have the power to establish a uniform rule of citizen naturalization, and provide revenues for national border security to prohibit illegal entrance into the sovereign nation or any sovereign state.
The National Congress shall have the power to protect the citizen's right of the Writ of Habeas Corpus, which shall not be suspended, unless in case of invasion, when the public safety may require it.
The National Congress shall have Power to dispose of and make all fair rules and regulations respecting the territory or other property belonging to the Democratic Republic of American States; and nothing in this Constitution shall be so construed as to prejudice any claims of the property of any state.

Article 2. Section 7. The War Powers of the National Congress.
Upon a presentment of a declaration of war by the President, the National Congress shall have the power to declare war and authorize the application of military power and action against foreign enemies, within 2 days of receiving the President's declaration.
No military action undertaken by the President may continue after 48 hours, without the consent of the National Congress.
The National Congress shall have the power to raise and support the military and armed forces, to provide and maintain a Navy, and to arm and provide a Coast Guard to protect and preserve the sovereign borders of the Democratic Republic of American States.
The National Congress shall have the power to provide for organizing, and arming, the National Guard, and reserving to the states respectively, the appointment of the officers, and the authority of training the National Guard, according to the rules and laws prescribed by the National Congress.
The National Congress shall have the power to make all laws which shall be necessary and proper for carrying into execution the national war and military powers.
The President shall be the Supreme Commander in Chief of all military personnel and resources.

Article 2. Section 8. Prohibitions and Limitations of Power of the National Congress.
The National Congress is prohibited from passing or enforcing any bill of attainder or ex post facto law.
The National Government shall be prohibited from making or enforcing any law that restricts the natural right of a citizen's freedom of speech and freedom of conscience."
The National Government and any state or local government is prohibited from making or enforcing any law which restricts the right of citizens to peaceably assemble, and to petition the National Government for a redress of grievances.
The National Government is prohibited from using agents of government or national resources to conduct searches and seizures of private citizen documents, in the absence of a true bill of indictment by a Citizens Grand Jury, and that any documents obtained from illegal searches and seizures, in the absence of a true bill of

indictment of a Citizens Grand Jury, are inadmissible in any national court.
The National Government, and every State government, are prohibited from making or enforcing any law which shall abridge the privileges or immunities of citizens of the Democratic Republic of American States; nor shall any State deprive any person of life, liberty, or property, without due process of law; nor deny to any person within its jurisdiction the equal protection of the laws.
Article 3. Section 1. The Authority of the Citizens House of Representatives.
The Citizens House of Representatives shall represent the interests and rights of citizens in each state.
The elected representatives are chosen every fourth year by the verified citizens of the several States.
No elected representative may serve more than two terms in the same office, nor more than 10 years in the same office, during a lifetime.
No person shall be a representative who shall not have attained the age of twenty one, and shall have been a citizen of the Democratic Republic of American States, for the previous 10 years, and who shall have been a resident of that State for the previous 10 years.
Each state shall have at least one representative. The total number of representatives shall not exceed one for every fifty thousand verified citizens.
The members of the House shall prepare the districts for representation based upon the criteria of compact geographical rectangular shapes, every 10 years,
based upon a census and enumeration of citizens in each state.
Direct Taxes shall be apportioned among the several States according to their respective numbers of verified citizens. The Citizens House of Representatives sets the tax rate, pursuant to the budget transmitted to the House from the Senate.
The House has the exclusive power to charter and regulate a system of national banks designed to promote interstate and international commerce and maximum rates of economic growth among all States.
The House imposes restrictions on the domain of power and authority of the system of national banks, and directs the domain of the bank's authority to promote the economic welfare of sovereign States and sovereign citizens.

The House has the exclusive authority to regulate the issuance of charters for interstate and international commerce.
The House may impose restrictions, sanctions and revocations of charters for trade practices that are contrary to the sovereignty and welfare of citizens or the states.
The House has the exclusive authority to propose laws to regulate and restrict the deployment of the use of artificial intelligence and human-like robots to insure that the deployment serves the financial interests and welfare of citizens.
Article 3. Section 2.
Vacancies in the Citizens House of Representatives from any State, shall be filled by an election of the citizens to be held within 4 weeks of the vacancy.
The Citizens House of Representatives shall choose their own rules of civil procedure and elect their own executive officers every 2 years.
Article 3. Section 3.
1. The Citizens House of Representatives shall have the sole power of initiating an impeachment of any elected representative or senior executive of the National Government whose position was filled by Congressional approval.
2. Upon a petition of 50% of the elected representatives, the House may convene a committee of impeachment to consider a true bill of indictment. The true bill must state the national felony committed and be ratified by 60% of the total number of representatives.

Article 4. Section 1. The Authority of the Senate of State Legislature Representatives..
The Senate of the Democratic Republic of American States shall be composed of one Senator elected from each state legislature.
The Senators represent the collective corporate interests of the state.
The Senators are chosen every fourth year by the legislatures in the several states.
No elected Senator may serve more than two terms in the same office, nor more than 10 years in the same office, during a lifetime.
No citizen shall be a Senator who shall not have attained to the age of twenty one, and shall have been a citizen of the Democratic

Republic of American States, for the previous 10 years, and who shall have been a resident of that state for the previous 10 years.
The Senate shall chose their own rules of civil procedure, and elect other presiding officers every two years.
Vacancies in the Senate from any state, shall be filled by an election of the legislature, to be held within 4 weeks of the vacancy.
The Senate shall have the sole power to try all true bills of impeachment, transmitted to the Senate from the House of Representatives.
The true bill of impeachment must state the national crime committed by the accused, including the crime of treason and the crime of espionage against private citizens of the Democratic Republic of American States.
A conviction of the accused by two-thirds of the Senate shall result in immediate removal of the officer from office, with a forfeiture of all accrued and future benefits of the office.
The Senate shall have the power to regulate commerce and approve trade agreements with foreign nations, which are negotiated by the President.
Article 5. The Office of President.
Article 5. Section 1. Term Limits and Election.
The executive power of the National Government shall be vested in a President of the Democratic Republic of American States.
The President shall hold the office for a term of four years, and, may serve a second term, if elected.
It is the constitutional duty of the President to preserve, protect and defend the natural and civil rights of citizens and to defend the sovereign borders of the nation from foreign and domestic threats.
No President may serve more than two terms, and no more than 10 years during a lifetime.
No Person except a natural born citizen, or a verified Citizen of the Democratic Republic of American States for the previous 10 years, shall be eligible for election of President; The President must be at least 35 years of age on the date of assuming office.
The President selects the candidate of Vice President, no later than August 1, of the year of the Presidential election.
The national election for President is held during the two days of the first weekend in November.

The final tally of votes cast must be counted by 12 pm on the Sunday of the election.
The presidential candidate with a majority of electoral college votes is declared the winner, by the House of Representatives, no later than November 15 of the year of the election. The number of electors for each State is equal to the whole number of Senators and Representatives to which the State may be entitled in the Congress. The Electors shall meet in their respective States, and are legally obligated to vote according to the popular vote of the citizens.
The term of office for the President begins December 1 of the year of the election.
Before he enters office on December 1, the President must recite, in a public ceremony, administered by the House of Representatives, the opening Paragraphs of the Declaration of Independence:

When in the Course of human events it becomes necessary for one people to dissolve the political bands which have connected them with another and to assume among the powers of the earth, the separate and equal station to which the Laws of Nature and of Nature's God entitle them, a decent respect to the opinions of mankind requires that they should declare the causes which impel them to the separation.
I hold these truths to be self-evident, that all men are created equal, that they are endowed by their Creator with certain unalienable Rights, that among these are Life, Liberty and the pursuit of Happiness. — That to secure these rights, Governments are instituted among Men, deriving their just powers from the consent of the governed, — That whenever any Form of Government becomes destructive of these ends, it is the Right of the People to alter or to abolish it, and to institute new Government, laying its foundation on such principles and organizing its powers in such form, as to them shall seem most likely to effect their Safety and Happiness.

Upon the conclusion of reciting the Declaration, The President swears the following oath of office:

I do solemnly swear that I will faithfully execute the Office of President of the Democratic Republic of American States, according

to the principles of government stated in the Constitution of the Democratic Republic of American States.
I solemnly swear to preserve, protect and defend the natural and civil rights of citizens and to defend the sovereign borders of the nation from foreign and domestic threats.
So Help me, God.
Article 5. Section 2. Removal.
In case of the removal of the President from Office, or of his death, resignation, impeachment, or inability to discharge the powers and duties of the Office, the Vice President assumes the office of President, no later than 24 hours after the removal of the President.
The House of Representatives, by law, may provide for the designation of an interim President, in the event that both the President and Vice President are not able to serve the Office. Within 24 hours of appointing an interim President, the House of Representatives shall set the time and conditions of the election of a new President, by a vote of valid citizens in each state, to be held within 30 days of the appointment of the interim President.
Article 5. Section 3. General Powers and Authority.
The President shall be the Supreme Commander in Chief of all branches of the Department of War, including the Army and Navy of the Democratic Republic of American States, and of the National Guard of the several States, when called into the actual service of the Nation.
The President may require the opinion, in writing, of the principal officer in each of the military departments, upon any subject relating to the duties of their respective
offices.
The President shall have power to grant reprieves and pardons for offences against the Democratic Republic of American States, except in cases of impeachment of any national official.
The President shall have power, by and with the advice and consent of the Senate, to make treaties, provided two thirds of the Senators present concur; and he shall nominate, and by and with the advice and consent of the Senate, appoint ambassadors, other public ministers and consuls, and all other Executive Officers of the Democratic Republic of American States, whose appointments are not herein otherwise provided for, and which shall be established by

law: but the Congress may by law vest the appointment of such inferior officers, as they think proper, in the President alone, in the executive officers of the executive departments.
The President shall have the power to fill all executive vacancies that may happen during the recess of the National Congress, by granting commissions which shall expire at the resumption of the session of the National Congress.
He shall, on January 21 of each year, present to the National Congress, the State of the Union, and recommend to their consideration such measures as he shall judge necessary and expedient for the next two years, including his proposal for the two year budget of the Democratic Republic of American States, to be ratified by the Senate no later than the day before the August adjournment in the year prior to the start of the 2-year budget cycle.
The President, Vice President and all civil officers whose appointment to office is confirmed by the National Congress, shall be subject to impeachment for treason against the sovereign interests of the nation or the sovereign interests of the states, espionage against verified citizens, bribery by a foreign government, or other national felony.

Article 5. Section 4. Veto Power of the President.
The President may veto a bill passed by both chambers of the National Congress, giving detailed explanation of the cause of the veto, including the specific provisions of the legislation which violate the public purpose of this Constitution.
The President may exercise the power of veto within 3 days of receiving the transmittal of the bill from the National Congress.
The Chamber of the National Congress which initiated the vetoed legislation may override the veto by a vote of 60% of the members of that chamber, within 7 days of the date of the veto.
A bill overridden by the chamber becomes enacted immediately upon the vote to override.
A bill not overrriden by the chamber is ineligible for reconsideration for a period of five years from the date of the vote to override.
Article 6. Section 1. The National Judicial Courts.
The national judicial courts shall consist of National District Courts and the National Supreme Court.

The Senate ordains and establishes National District Courts in each state, and provides the two year operating budget for each District Court, every two years.

All judges of the national judicial courts shall hold a term of office for six years, and may serve one additional term, if approved by the Senate.

No judge may serve more than two terms in a single court system, nor more than 18 years in both courts, in a lifetime.

Vacancies on either the District Courts or Supreme Court are filled by nominations by the Senate, and confirmed by a majority vote of the House of Representatives. The Senate is obligated to nominate judges within 7 days of a vacancy, and the House must confirm or reject the nomination within 7 days of obtaining the nomination from the Senate.

Article 6. Section 2. National District Courts.

The judicial power of the District and Supreme Court extends to cases arising under the Constitution of the Democratic Republic of American States.

The District Court is a trier of facts in criminal and civil cases arising under this Constitution.

In all cases arising in the District Court, the principles of justice are the equal application of the law to all citizens and substantive due process.

The trial of all national crimes shall be by jury, upon a presentment of a true bill of indictment to the District Court, by a majority vote of an impaneled Grand Jury of 18 citizens, in the state where the alleged crime occurred.

A person charged in any state with treason, a national felony, or any other crime against a Congressional law, who shall flee from justice, and be found in another state or foreign nation, shall on demand of the judicial authority of the National District Court, be delivered to the state having jurisdiction of the crime.

The District Court tries cases of treason of citizens against the Democratic Republic of American States, or against any State.

The National Congress shall have the power to declare the punishment of treason, including the penalty of death.

Appeals of judicial decisions from the District to the Supreme Court must state the specific text of the Constitution that is being appealed.
A majority of the Supreme Court may agree to hear an appeal.
A decision by the Supreme Court becomes the supreme law of the land for issues pertaining exclusively to the Constitution of the Democratic Republic of American States.
This Constitution, and the laws made by the National Congress, or which shall be made, under the Authority of the States, shall be the supreme Law of the Land for laws and cases exclusively pertaining to the National Government.
Full Faith and Credit shall be given in each state to the public acts, records, and judicial proceedings of every other state. And the Senate of the National Congress may by general laws prescribe the manner in which such acts, records and proceedings shall be proved, and the effect thereof.
A judge, or any staff of either the District Courts or the Supreme Court may be impeached, for cause, under the same provisions of impeachment of the Congress and the President.
Article 6. Section 3. Citizen Grand Jury.
The Chief District Judge manages and administers the Citizen Grand Juries in each district, provides for their operating budget, impanels them and instructs the members that their mission is to serve as a barrier to oppression and tyranny.
Article 6. Section 4. Qualifications.
All national court judges must be at least 45 years of age, and have been a practicing, licensed attorney at the state or national level, for a period of 20 years, prior to the nomination to the Court.
The mandatory retirement age of all National judges is 70 years of age.
Article 7. Admission of New States and Removal of States From the Union.
Upon a petition for admission from a state legislature, transmitted by the Governor to the Senate, new states may be admitted by the Senate into this Union.
The Senate may determine the geographical area and jurisdiction of a new State, including partial jurisdictions of states not currently a member of this Union.

Verified citizens of a partial jurisdiction in any state not in the Union may petition the Senate based upon a certified referendum of 66% of the citizens in the proposed jurisdiction.
Prior to their admission to the Union, as a condition of admission, the state or partial jurisdiction, seeking admission must deposit a full year of their projected taxes into the National Treasury, as determined by the Senate.
Upon a resolution presented by a Senator of any state, the national Congress may consider the removal of an existing state member of the Union.
The grounds for removal are failure to abide by the rules of this Constitution.
A vote of 2/3 of the representatives of both chambers is sufficient for permanent removal from the Union, effective immediately upon the vote.
Any state may secede from this Union by a petition ratified by a majority of the state legislature, presented to the National Senate.
The Senate must act upon the petition to grant secession within 14 days.
The grant of secession is irrevocable and permanent.
Notwithstanding the permanency of secession of a state, verified citizens of a partial geographical territory of the former state may petition the Senate for admission as a new state.
A citizen of the Democratic Republic of American States may emigrate to a non-member territory or state by a petition of citizenship revocation, executed and delivered to the citizen Grand Jury of the emigrant's residence..
A citizen revocation of citizenship is irrevocable and permanent.

Article 8. Amendments.
Upon a petition from any state legislature to the Senate, a resolution for amendment of this Constitution may be considered by both Chambers of the National Congress.
The resolution must be voted upon within 14 days of amendment submission to the National Congress.
An amendment to the Constitution, ratified by both Chambers of the National Congress, must be submitted to the citizens of the various states, within 5 days, and a majority vote of all citizens, in all states,

ratifies the amendment, which becomes effective immediately, upon citizen ratification.
A failed amendment of a citizens ratification may not be reconsidered by the National Congress for a period of 5 years after the date of the citizens referendum.

Article 9. Ratification of this Constitution.
This constitution will be ratified upon a majority vote of verified citizens in 9 states.
Any state that seeks admission to the Democratic Republic of American States after initial ratification by nine states follows the procedures outlined above, in Article 8. Admission of New States: The Governor of the state seeking admission to The Democratic Republic of American States shall transmit the petition for admission to the National Senate for the Senate's decision of approval of admission of the state into this Union.

Chapter 1. Constitutional Solutions to The Great American Betrayal of U. S. Citizens.

In Chapter 5, (The American Economic Transition to Predatory State Capitalism), we explain the chronology of economic events that transitioned the American economy from the era of monopoly capitalism (1945 – 1990, the Boomers), to the era of the predatory state capitalism (1990 – 2025, Gen Z).

In the historical chronology of events, after World War II, centralized political power became increasingly insulated from citizen consent while serving elite corporate and financial interests.

The economic changes in the U. S. domestic regional interindustrial supply chain linkages, in the latest era of predatory capitalism, are irreversible and those changes have permanently altered the initial American political principles of a constitutional representative republic.

We describe the era after 1992 as The Great American Betrayal, because ordinary, common citizens were betrayed by their elected representatives to protect and defend the welfare and freedoms of citizens.

The dilemma for red state citizens is that Madison's constitution does not provide mechanisms or procedures to dislodge the unelelcted, unaccountable corporate powers from their privileged positions.

In Chapter 6. (How Modern American Crony Capitalism Prevents the Emergence of A Beneficial Social Order), we explain that the American constitutional republic has been replaced by a global corporate crony capitalist system, where elected representatives represent the financial and corporate interests, and do not represent the interests of the citizens who elected them.

In the era of predatory capitalism, the political and financial institutions in the global "rules-based" economic order become so far removed from the consent of common middle and working class citizens that they have no legal or political recourse against government transgressions and corporate exploitation.

We agree with the analysis of Sundance, at the website, "The Last Refuge," that the U. S. President no longer controls the activities of the global military intelligence community that enforces the global rules-based military-industrial order.

Sundance writes,

"In the growing awareness of the American electorate, the President of the United States does not control the Intelligence Community. President Putin continues the war in Ukraine; because ultimately he knows President Trump does not control the elements that facilitate the Ukraine military…Something needs to change. That something is generally that President Trump has to either:
1. admit publicly he does not control the U.S. Intelligence Community (very ugly); or
2. take control of that intelligence community (even uglier). (A Significant Geopolitical Problem for President Trump and Us, July 10, 2025).

We disagree with the solution proposed by Sundance that the President must admit that he no longer controls the military-industrial complex.

A better solution is for red state citizens to conclude that the system of government in the U. S. is irrevocably damaged, and to begin creating a new, and better constitutional order.

We argue that the unelected, unaccountable global corporate regime has failed the citizens and that red state citizens bear the responsibility for creating a new beneficial economic constitution.

We agree with Richard C. Cook, who describes how the U. S. Intelligence Community gained unelected, unaccountable power in the transition to the global predatory state.

Cook writes,

During the 1980s-1990s, "Straussians," known collectively as "Neocons," joined with the denizens of the U.S. military-industrial complex like Senator Henry "Scoop" Jackson, Donald Rumsfeld, and Dick Cheney, along with Rockefeller/Rothschild-dominated Big Finance to take over the U.S. government. Instrumental was David Rockefeller, who founded the Trilateral Commission to extend and rule over global finance…The 1980s and 1990s saw the banking elite behind Federal Reserve Chairman Paul Volcker crash the producing economy. The nation saw the shipping of millions of American jobs to China and Mexico, deregulation of the banking industry to allow predatory policies like leveraged buyouts and stock buybacks, destruction of the consumer-friendly Savings & Loan industry, the cancerous growth of derivative speculation, the invasion of Iraq, and the plunging of a newly-looted Russia into depression after the 1991 fall of the Soviet Union. (The Dark Forces in Control of the Anglo-American-Zionist Empire Are the Source of the World Crisis. 2025).

The Great American Betrayal was a planned, well-organized coup of the U. S. Government by the dark forces described by Cook, in order to direct income and wealth to a very small set of global corporate and banking elites.

The social and economic consequence of the Great Betrayal was a bifurcation of the American society, in both metro regional geographical terms and in terms of social class income inequality.

In other words, the American society split into a two-class social structure, with about 10% of the upper income classes benefitting from the transition to the predatory global economic order, and the other 90% of the population not benefitting from the globalization of the world economy.

The common citizens were betrayed by the corporate propaganda that a global economy would benefit all citizens, via lower consumer prices.

As the transition to the predatory state capitalism progressed, U. S. metro regions began splitting into two distinct types of metro regions.

Some of the U. S. cities that were integrated into the global economic corporate value chains benefitted from the globalist transition, while most of the citizens in cities, in what Harald Bathelt calls the "American Hinterlands," did not benefit. (Relational Hinterlands in the USA Have Become Disconnected From Major Global Centres, October 2023).

After 1990, the national share of wealth for the top 10% of the U. S. population increased from around $20 trillion to around $60 trillion, while the net worth of the middle and lower income classes barely increased.

Chapter 1. Diagram 1. U. S. Household Net Worth, 1990 – 2025.

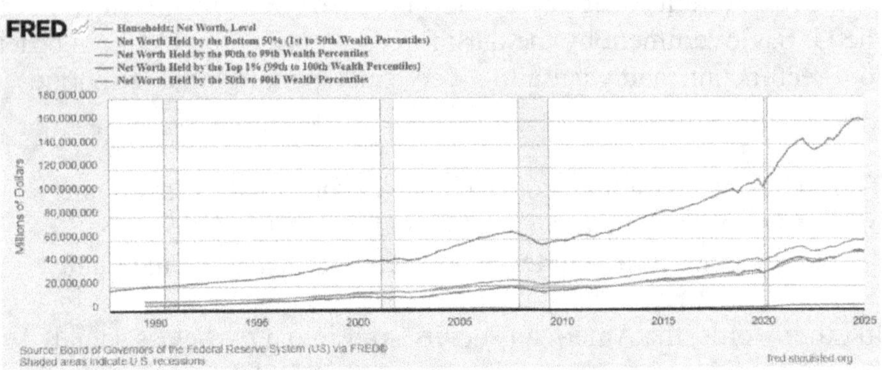

After 1990, the retail consumption by the U. S. wealthy social classes propped up a national economy that depended on retail spending because the U. S. industrial sectors that had fueled economic growth, during the monopoly capitalism era, had been exported to Asia, in the transition to the Predatory State.

Chapter 1. Diagram 2. Retail Consumption by the American Rich.

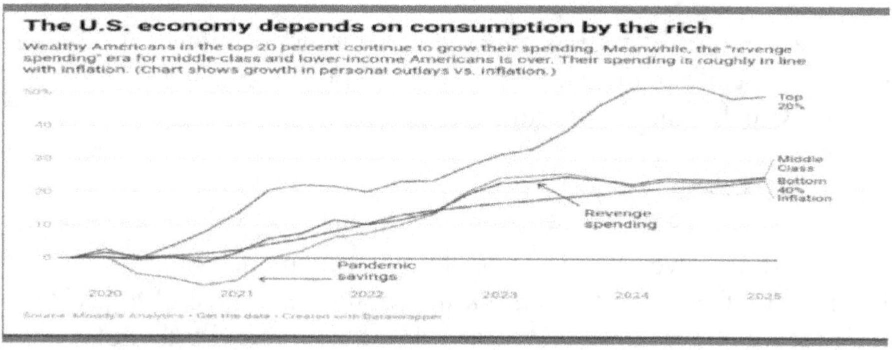

Image Credit: Moody's Analytics.

After 1990, retail consumer spending makes up about two-thirds of U. S. GDP, meaning that retail sales largely determine whether the U. S. economy is growing or slowing.

Retail spending by the wealthy social classes is fueled by the Fed's manipulation of money supply and government debt.

The Fed is trapped in its boom-bust cycle. The Fed must keep inflating assets to maintain the mirage that consumption creates economic growth, but the Fed boom-bust cycle further concentrates wealth in the top 10% of the society.

As Steve H. Hanke, professor of applied economics at the Johns Hopkins University, explains in his interview with Tyler Durden, in the transition to the global predatory state, wealthy citizens made out like bandits, in the transition to the predatory state globalist order. (The Fed Pours Jet Fuel On The Inequality Gap, 2025).

Hanke states,

"[The U. S.] monetary system is fundamentally broken, and it's rigged to benefit the asset-rich elite at the direct expense of the working and middle class… Billionaires made out like bandits, [because of the Fed] In January 2020, billionaire wealth was 14.1% of GDP. Today it's 21.7%. That's the Fed. That's monetary policy."

As we explain in Chapter 4, the Fed's econometric models are flawed and are used as subterfuge to promote the predatory capitalist system, which benefits the ruling class elite.

Hanke continues,

"the Fed didn't even know it was doing that…money has disappeared from economic thinking. [at the Fed] most of today's macroeconomic models, especially at the Fed, literally do not include the money supply as a variable. There's no M1, no M2, no M3. It's just not in the [Fed's] model."

A better economic constitution would remove the pretense that seven wealthy private bankers, meeting in secret, can somehow divine the "correct" interest rate through models and projections

A better economic constitution would allow a beneficial future order to emerge by allowing citizens in financial markets to aggregate their knowledge and expectations about real economic conditions.

Market-derived interest rates, in conjunction with written constitutional rules on money supply creation, would allow a more beneficial economy to emerge.

After 1990, over 80% of the entire U. S. labor force is employed in 7 retail consumer spending economic sectors, such as restaurants, hotels, and hair salons.

Those occupations are commonly called the "gig economy," which have no paths of upward occupational mobility, and no health or retirement benefits.

David Autor has documented the polarization of the U.S. labor market into high-wage and low-wage regions, caused by a decline in capital investment in U. S. technology. (David Autor et al., The Polarization of the U.S. Labor Market. 2006).
Before 1990, during the era of monopoly capitalism, low wage regions and states had income convergence with the high wage regions because their income and employment economic multipliers were connected in U. S. industrial supply chains.

After 1990, the polarization in the U. S. labor markets intensified, because U. S. domestic employment supply chains were eliminated in the transition to the global predatory state.

As capital investment in technology new ventures ceased to exist, the U. S. labor market evolved into a service gig economy, dependent on retail consumption by wealthy citizens.

Retail sales and consumption by wealthy citizens does not generate economic growth, and does not have strong inter-industry income and employment multipliers that distribute the benefits of economic growth to all social classes.

The only economic force that generates economic growth is capital investment in technology, and in the coming era of artificial intelligence and human-like robots, capital investments in ideas generated by tacit knowledge in human social networks will become even more critical to sustain U. S. domestic economic growth.

In the predatory capitalist system, codified knowledge becomes more important than tacit knowledge in the creation of technology innovation.

Codified knowledge is amenable to artificial intelligence programming because AI is based upon accumulated human knowledge, which already exists in books and documents.

Codified knowledge, in the form of patents, databases, digital platforms, is more easily controlled by the corporations than the creation and spread of tacit knowledge, which may cause knowledge to leak off the plate of the corporations and fall into the hands of new venture entrepreneurs.

The intermediate demand industrial production networks, which were the incubator nurseries for technology innovation in U. S. metro regions, no longer exist in the United States, and from the perspective of the authoritarian one-world government of the ruling class, it is essential that those tacit knowledge networks never again exist in the American society.

The spread of tacit knowledge cannot be controlled by the large corporations, and uncontrolled tacit knowledge creation is a threat to the smooth operation of the New World Order in directing the global flow of income to themselves. (Laurie Thomas Vass, Updating Schumpeter's Gales of Creative Destruction: Exploiting the Vulnerability of New World Order Corporate Globalism With Regional Blockchain Entrepreneurial Economic Growth, 2022).

The key causal factor of American new venture creation in tacit knowledge creation is an individualist social moral value that allows any individual to create a new venture and to obtain future rewards in profits and income.

That type of American individualist social culture is a threat to the global ruling class, which is why the totalitarian collectivist society of China is so attractive as a model to the U. S. corporate ruling class, in implementing a world where all citizens look and act the same.

The implementation of that future collectivist global society depends on corporate control over technology innovation inside of the vertically integrated global value chains, where codified technological knowledge is insulated from open, uncontrolled flows of tacit knowledge in the 350 metro regional intermediate demand industrial clusters that existed, prior to 1990.

Capital investment in domestic technology entrepreneurial ventures created economic growth, before 1990, but no longer contributes to national economic growth because capital investment in the 9 U. S. high tech industrial sectors was outsourced to Asia.

After 1990, the real enemy who organized and conducted the takeover of the U. S. Government and betrayed American middle and working class citizens was not some foreign government or alien force.

We agree with Doug Casey, an investment advisor and the author of articles at International Man.

Casey writes,

"But the real enemy is not some foreign power, but the fact that the US has turned into a dysfunctional multicultural domestic empire, which is likely to suffer serious financial, economic, social, and political problems over the next years…The real enemy is US military contractors—the so-called defense companies. They've learned to fight wars by hiring lobbyists instead of engineers. They take decades to build planes like the F-35, which are already obsolete by the time they're in production." (On Why The Military-Industrial Complex Always Wins, July, 2025).

Casey is correct in his analysis that a future successful nation requires a citizenry that shares moral and cultural values in Buchanan's constitution of fair rules.

Casey writes,

"Successful countries have a citizenry that shares common values and loves their culture. Those things pretty much disappeared as the US mutated into a welfare-warfare state."

The cultural and moral differences between red state and blue state citizens are irreconcilable, and we argue that a civil dissolution, into two separate nations, is the best solution to the differences. (Laurie

Thomas Vass, A Civil Dissolution: The Best Solution to America's Irreconcilable Ideological Conflict, 2023).

The bifurcation in social classes in the U. S., caused by the growing income and wealth gap, has caused the Gen Z citizens to embrace communism, because the original social contract, of 1776, no longer works. (Laurie Thomas Vass, The American Millennial Attraction to Socialism: Comparing the Economies of Chinese Communism, Crony Corporate Capitalism, European Crony Socialism, and the American Free Enterprise Innovation Economy, 2020).

As a consequence of the evolutionary mutation of the nation into a welfare-warfare state, a near majority of young citizens no longer embrace the principles of an individualistic constitutional representative republic government, created in 1776.

Ben Shapiro writes,

"America has a major problem: nearly half of Americans, 42% don't believe in America. According to Gallup, just 58% of adults say they are either "extremely" or "somewhat" proud to be American. That number has been in steep decline for a decade: In 2004, that number was 91%, and was still 81% as of 2016… Democrats, who plummeted from 80% to 36% during that same period (2004 – 2025), Furthermore, Americans' age correlates highly with levels of American pride: just 58% of Millennials (the children of the Boomers) and 41% of Generation Z (the children of Millenials). (The End of Patriotism? 2025).

After the 1990 transition to the predatory state, young Americans cannot afford to get married or buy a house. The ability of citizens under 30 to both be married and own a home dropped from around 45% to under 15%, in 2025, which mirrors the decline in Gen Z allegiance to American social contract.

Chapter 1. Diagram 3. Generation Z Erosion of Attaining Benefits of Original American Social Contract.

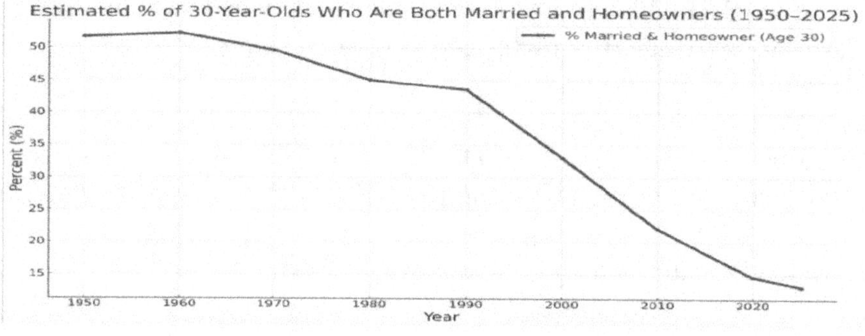

Image Credit: Josh Stylman, The Boomer Mirage, published in ZeroHedge, 2025.

As Tyler Durden, of ZeroHedge, comments about the Stylman chart,

“It [Stylman’s chart] shows the slow evaporation of the [American] social contract. For one generation, [Boomers] adulthood was a starting point. For the next, [Millenials] a struggle. For the latest, [Gen Z] an abstraction—marketed endlessly [by corporate media] but almost never attained. What began as a rite of passage [for Boomers] has become a paywalled simulation.” [for Gen Z].

Durden explains that the Boomer years were a result of the U. S. economic dominance in the world, based upon the U. S. dollar as the global currency, (World War II Bretton Woods Agreement), that was never sustainable, and never to be repeated.

Durden writes,,

“The post–World War II boom was never sustainable… America has become a "club promoter" for the global [U. S.] dollar system, offering relaxed entry requirements that have drawn hundreds of billions into U.S. treasury-backed stablecoins…The [American] institutions that promised stability—education, government, media, finance—mutated into extraction machines [of] industrial monopolies before globalization kicked in, dollar hegemony that exported inflation globally, and a demographic pyramid with more workers than retirees. It was a golden window, not a golden age. And when the [Boomer] window closed, the illusion had to be maintained —through leverage, narrative, and ever-increasing sacrifice from the generations that followed."

We agree with the analysis of Durden that the Boomer era will never be replicated, after the transition to the Predatory Capitalist State.

Durden advocates starting over, as we do, also.

Durden writes that what is needed in the U. S. is a new social contract.

"A new structure, grounded in truth, agency, and actual sovereignty. [Stylman's] chart that documents the death of the old dream becomes the blueprint for something better—if we're honest enough to read what it's really telling us."

The constitutional solution that we advocate is a metro regional economic entrepreneurial growth strategy, combined with citizen liberty to create the emergence of a beneficial society, in a decentralized state-sovereignty political constitution.

As we explained in "The New Three-Legged Stool of American Economic Growth," (2008),

"The series of speculative bubbles in the past 15 years have tended to obscure a dark economic fact that America's ability to innovate has been seriously damaged by the open border, [Fed] bubble strategy. During the 15 year era of bubbles, the formerly integrated American economy was replaced by two economies: a global market made up of 1500 large corporations, and the rest of the domestic economy, not plugged into the global economy. The major issue for workers in the domestic [U. S.] economy is that while open borders work great for the 1500 global corporations, and all of the diminishing number of staff who work there, it does not work so great for the remaining 90% of Americans. The two economies are not integrated and the benefits of free trade, consequently, are not widely distributed in the American society."

In addition to the social class income and wealth bifurcation in American society, after 1990, a bifurcation, or economic disconnect, occurred in the economic vitality of American metro regions.

Dean Stansel asks the right question in his article, "Why Are Some U. S. Cities Growing While Others Are Shrinking?" (2010), but gives the wrong answer.

Stansel compares and contrasts communistic command and control economies with a capitalistic laissez faire economy. He suggests that the main reason why U. S. cities have stopped growing is related to an absence of "private property rights."

Stansel writes,

"One of the most common findings relates to how economic activity is organized. For example, capitalist countries (those in which economic activity occurs on the basis of voluntary exchange within private markets) tend to grow faster than socialist countries (those in which economic activity is organized by government). The existence of private property rights in capitalist countries helps create stronger incentives for individuals to be productive."

But, the absence of private property rights in American cities is not the answer to the question of why some cities are prosperous and other cities are dying, economically.

The better answer, after 1990, is the absence of private capital investment for entrepreneurial technology ventures, and an absence of shared moral and cultural values that allow citizens to obtain the future prosperity that their brains are imagining.

Harald Bethelt, of the University of Toronto, provides a more accurate and realistic explanation for why some U. S. metro regions are growing, while other regions are dying, economically.

Bethelt explains that, after 1990, cities in the hinterlands became economically disconnected from their former trading partner cities, throughout the U. S. geography.

The former U. S. trading partner firms in cities were re-located to cities in China, as a part of the Great Betrayal.

The interindustrial supply chain linkages among firms within metro regions was destroyed, and as those industrial linkages were destroyed, so were the regional social tacit knowledge networks.

Maximilian Buchholz and Harald Bathelt write,

"Research identifies strong concentrations of economic activity in dynamic, major city regions, whereas shifts in economic linkages between these and smaller, less-advantaged city regions have been less investigated. Using data on firms' investment/disinvestment decisions between 1993 and 2017, we show that the majority of 'relational hinterlands' (smaller, non-contiguous city regions with at least 1 investment tie to a global centre in 1993) in the USA have become disconnected from major US 'global centres' (globally integrated city regions)." (Relational Hinterlands in the USA, 2023).

They cite a correlation between the growing disconnect between global metro regions and hinterland cities and the growing income inequality in the U. S. (Income Divergence and Global Connectivity of U.S. Urban Regions, 2020).

They write,

"This paper suggests OFDIs (U. S. capital investment in foreign nations) have contributed to income divergence across U.S. cities… Between 1979 and 2016, the U.S. Gini coefficient (a statistical measure of income inequality) grew from 34.6 to 41.5 (World Bank, n.d.), reflecting rising interpersonal inequality. However, inequality is not only on the rise at the personal level, but also geographically… between 1969 and 2017, showing that inter-regional inequality across

U.S. cities has undergone a substantial and sustained increase since the 1990s."

As the transition to the predatory capitalist state continues over time, and as income inequality continues to increase, the hinterland metro regional economies continue their slide down the ratchet of economic decline that we describe in Chapter 2. (Visualizing The U. S. Economy As Complex Adaptive Systems), the potential for future economic growth in the hinterland regions dissipates, as would energy dissipate in Prigogine's natural system.

As the hinterland regions continue their slide through the ratchet points towards the distant future attractor point, the bifurcation in the labor market intensifies, with decent, high-wage jobs occurring in the major global cities, and low-wage gig service jobs occurring in the hinterlands.

Chapter 1. Diagram 4. Diagram of Regional Economic Decline.

Diagram 6. Economy Breaking Away From Equilibrium In Time Period One to Potential Attractor Point of Economic Decline in Time Period Two.

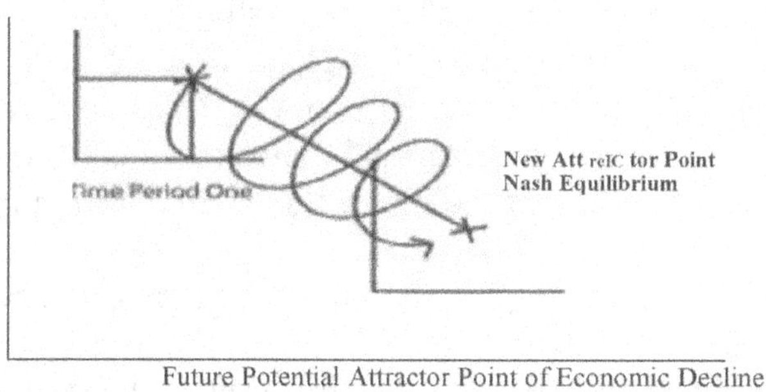

Diagram 4 from Chapter 1. Theory of Technology Evolution.

Buchholz and Bathelt cite the importance of tacit knowledge networks for corporations for their location strategy for implementing the global predatory capitalist order.
They write,

"In the so-called "knowledge economy" firms [global corporations] make investments across the globe to gain knowledge about different technologies and production processes, and to access new markets."

After 1990, the hinterland metro regions did not replace their tacit knowledge networks, gained during the Boomer era, and as a result, the hinterland metro regions lost both economic vitality and decent jobs.

They continue,

"The recent history of US "hinterland" cities, finding that since 1993, their economic – especially manufacturing – and social connections to larger global cities have declined…these cities did not replace these lost connections with links to other locations, and that these declining links are likely to have compounded the trend of rising socioeconomic disadvantage in these cities."

As we explain in Ending The Predatory Corporate Capitalist War on the American Middle Class: The American Entrepreneurial Alternative to Totalitarian Corporate Globalism, (2024), the global corporations absorbed the formerly open tacit regional knowledge networks internally in their vertically integrated global value chains, thus cutting off citizens in hinterland metro regions from the flow of tacit knowledge creation at the top of the deal creation pipeline.

Part of the Great Betrayal propaganda lie used by corporate media, in 1990, to implement the predatory order was that production efficiency in the slave labor markets in China would translate into lower retail consumer prices in the domestic U. S. economy.

What happened, instead, is that the vertically integrated corporate value chains absorbed the surplus slave labor value, as corporate profits, and did not pass along the cost savings to American consumers. (Pol Antràs and Davin Chor, Global Value Chains, 2021).

The rate of domestic U. S. inflation is a combined effect of the Fed's manipulation of money supply to prop up consumer spending, and vastly increased profits for the 1500 corporations that do business in China, directed by the lobbying efforts of the U. S. China Business Council.

The USCBC is a private, nonprofit organization of approximately 200 American companies that do business with China.

As they modestly state on their website, the mission of the USCBC is to "Help Shape the World's Most Important Relationship."

Their membership overlaps with the members of the U. S. Business Roundtable, which provides added political muscle to implement their political activities in Washington.

About 75% of the 200 USCBC member companies are also members of the Business Roundtable, which has branch affiliates in major metro regions in the United States.

We place the political power of this small group of corporations into a political theoretical framework called global corporate cronyism.

In other words, the political forces inside the U. S. domestic political structure, after 1990, that conducted the coup to implement the predatory capitalist state are the "dark enemies cited by Richard Cook, above. ((The Dark Forces in Control of the Anglo-American-Zionist Empire Are the Source of the World Crisis. 2025).

Todd Zywicki explains the 3-step political process in this transition to the predatory capitalist state. (Rent Seeking Crony Capitalism, and the Crony Constitution, SSRN, 2015.).

- First, the U. S. government collects taxes to fund global military operations. The U. S. military industrial complex sells military equipment to both the U. S. military, and also to foreign governments, who are members of the WTO western trading alliance.
- Second, the special interest military lobbying system wheedles government elected representatives for a piece of

the tax revenues when the government pays for both the domestic and foreign military equipment.

- Third, during the rent seeking negotiations between lobbyists and elected representatives, the rent extractors set their price for rent extraction, in exchange for government protection of the large corporation in U. S. foreign policy.

Stephen Haber emphasizes the legal change in property rights granted to the global corporations, in their successful lobbying efforts to that skew the benefits of global trade exclusively to those corporations and elected representatives. (Stephen Haber, Introduction: The Political Economy of Crony Capitalism, 2015.).

Haber states,

"The preferential subsidies, monopoly rights or protection from international competition benefits global corporations by establishing a legal system that provides access to bank credit,, property rights protection between incumbents and new entrants and favorable trade agreements, like NAFTA."

Diez, et al., also describe the relationship between the large corporation's power to markup prices over marginal costs and monopoly power in a very small set of U. S. corporations.

They write,

"For 2016, the U.S. firms in the sample have sales equivalent to 79 percent of U.S. GDP. We find a strong positive relation between markups and broad measures of profitability at the firm level, suggesting that the rise in measured markups has been associated with increased market power. On average, for firms in the United States and other advanced economies, a 10 percentage point rise in markups is associated with, respectively, 19 and 13 percentage point increases in the ratio of dividends to sales…As of 2016, higher markups are associated with lower investment for 8, 17, and 6 percent of U.S. publicly listed firms, across the three specifications,

respectively." (Federico J Díez,et al., Global Market Power and its Macroeconomic Implications, IMF Working Paper, 2018).
Diagram 5, below, describes that the increase in average corporate markups is related to the concentration of GDP market share of sales in a very narrow spectrum of large corporations.

Chapter 1. Diagram 5. Evolution of Global Corporate Average Markups Over Marginal Costs of Production.

Figure 1: The Evolution of Average Markups (1960 - 2014). Average Markup is weighted by marketshare of sales in the sample.

Image credit: Jan De Loecker and Jan Eeckhout, The Rise of Market Power and the Macroeconomic Implications, NBER Working Paper 23687, 2017.

The rate of markups over marginal costs of production is "pure profits," and is not in any way derived from competition in prices. The pure profits are entirely related to unelected, unaccountable political power.

The income that was previously distributed to U. S. middle and working class citizens, before 1990, in the intermediate demand networks, no longer is obtained by U. S. citizens because the large corporations have successfully diverted 90% of the intermediate demand income, to themselves.

The increase in normal market profits, and the increase in pure profits, after 1990, in the vertically integrated global value chains, are not re-invested in the domestic U. S. economy.

The Chinese command and control collectivist society steals the U. S. technology and invests their share of value-added by creating Chinese firms which contribute to the nine Chinese "champion" industrial sectors in China.

The stolen U. S. technology does not lead to entrepreneurial new venture creation in U. S. metro regions because the tacit knowledge creation and diffusion networks were destroyed when the large corporations moved the intermediate demand production networks to China.

To cite our analogy, in Chapter 2, to Prigogine's emergence of order in natural systems, the predatory capitalist state restricts information flow and knowledge dissipation, which generates increasing internal economic system complexity without allowing the adaptive capacity of citizens to manage, for their own benefit, that complexity, for the emergence of a beneficial social order.

Our beneficial economics application of the economy as a complex adaptive system, differs fundamentally from the complexity economics developed by Brian Arthur, of the Santa Fe Institute, and also differs from Posner's model of seeking the exclusive goal of economic efficiency in government policies and judicial interpretations of economic class conflict.

Arthur presents complex adaptive economic systems as moral value-neutral processes where order emerges through deterministic algorithmic relationships, consistent with the differential math of general equilibrium theory.

In contrast, in our application of the emergence of beneficial economic order requires conscious moral choices by citizens who deliberately create and maintain trust ecosystems through adherence to fair constitutional rules and ethical behavior.

In the absence of including the moral value of trust, Arthur's theory does not address how technological evolution affects the U. S. social class structures or how the power dynamics of crony capitalism influence which technologies emerge.

Arthur's "value neutral" approach is like claiming that the outcome of a rigged casino game is just like the emergence of "natural market forces."

In beneficial economic theory, technology evolution is not morally neutral.

The constitutional "rules of the game" determine which technologies receive capital investment, who benefits from their development, and how the resulting economic benefits of economic growth are distributed to social classes.

While Arthur's concept of technology evolution includes "economic phase transitions," similar to both Prigogine's and our concept of bifurcation points, Arthur's application of complex adaptive theory leaves out entirely an explanation of how transition points intensify social class conflict, which affects how humans modify their behavior to adapt to the new technological change.

In beneficial economic theory, the trajectory of the economy, after technological disruption, depends on whether the constitutional rules favor elites or enable broader social class distribution of economic benefits.

Under "fair constitutional rules," and that incorporate the moral social value of trust, technological evolution creates the emergence of widely shared prosperity; under "unfair rules," it concentrates wealth and further entrenches class divisions.

Under "unfair rules," the diffusion of valuable tacit technological knowledge remains concentrated among elite networks, preventing broadly beneficial market emergence through the human agency of adaptive behavior.

In contrast to Arthur, our application of the economy as a complex adaptive system, emphasizes the following points:

- The importance of regional tacit knowledge networks in a regional decentralized metro geographic market framework, where tacit knowledge creation and diffusion happen through localized networks rather than the controlled codified global corporate networks.
- Constitutional rules for metro regional market autonomy that emphasize regional economic self-determination and self-government.
- The inclusion of the moral value of trust in economic exchange and capital investment in close geographic proximity.
- The incorporation of citizen participatory democratic procedures that allow for human behavior to adapt to changes in technology.

Richard Posner's judicial economic efficiency model is similar in concept to the attainment of social order based upon the neo-classical general equilibrium end state of a price-competitive economic equilibrium. (Richard A. Posner, An Economic Approach to the Law of Evidence, 1999).

Posner's Economic Efficiency Model is based upon the goal of social wealth maximization and the assumption that production efficiency leads to aggregate economic gains.

Posner incorrectly assumes that economic efficiency is obtained, if, and only if, the social class winners of increased production could, theoretically, compensate the losers.

There are two philosophical flaws in Posner's logic.

First, he does not require that the winners actually compensate the losers. All that Posner requires is that efficient production leads to an economic surplus that could be paid to the losers.

For example, in our application of the transition to the global predatory state, the corporate winners of global trade did not benefit the 90% of the middle and working class losers.

The use of slave labor in China was "efficient" in Posner's model, but his efficiency criterion lead to economic misery for the great majority of American citizens.

The second philosophical flaw in Posner's logic is that he assumes price competition in the attainment of social order leads to equilibrium.

As we described above, in the transition to the global predatory state, the internal corporate value chains insulated large corporations from price competition, so that the benefits of economic efficiency are absorbed by the pure profits of the corporations, and never translate into social welfare benefits for the majority of U. S. citizens.

In our concept of the economy as a complex adaptive system, the market is simply the mechanism of exchange based upon the macro rules of the constitution and the micro rules that govern market exchange between individuals.

Posner's economic efficiency model, applied to judicial interpretations of the law, violates the basic tenets of the Pareto's Efficiency criterion that one person be made better off without harming the welfare of other citizens.

In Posner's application, one person is made better off from the transition to the predatory state, while 90% of the population is made worse off, and has no recourse against the powerful forces that inflicted the harm.

Both Posner's model of production efficiency and Arthur's model of value-neutral processes where order emerges through deterministic algorithmic relationships, conceal a deeper ideological bias that perpetuates the existing top-down, ruling class benefits of the status quo social class conflict in the American society.

Neither model presents a realistic explanation of the drift to the global corporate predatory state.

Both economic models perpetuate:

- The Federal Reserve continuing to manipulate interest rates and money supply.
- Corporate globalists extracting wealth from regions and citizens in the hinterlands.
- Financial elites using their institutional positions to maintain the status quo.
- Government-corporate partnerships that "lock" citizens into a static economic system, which has no upwardly mobile career paths.

In contrast to Posner and Arthur, our model of beneficial economics provides a bottom-up, citizen participatory social order to emerge from human behavior adaptation to technological change.

Our model of the emergence of a beneficial social order is based upon:

- Regional trust networks making capital investment decisions for new technological ventures.
- Local entrepreneurs creating new ventures through face-to-face trust relationships.
- Citizens crafting better economic constitutions, which contain fair rules, and the goal of a beneficial society in the Preamble.
- Decentralized metro regional blockchain networks that facilitate regional economic growth and citizen participation in social and economic policy decisions.

Our constitutional solutions to the Great American Betrayal of U. S. citizens begins with citizens in red states taking the initiative to craft a constitutional decentralized state-sovereignty political framework in a metro regional entrepreneurial capitalist society.

Following the advice of James Buchanan, the better economic constitution contains both protective and productive rights that allow citizens in red states the liberty to define their own future prosperity.

Chapter 2. Visualizing The U. S. Economy As A Complex Adaptive System.

The theory of beneficial economics rests upon a fundamental reimagining of the role of market exchange in creating a stable future social order.

This new perspective on the consequences of market exchange relies on applying recent research on the emergence of order, out of chaos, in the physical sciences.

Like chemistry and physics, markets are also dynamic systems characterized by exchange that often exhibit chaos after a shock to the system.

In chemistry and physics, the units which are exchanged are energy and material transfers.

In beneficial economic market exchange, the units that are exchanged are moral values and knowledge among market participants in social and market relationships.

Economic markets are like living ecosystems, where countless individual actions create organized patterns that no person, or set of political elites, designed in advance.

Economic markets are similar to how ants build complex colonies without a blueprint or a single powerful leader. Scientists call these self-organizing networks complex adaptive systems.

In the new theory of beneficial economics, citizens meet each in markets in order to transact business and exchange values, guided by their own ideas of what behavior is the best choice.

Beneficial future social order only emerges out of market exchange under certain rules, similar in physical sciences to rules, or laws, like the law of gravity, or the second law of thermodynamics.

If the rules of market exchange change, then the type of social order that may emerge also changes.

Under one set of constitutional rules, an unfair market order may emerge.

Under a different set of rules, a more fair market order may emerge.

As an alternative to viewing economics through the traditional lens of general equilibrium, where resources find optimal allocation through price mechanisms, beneficial economics sees markets as complex adaptive systems that generate social order through the human market relationships, many of which are not price based.

The role of prices in allocating scarce resources is just one of many important variables in a more realistic theory of how humans engage each other in social cooperation and social conflict.

The philosophical difference between general equilibrium theory and beneficial economic theory is that general equilibrium is based upon the idea that all complex market events can be reduced to the most elemental factor, such as the role of price, in a single instant of time.

Market exchanges in traditional economics are modeled, in mathematics, as simple, predictable linear systems, which have an expected end point.

The predicted end point of general equilibrium, after a shock, is a return to equilibrium.

The math models used in general equilibrium are like investigating a ball rolling back to the bottom of a bowl no matter where you place it. The math models are designed to always end at the bottom of the bowl.

The type of math models used to investigate the return to equilibrium are called, "differential equations, and regression statistics."

In the linear theory of general equilibrium, a small change in price leads to a very small, or marginal change, in supply and demand, leading to the re-establishment of the prior equilibrium conditions, when all second derivatives of marginal market adjustments reach zero, at the same moment in time.

General equilibrium models do not begin with observations of how humans in society interact.

Rather, general equilibrium begins with differential math models and concludes that if the real world acted like the imaginary world of the models, that the real world markets would act like the imaginary world.

Beneficial economics views market exchange as a non-linear, nonequilibrium, and dynamic system, which cannot be modeled as the second derivative of a differential equation.

Beneficial economics begins with observations of how humans interact with each other, and then applies the insights from physical science to explain how humans in markets react when conditions in the market change.

In non-linear complex systems, a small change may lead to large disruptive changes throughout the system, whose ultimate effects may not be known, before the small change occurs.

Rather than re-adjusting to the prior equilibrium, a small change in the non-linear market may lead to chaos, such as occurred in the U. S. economy after the 2008 financial meltdown.

After the small change in a non-linear market system occurs, the prior conditions can never be regained. In other words, in the non-linear market economic theory, the effects of a small change to the system are irreversible.

As applied to general equilibrium, the condition of irreversibility means that the prior equilibrium can never be regained because the market economy which emerges is completely different than the prior economy.

For example, the weakness in general equilibrium theory was exposed by Robert Solow, in the mid-1950s because the theory could not explain how changes in technology, over 3 decades, caused economic growth.

Changes in technology changed the entire U. S. economic structure, and after technology innovation, no one in the U. S. wanted to buy horse buggies, or use the yellow pages, again.

Technology innovation in one small part of the market economy causes the entire future market to change in all other parts of the market by creating new future markets, and new relative prices, that did not exist in the prior period of time.

Those new future markets, in beneficial economic theory, act to distribute new flows of income, which did not exist in the prior period.

The human agents in future markets adapt and adjust, in an evolutionary way, to the new flows of future income, which changes both human interactions in the market and inter-industrial production relationships in the supply and demand networks.

In the beneficial economic market, the introduction of a radical new technology, or radical new knowledge, may change the entire institutional government and legal framework of the market society, which then entails subsequent changes in income and wealth distribution in the market environment.

Beneficial economics takes the perspective that market exchange is a human social interactive event, which cannot be explained by price, alone. The more important factors are the human brain's anticipation of future events, and the type of legal and market institutions that form the environment for exchange.

In beneficial economic theory, agents in the market follow moral and legal rules of exchange, which all agents agree to follow, prior to entering a market exchange. Their prior agreement and consent to follow rules of exchange extends into the future, long after an exchange has taken place.

Just as flocks of birds create stunning patterns of order, economic participants in market exchanges, after the introduction of new technology, create sophisticated reoccurring patterns of behavior, based upon agreement to follow the pre-existing constitutional rules.

If market exchange is re-imagined as a complex adaptive system, then:

1. Stable beneficial social order emerges spontaneously from fair constitutional rules that guide individual behavior in market exchange.
2. Small changes in the constitutional rules can create dramatically different economic outcomes, including changes in the social distribution of income and wealth, after market transactions have occurred.
3. Knowledge creation and diffusion become the primary drivers of prosperity, not the current emphasis in general equilibrium, on efficient resource allocation in production.
4. Decentralization of market exchange to regional metro markets becomes the main focus of investigation of social order emergence, as it allows agents in the market to use tacit knowledge and the moral value of trust for agents to gauge the future potential benefit of entering into a market exchange, both before, and after an exchange takes place.

This understanding of markets as complex adaptive systems, when operating under fair constitutional rules, generates a more stable social order, and equitable income distribution because all citizens give their consent to follow the unwritten fair rules, which apply to everyone.

Unlike the role of prices in general equilibrium theory, the theory of beneficial economics places the greatest emphasis on understanding the ecosystem rules governing exchange relationships.

Market exchange has rules of the game, generally called constitutional rules, just like a card game has rules. A change in the ecosystem rules changes the strategy and outcomes of the participants in the market exchange.

As John Holland notes, in Emergence: From Chaos to Order, (1998),

"The state of a [market] system, when properly defined (whether for games, neural nets, or physics), subsumes all aspects of past history that are relevant to future possibilities…A general setting [of the market] for the study of emergence should make the rules governing economic exchange [of the market] as straightforward, for markets, as it is for games.

Many other economists have made the mental connection between market exchange and the emergence of stable social order, based upon the existence of constitutional rules of exchange.

In 1776, Adam Smith, in The Wealth of Nations, had this same insight, based upon his analysis of the social class structure of the English economy, at that time. Smith's explanation for the emergence of beneficial social order arising from market exchanges was the "invisible hand."

The invisible hand worked in a social framework of what C.B MacPherson (1964), described as a possessive individual market.

Under a different social class structure, for example under feudalism, the beneficial effects of the invisible hand may not occur.

Hayek (1960), and Buchanan, (1991), more recently, have also shared this same insight about the emergence of stable social order as a result of market exchange, based upon the voluntary social agreement of citizens to obey the rule of law.

What is new about beneficial economic theory is that the recent insights of complex adaptive systems, in physical sciences, are applied to social science, in the areas of economics, sociology, and the political theory of participatory democracy.

Rather than seeing the market economy as an equilibrium system that returns to the prior equilibrium, after a shock, beneficial economics views the market economy as a non-equilibrium system, which allows social order to emerge in the future.

The future order emerges after changes in the macro economic and macro social exchange networks, as a result of self-organization of the humans engaged in market exchange.

It is the behavior of humans adapting to the new future markets, as they change their behavior, during the transition from the old market to the new future market, which allows the new future market to emerge.

It is the changing behavior of humans in the market, during the transition phase from old to new, that causes Smith's invisible hand to work.

At the most micro economic level of an individual exchange, after the appearance of new technology, quantum-mechanical uncertainty arises about the future market and where in that future market, the people in the exchange may find themselves.

At that moment of uncertainty, the participants to the exchange rely on the stability of constitutional rules, and the moral value of trust, to engage in an exchange that may take years to complete, such as a capital investment in a new technology venture.

In other words, the theory of beneficial economics has both a macro economic framework, grounded in the analogy to complex adaptive systems at the macro level, and part of the theory is grounded in the cognitive neurological function of the human brain, at the micro level, in an environment of uncertainty, when the brain anticipates the behavior of other humans.

The most important function of the human brain at the moment of uncertainty in market exchange is the decision to extend trust, in the absence of evidence that trust will be reciprocated.

Generally, the moral value of trust occurs in local or regional economic settings, within an envelope of 50 miles, because trust is usually based upon the human brain's anticipation of the behavior of other humans, in face-to face human market transactions, governed by common cultural values, as codified in constitutional rules and adherence to the law of contracts.

The application of complex adaptive theory to market exchange begins with the definition of two terms, dissipative structures and social self-organization in open, non-equilibrium market ecosystems.

The concept of dissipation in complex physical systems means that matter and energy disperse, or dissipate, throughout the system, after a change. As the matter, or energy, disperses through the system, the force of dissipation changes the entire system.

For example, dropping a green drop of ink into a jar of yellow ink may result in the entire jar of ink turning an entirely different color, like blue.

As the drop of green ink dissipates in the jar, the original yellow color changes, so that after dissipation, the jar is a completely different color, which is an irreversible change.

This same idea in beneficial economics is called knowledge diffusion, because the appearance of new knowledge in an open, non-equilibrium economy disperses among the participants in the market.

After the diffusion of new knowledge in a market, the images and insights created by the human brain are altered. The old way of thinking and imagining the future changes, and those new images in the brain are irreversible.

One way to apply the physical science concept of dissipation to knowledge diffusion in a market is to think about how a disease moves through a population, infecting new patients.

Epidemiologists call this diffusion of disease a contagion, and speculate that the density of the humans in the ecosystem of the human's habitat influences the rate of contagion.

The diffusion of knowledge in markets is not random, as it is in Darwin's evolution of species.

The search for new knowledge is purposeful and results in behavior adaptations of human behavior in the immediate time period following the introduction of new knowledge.

As applied to beneficial economics, there is both a feed forward effect from the production side of knowledge creation, and a feedback effect in knowledge diffusion, and in this sense, knowledge diffusion exhibits a certain type of evolutionary "Lamarkian" characteristic.

Unlike random selection for the survival of the fittest, where changes happen by random accident, market evolution happens through purposeful human adaptation to the new environment, as people deliberately change their behavior based on new knowledge and information.

Popper (1981, 1989) calls this passive Darwinism, in contrast to exploratory or active Darwinism in which living organisms actively explore the environment for more favorable eco-niches and modes of survival: 'a selection pressure that moulds it to fit better into that new habitat, into that new way of life which it has actively chosen, and which it has preferred' (Popper, 1981:42).

Some market environments have social networks that share norms and culturally-based systems of interpretation of rules, where the diffusion of knowledge occurs more rapidly, than other types of social market environments, with different social networks and legal rules.

The theory of beneficial economics seeks to explain how certain social environments act to inhibit or limit the diffusion of knowledge, which explains why some regional markets experience economic growth, while other regions may experience economic decline.

In the application of the concept of dissipation in physical sciences, Ilya Prigogine (pronounced pree-go-gene), states that it is the force of dissipation, or the flux of matter and energy, through the system, after a change, that is the driving force for generating order out of chaos.

Prigogine won the 1977 Nobel Prize in Chemistry "for his contributions to non-equilibrium thermodynamics, particularly the theory of dissipative structures."

Prigogine's theory serves as the source of authority for applying physical science concepts of non-equilibrium to the theory of beneficial economic theory.

Prigogine and Stengers write, in Order Out of Chaos: Man's New Dialogue With Nature, (1984), that dissipative systems produce a "unique and irreversible " 'historical path along which the system evolves.

In the application to market exchange, knowledge diffusion creates a new path, or new economic trajectory, from the initial position of the economy, to a distant future attractor point, which is both uncertain and irreversible.

Prigogine and Stengers note, that after dissipation occurs in a nonlinear, non-equilibrium, open system, "the old universal laws of science" are not universal any more.

In the application to beneficial economics, the initial economic position, described as an economy in short-term equilibrium, can only be described as remaining in temporary equilibrium, because after new knowledge diffusion, the old rules of price-based equilibrium do not apply, anymore.

Prigogine and Stengers call this period of energy transition from the old order to the new order, a revolutionary moment, or also a "singular moment" where the physical system approaches a "bifurcation point."

At the bifurcation point, they write,

“it is inherently impossible to determine in advance which direction the change in energy will take: whether the system will disintegrate into "chaos" or leap to a new, more differentiated, higher level of "order" or organization.”

At certain critical moments, economic systems reach a crossroads where the trajectory of the economy must follow one path or another. The social and economic forces, at the bifurcation point, are too strong to allow the economy to remain at the static point.

The trajectory of the economy, as it approaches the bifurcation point, is like water reaching a fork in a river. The force of the water forces the water to move in one direction, and that movement of water permanently shapes its future flow of water in the river.

What beneficial economic theory adds to Prigogine’s theory of a bifurcation point is that the emergence of a future beneficial market only occurs under a specific set of fair constitutional rules, given a certain rate of knowledge creation and knowledge diffusion, in the regional social networks.

At the moment of market bifurcation, it is unknown and uncertain what future path the market may follow.

Under a different political and institutional framework, based upon unfair rules, the future market may be characterized by economic chaos and social class conflict over the distribution of income.

At the moment of bifurcation in market economies, the economy may continue on an upward trajectory to another future distant attractor, or the economy may descend, through downward ratchets, characterized by the absence of new knowledge creation and knowledge diffusion.

As Prigogine notes,

"Small inputs [in the open physical system] yield huge, startling effects. The entire system may reorganize itself in ways that strike us as bizarre."

In the application of complex adaptive physical systems to beneficial economics, small technological innovations in one part of the market may produce large changes throughout the market structure, that cause the trajectory of the economy to move to a new distant attractor point, that may seem bizarre, such as the appearance of human-like robots which work in manufacturing plants.

Prigogine describes this moment of bifurcation in chemistry as two distinct paths, both starting from a single moment in time.

Chapter 2. Diagram 1. Diagram 1. From Prigogine Order Out of Chaos, p. 296.

they may represent either of the two nonuniform distributions of chemical *X* in space, as represented in Figures 12 and 13.

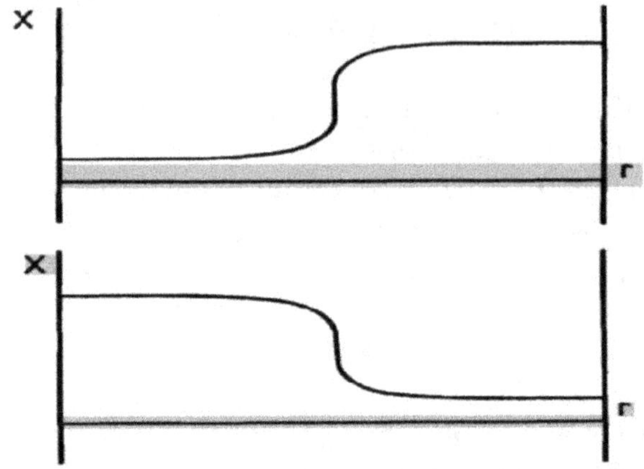

Figures 12 and 13. Two possible spatial distributions of the chemical component *X*, corresponding to each of the two branches in Figure 11. Figure 12 corresponds to a "left" structure as component *X* has a higher concentration in the left part; similarly, Figure 13 corresponds to a "right" structure.

This same idea of Prigogine's moment of bifurcation, in beneficial economics, is described in Diagram 2, taken from Theory of Technology Evolution, (Vass, 2019), as a regional economy breaking away from the initial point of temporary equilibrium to a higher level of economic exchange, in time period two.

Chapter 2. Diagram 2. Regional Economy Breaking Away From Equilibrium. From Theory of Technology Evolution, 2019.

Diagram 4.3. Regional Economy Breaking Away From Equilibrium

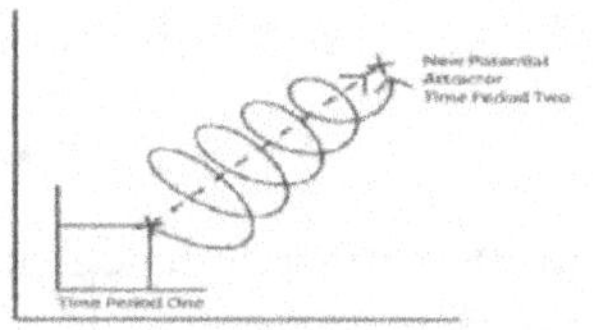

At time period 2, the regional economy can be described as being in a second time period phase of bifurcation, the future trajectory being uncertain.

Diagram 3 describes the pathway of the regional economy, on a downward trajectory, as a result of the loss of knowledge creation and knowledge diffusion

Chapter 2. Diagram 3. Regional Economy Breaking Away to Economic Decline. From Theory of Technology Evolution, 2019.

Diagram 6. Economy Breaking Away From Equilibrium In Time Period One to Potential Attractor Point of Economic Decline in Time Period Two.

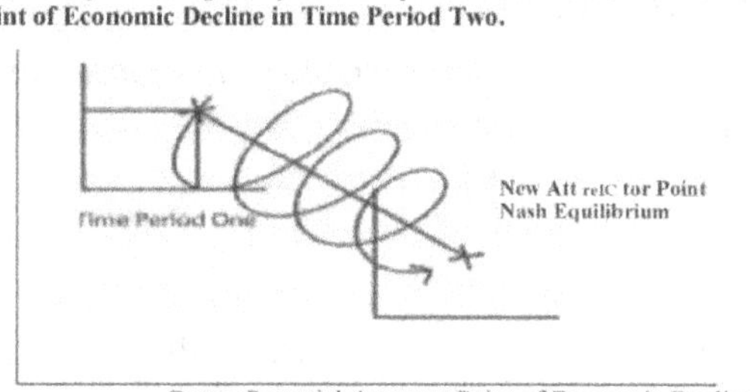

Future Potential Attractor Point of Economic Decline

Prigogine's term "moment of bifurcation" must be interpreted in geological, evolutionary time.

Regional markets sometimes become static, in a situation where everyone is stuck in a pattern that makes it hard to break out of an existing bifurcation point.

At that condition, no one person can improve their situation by changing their own behavior, so the market system becomes locked in place.

In the application to beneficial economics, a regional economy can rest in a stationary, suboptimal state for decades at a time, in what economists describe as a "Nash Equilibrium."

The force that knocks the static market out of the Nash Equilibrium is the creation and diffusion of new knowledge, which acts to provide new brain images for humans on how to change their behavior.

This stationary resting place can endure for many years, because the rate of knowledge creation and knowledge diffusion within the regional social networks is not great enough to move the regional economy to either a higher point of market exchange, or to remain at a lower point of a Nash Equilibrium.

Applying the evolutionary metaphor from physical science to beneficial economics, Motoo Kimura, in The Neutral Theory of Molecular Evolution, (1983), would describe the Nash Equilibrium as the regional economy having entered a period as "nearly neutral" genetic drift.

In the absence of knowledge diffusion, in the regional economy, the economy just drifts along, like a car idling in neutral, at a stop light.

At some point, the traffic light may turn green, with the creation and diffusion of knowledge.

Or, alternatively, the economy may move from neutral, to begin a slow descent towards a distant future attractor point of economic decline.

At some point of time around the economic bifurcation point, the market can be seen as either growing or dying, caused by the creation and diffusion of knowledge.

In either the case of economic growth, or regional economic decline, the economy can be visualized as being in Prigogine's state of "far-from-equilibrium," on a trajectory towards a distant future attractor point.

The same idea of Prigogine's far-from-equilibrium , in beneficial economics, is called "distant future attractor point."

The future distant attractor point acts as a possible force of attraction, similar in concept to the idea that the ellipse of a planet around the sun is caused by the force of gravity.

Prigogine writes,

"Matter (energy) near equilibrium behaves in a "repetitive" way. On the other hand, far from equilibrium there appears a variety of mechanisms corresponding to the possibility of occurrence of various types of dissipative structures… near-bifurcations systems present large fluctuations. Such systems seem to "hesitate" among various possible directions of evolution, and the famous law of large numbers in its usual sense breaks down. A small fluctuation may start an entirely new evolution that will drastically change the whole behavior of the macroscopic system."

The reason why Diagram 3, above, describes the uncertain pathway of the economy towards the distant future attractor point as oscillations around the mean trajectory is that, at any moment in time, the force of attraction may vary, or even disappear.

As Prigogine states,

"Instead of remaining stationary, the concentrations of X and Y begin to oscillate with a well-defined periodicity. The oscillation period depends both on the kinetic constants characterizing the reaction rates and the boundary conditions imposed on the system as a whole (temperature, concentration of A., B, etc.)."

In the application to beneficial economics, the rate of knowledge creation, and the social-institutional networks of knowledge diffusion, are the forces which move the regional economy towards the distant future attractor point, after a shock, or disruption in the regional ecosystem.

If the force of attraction of the future distant attractor point remains constant through time, the trajectory of the economy narrows its pathway, in smaller oscillations around the trajectory, eventually leading the economy to come to a resting point, at the future distant attractor bifurcation point.

Prigogine writes about this uncertain pathway of the physical system as "intrinsically indeterminate."

He writes,

"However, a trajectory may become intrinsically indeterminate at certain singular points. For instance, a rigid pendulum may display two qualitatively different types of behavior… An infinitesimal perturbation would be enough to set it rotating or oscillating… the motion may become so complex, the trajectories so varied, that no observation, whatever its precision, can lead us to the determination of the exact initial conditions. But at that point the duality on which classical mechanics was constructed breaks down. We can predict only the average behavior of bundles of trajectories."

The analytical tools used to investigate the possible short-term future trajectory of the regional economy shift from deterministic mechanical regression analysis and differential equations, more suited for equilibrium analysis, to more probabilistic statistical tools.

The analytical probabilistic tools are useful for describing economic movements in the short term of 3 to 5 years.

Markets don't move quickly towards a single fixed point of equilibrium, but move slowly towards multiple possible future states, all of which have different probabilities, based upon how humans are adapting to the new knowledge.

For example, in complex natural systems, like the weather, weather forecasters show multiple possible hurricane paths, rather than a single predicted path. The introduction of a new high pressure system, or some new, unexpected atmospheric condition, may change the earlier projected path of the hurricane.

A better analytical tool for investigating the path of the regional economy begins by continuously updating the condition of the economy, as new information arrives to the analyst, in order to adjust expectations on what may happen in the immediate future phase of the economy.

Using "future probabilities" as a tool of beneficial market analysis allows for the inclusion of chaos, or uncertainty, as an outcome of the market's trajectory, that may be on a downward trajectory of economic decline.

The goal of the future probabilistic statistical method is to provide an educated guess whether the rate of creation and diffusion of knowledge is leading to a future distant attractor point of economic growth, or that the regional economy is on a downward trajectory, through ratchet points, caused by the absence of knowledge diffusion.

For example, in the immediate economic future, the probabilistic methods could indicate how a capital investment in a new technology venture may affect the future trajectory of the economy towards a distant future attractor point.

The capital investment in a new technology venture may have the effect of changing the regional intermediate supply chains, which would tend to increase the rate of the creation and diffusion of new knowledge through those new social knowledge networks.

New regional supply and demand networks may emerge as a result of the capital investment, as the new venture begins buying and selling relationships that did not exist in the prior time period.

The new capital investment acts to change the entire social and market ecosystem, just as the drop of green ink in a yellow ink jar changes the entire color of the ink in the jar.

The future regional economic structure will never be the same, after the capital investment in the new technology venture.

In other words, the regional economy can never return to the point of the prior equilibrium, after the capital investment because human behavior has changed and adapted to the new knowledge, as the market becomes a new environment.

Stuart Kauffman, in At Home In The Universe (1995), suggests that the capital investment in a new technology venture in the region is, biologically, like co-evolution between the technology itself, and the evolution of human behavior, as the humans adapt to the appearance of technological novelty.

Kauffman writes,

"technological evolution is actually coevolution. Entry of the car drove the smithy (horse shoes), to extinction and created the market for motels. You make your living in a "niche" afforded by what I and others do. The computer-systems engineer is making a living fixing widgets that did not exist 50 years ago. The computer shops that sell hardware make a living that was impossible to make 50 years ago."

John Holland (1995), applies this idea of human adaptation to the new environment to a regional metropolitan economy.

Holland writes,

"Yet these cities have no central planning commissions that solve the problems of purchasing and distributing supplies. Nor do they maintain large reserves to buffer fluctuations; their food would last less than a week or two if the daily arrivals were cut off. How do these cities avoid devastating swings between shortage and glut, year after year, decade after decade?.. Adaptation, in biological usage, is the process whereby an organism fits itself to its environment. Roughly, experience guides changes in the organism's structure so that as time passes the organism makes better use of its environment for its own ends… the city can be seen as a complex adaptive system composed of interacting agents, [whose behavior can be] described in terms of rules. These agents adapt by changing their rules as experience accumulates. In cas, a major part of the environment of any given adaptive agent consists of other adaptive agents, so that a portion of any agent's efforts at adaptation is spent adapting to other adaptive agents [humans]."

In other words, the major force that moves a regional market towards a distant future attractor point is related to how the human brain uses new knowledge to anticipate the behavior of other humans, as the market conditions change.

In the example of a capital investment in a new technology venture in a metro region, the investment creates new flows of income and wealth, and humans then use the new knowledge about income flows in order to adapt their behavior to the changed market environment.

Kauffman (1995), explains that the new regional economic structure, after the appearance of technological novelty, has the appearance of an economic web of inter-relationships of humans, as they adapt to the changed environment.

Kauffman writes,

"You have, in short, the start of a model of an economic web where the web structure drives its own transformation. The web of technologies expands because novel goods create niches for still further new goods. Our symbol-string models therefore become models of niche creation itself. The molecular explosion of supracritical chemical systems, the Cambrian explosion, the exploding diversity of artifacts around us today—all these drives toward increased diversity and complexity are underpinned by the ways each of these processes creates niches for yet further entities. The increase in diversity and complexity of molecules, living forms, economic activities, cultural forms— all demand an understanding of the fundamental laws governing the autocatalytic creation of niches."

Holland applies the idea of new knowledge flows in the region to how the changing networks in regional intermediate production supply and demand networks change, after the capital investment.

Holland writes,

"There are two properties of flows, well known from economics, that are important to all complex adaptive systems, (CAS). The first of these is the [income and job] multiplier effect (see, for example, Samuelson, 1948), which occurs if one injects additional resource [ie., a capital investment] at some node. Typically this resource is passed from node to node, possibly being transformed along the way, and produces a chain of change."

In the theory of beneficial economics, the human brain's anticipation of the behavior of other humans, during the transition time from old to new markets, creates economic uncertainty on the best course of behavior.

At the macro level of economic analysis, the future uncertainty creates chaos, such as market crashes or social conflict.

Holland applies this idea of economic chaos to reoccurring speculative bubbles and market crashes, such as occurred in the Year 2000 speculative period.

Holland writes,

"In particular, we felt that the anticipatory speculations produced by the [brain's] internal models of such agents would generate speculative bubbles and subsequent crashes. In other words, we felt that learning, and the imperfect internal models it produces, would automatically generate realistic dynamics without the introduction of exogenous variables...The interactions of agents in cas are governed by anticipations engendered by learning and long-term adaptation."

As Holland notes, some metro regional markets are characterized by knowledge and information flows which allow humans to gain a common understanding of the possible future direction of the economy.

Holland (1998), describes the example of a single human brain anticipating the behavior of other humans in an uncertain environment as the neurons all lining up in the brain to provide coherence on the correct decision or best behavior to adopt.

As the same type of neurons line up in other human brains, a type of social quantum coherence emerges about the type of market that may be emerging in the future.

Holland writes,

"Observations [of the human brain] shows that the combination of variable threshold and high [neuronal] firing rate causes some of these active CP neurons to begin to fire in a synchronized lockstep; they begin to reverberate. Neurons not participating in this lockstep group tend to be in the very high threshold part of the variable threshold when pulses arrive, so they do not fire. The result is a "weeding-out" process that favors neurons that belong to the lock-step group… Situations not previously encountered [like a new capital investment or a new source of knowledge]…Situations not previously encountered can, despite their novelty, cause well-developed [neuronal] assemblies to be sequenced or pieced together in new ways. The assemblies become building blocks, responding to familiar elements in new situations."

As more and more human brains begin to process the same neuronal images, the common understanding of all the humans in the region allows humans to coordinate their market behavior because they all see the same future reality.

Other types of regional markets may have restrictions or limits on how new knowledge is transmitted among the agents in the regional ecosystem, which perpetuates chaos and social class conflict.

Holland (1998), describes the social awareness of the new regional environment as "emergent," meaning that the social coherence about the future does not occur rapidly.

Human brains process images differently, and social information networks of knowledge diffusion may act to limit or inhibit new information flows.

In addition, there are social class political forces which act against the awareness of the new future economy because that future economy may disrupt the status quo distribution of income and political power in the region.

Holland describes the framework of the ecosystem as a mechanism of diffusion, and in the application of complex adaptive systems to beneficial economics, the market exchange is the mechanism of diffusion that allows for emergence of social order.

By examining the mechanisms of emergence in physical science, Holland seeks to explain the "laws of emergence."

Holland writes,

"mechanisms for mediating interactions, as when a photon causes an electron to jump from its orbit around an atom. Mechanisms so defined provide a precise way of describing the elements (agents), rules, and interactions that define complex systems. The setting that results gives us a common way of describing the diverse rule-governed systems that exhibit emergence…we should be able to extract some of the "laws of emergence."

As an example of emergence, Holland describes how an economic market may be characterized as having laws of emergence.

Holland writes,

"Think of a market. The negotiations (among agents in the market) that determine the state of the market depend on the (cognitive neurological) objectives and strategies of individual agents—the buyers and sellers—as they enter and leave (market interactions). Large markets, like the stock and commodity markets, are notorious for their complexity and unpredictability. Even simple models of a market, with buyers and sellers severely limited in their actions, exhibit complicated dynamics (see Arthur et al., 1997). There are sudden shifts in activity and price levels, with occasional crashes and bubbles. The (probabilistic) model (of a complex) market may go on for a thousand simulated days with only minor fluctuations, and then shift suddenly into a new regime, much like a real market. All of this is well beyond the most dedicated pencil-and-paper explorations, be they calculations or mathematical analysis. (differential equations or regression statistics)."

For Holland, it is the novelty, or new conditions in the market, which alter the cognitive neurological image processing in the brain, when agents are confronted with new technology or new information.

By examining what humans do when confronted by a new situation, in the market mechanism, Holland seeks to apply laws of emergence that cause social order to emerge.

He writes,

"Situations not previously encountered can, despite their novelty, cause well-developed (neuronal) assemblies to be sequenced or pieced together in new ways. The assemblies become building blocks, responding to familiar elements in new situations…humans effortlessly parse unfamiliar scenes into familiar objects, an accomplishment that so far eludes even the most sophisticated computer programs."

For Holland, quantum neurological coherence in a single human brain can possibly act to provide a building block for other human brains, leading eventually to quantum social coherence, as more humans perceive the new future market.

Philosophers generally call this emergent social coherence as intersubjective verification of reality, as more brains see and imagine how to act in their common understanding of the new future market.

The future market emerges spontaneously, as agents adjust, and coordinate, their behavior to the new future market.

Michael Polanyi (pronounced Pole-an-yee), (1941, 1951). describes this market behavior adjustment process as a "dynamic order" grounded on freedom and spontaneously emerging from mutual adjustment of free actions."

In other words, according to Polanyi, the essential prerequisite of the market, which allows spontaneous social order to emerge, is individual freedom of agents in the market to adjust their behavior to the new reality.

In communistic collective economies, individuals do not have freedom from coercion or repression to adjust their behavior to the new reality, because government elites control human behavior.

In corporate capitalist social class societies, the ruling class nobility of wealthy citizens may limit or oppress citizens from gaining new information, or limit the ability of citizens to adjust their behavior to the new market reality.

The element of freedom and liberty of citizens to adjust their behavior to the new reality will be explored in Chapter 6, (The Emergence of American Beneficial Social Order Under Buchanan's Fair Constitutional Rules and Kant's Moral Values).which reviews the work of Friedrich Hayek and James Buchanan, on the emergence of spontaneous market order.

In beneficial economic theory, the market is the mechanism through which new knowledge is created and diffused.
The beneficial market mechanism neither maximizes nor minimizes social welfare. The beneficial market simply allows participants to pursue that which they value by trading and bartering with other citizens.

Under certain types of cultural values and constitutional rules, the social order which emerge from citizens pursuing their own values may be seen as a fair system.

In the Market As A Creative Process, (1991), James Buchanan and Viktor Vanberg provide the intellectual framework for reimagining of the role of market exchange in creating a stable future social order by applying recent research on emergence in the physical sciences.

They write,

"If the market is genuinely perceived as an open-ended, nondetermined evolutionary process in which the essential driving force is human choice, any insinuation, however subtle, of a (general equilibrium) telos toward which the process can be predicted to move must be inherently misleading. There is, in our view, no systematically sustainable middle ground between a teleo- logical (equilibrium) and a nonteleological (complex adaptive system) perspective. And all conceptualizations of the market process that suppose, whether explicitly or implicitly, a "something" toward which the process is moving are, by this very fact, teleological, whether the "something" is specified as an equilibrium or, otherwise."

The key variable in beneficial economics is the creation and diffusion of knowledge, within a defined geographical territory.

As Buchanan and Vanberg note,

"Only a decentralized market structure of economic interaction can exploit fully the knowledge of localized circumstances required to allow a definition of the ultimate valuation that is placed on resource use. Only the market can allow persons the effective liberty to discover the particular localized eccentricities that give form to value."

It is the processing of images and imagination of the human brain, under fair constitutional rules, that allow human coordination of behavior during the transition from the old market to the new market that allows spontaneous social order to emerge.

Chapter 3. How A Person's Brain Naturally Creates Social Order Through Their Everyday Market Choices

Just as Prigogine observed that, at the macro level of physical science systems, order emerges spontaneously from chaos, a similar pattern of spontaneous order emerges at the micro economic level of a brain's market decisions.

In Prigogine's physical science model, coherence arises naturally through a process of energy dissipation and the exchange of material forces that result in spontaneous order.

The brain's decision-making process mirrors the larger complex adaptive systems Prigogine described, but on the scale of individual neurons and neural networks.

Prigogine suggests that the brain's neuronal cognitive functions during deep sleep may be described like quantum physics, where the action of neurons are attracted to a distant attractor. (Exploring Complexity, Ilya Prigogine, European Journal of Operational Research, 1987).

Prigogine writes,

"The brain's operation at the highest level of cognition is more like quantum physics than mechanical relativity theory because the brain is shuffling and sorting thousands of [neuronal] images… the movement [of neurons] is discontinuous, [like] entities such as electrons that have both wavelike, particle-like properties, and that they interact in non-causal, non-local ways that violate the requirements of separateness and independence of fundamental constituents basic to any mechanistic approach…Obviously, the dynamical complexity of the brain cannot be an accident. It must have been selected for its very instability."

As described in quantum theory, neuronal activity is discontinuous, and neuronal charges interact in non-causal, non-local ways that violate the scientific rules of mechanical relativity science.

The brain has an estimated 86 billion neurons, or nerve cells. Each neuron is capable of forming linkages to other neurons, across tiny spaces, called synapses. These connections between neurons can change shape over time, a property called “plasticity,” by scientists.

Any single neuron can form up to 10.000 synaptic connections with other neurons. The neurons emit very small electrical signals across the synapse. This electrical signal, or charge, acts like a communication mechanism between neurons.

Each neuron has a unique cytoskellatal form, composed of proteins. One type of protein in the cytoskelleton can assume two different shapes, through a slight bending action. Each shape corresponds to an electrical charge, either positive or negative.

It is this change in electrical charge that is propagated down the length of the neuron’s axon, or stem, to the point of linkage to the next neuron.

The electrical charge is carried across the synapse via chemical substances, called neurotransmitters. One of the neurotransmitters, magnesium, performs the task of maintaining the same electrical charge from neuron to neuron.

This task by the neurotransmitter preserves the polarity of the signal as it is broadcast through the different neural circuits.

Many of the brain’s neural circuits are specialized in function, and, like the language circuits, are formed before birth.

Other neural circuits are formed during a lifetime, and can change shape over time. Depending on the interactions between the chemical and electro physical forces when a neuron is transmitting a signal, the neural circuits can become more permanent by depositing a small trace of calcium.

These more permanent circuits are related to both the brain's memory function, and the insight/imagination function. The more permanent brain circuits are comprised of neural networks that tend to be located in particular areas of the brain.

The transmission of the electrical current by a neuron is called "firing." The frequency of the firing refers to the number of times the current oscillates, or vibrates, in a millisecond.

Neurons are always firing at some level, or resting frequency. Generally, the neurons in the same vicinity are also firing at this same frequency. When images are being processed and sorted, the frequency level of the neuronal firings changes, generally by increasing.

An image being processed in the brain represents a type of global coherence in frequency among neurons in one area of the brain with neurons in other parts of the brain. What this collective quantum coherency represents is a similar shape and function within the neuron's cytoskellatal structure.

The process of generating images is an on-going activity of the brain, related to the mission of guiding the individual through the external environment by selecting images based upon their survival potential.

The behavior of neuronal process in the brain is a mirror image of Prigogine's macro complex systems of flowing energy dissipation patterns, based upon mutual interaction and interdependence that appear initially as chaos, but eventually lead to the emergence of brain neuronal order.

At the micro individual economic level of decision-making, the market economy is linked to the evolution of the human brain's ability to imagine and anticipate future scenarios, especially when the brain is confronted with a new circumstance that creates risk and uncertainty in decision-making.

The two philosophical traditions of macro and micro economic spontaneous order are largely aligned, and interdependent, as both traditions emphasize emergent order, decentralized processes, and the interplay of individual actions leading to collective social outcomes

The primary philosophical difference in the two traditions is that Prigogine's macro philosophy is based upon the laws of quantum physical science, while the philosophy of the brain is based upon the theory of Eccles and Popper of how mental images arise from the non-material insight and imagination functions of the brain.

The two philosophies are interrelated because Prigogine's macro-level emergence, as applied to market decisions, is dependent upon micro-level emergence of beneficial social order, under a certain set of constitutional and cultural rules.

For example, at the macro economic level, Prigogine's philosophy could be seen as a farmers' market, or a flea market, where order emerges from agreed upon market rules, seen as buyers and sellers bartering over price.

Every time the mental images in the brain leads to a micro economic exchange at the farmers' market, that decision creates a ripple effect, at the macro economic level, just like a stone thrown into a lake creates an expanding ripple effect.

As applied to the brain's market decision-making, Prigogine's complex adaptive philosophy is related to the brain's insight and imagination cognitive mental function, which allows the brain to anticipate future, never-before-seen events.

The future reality being imagined in the brain is not based in material-deterministic empirical laws of mechanical science. As Prigogine suggests, a better interpretation of the brain's image-making may be based upon quantum physics.

The brain's creative mental imagination ability evolved to provide both self-conscious insight and conscious awareness to anticipate what other humans may do.

Eccles and Popper make a distinction between the biological evolutionary processes of the brain and the cultural evolutionary effects on the brain. (The Self and Its Brain, 1977).

The biological evolution of the brain was not a uniform progression, through time, of adding new imaging functions.

Some parts of the brain were added, while other parts of the brain were discarded. Some early homind species had different brain sizes and brain functions, at the same moment in history, as other human species.

In biological evolution of the brain, according to Darwin's thesis, the biological raw material of an organism is established by genetic mechanisms, involving chemicals and natural forces such as gravity and electricity.

The environment in which the organism happens, by chance, to exist, gives direction to the evolution of the raw biological material by selecting the best combination of material.

For example, William Calvin, in The Cerebral Symphony, (1990), notes that very slight random variations in genetic materials in the brain could yield very slight advantages in natural competition, yielding new functions and abilities that were eventually selected over other possible functions and abilities of the brain.

What at first glance may appear to be the obvious purpose of an organism, upon closer examination, turns out to be not so obvious.

The purpose of an organism could be for some function different from what is first suspected. In the case of the human brain, the unexpected result in purpose is best illustrated by the development of language.

It first seems obvious that the language function of the brain is to promote communication between humans. Upon closer examination, the evolution of language appears to be more for the function of creating and interpreting mental images.

Brains continually spin out the private images of an individual's mental world. The symbols and images of language are like the computer software programs that interpret the meaning and significance of the brain's mental sorting and filtering function.

According to Roger Lewin, in The Origins of Modern Humans, (1984),

"language was the medium that interpreted the internal world of inner reflection."

Following Darwin's second principle of evolution, the environment of some early hominid species caused very slight variations in some of the brain's processes of creating images.

The slight variations in brain function allowed a single individual to imagine what another human was thinking, and to use that image to predict the behavior of the other human.

Some other early hominid species did not develop this same brain function of mental imaging, and those species no longer exist.

In terms of evolutionary history, the physical development of the larynx, which promotes speech, came much later in time than the mental imaging function in the brain.

The ability of the larynx to promote speech communication seems to be an evolutionary by-product of the brain's earlier ability to imagine the behavior of another human.

In his book, Evolution of the Brain, (1991), John Eccles states that the language areas of the human brain are well defined and developed before birth. He describes the development of the language areas of the brain as a genetically coded process in which the neural connections are formed and encoded in the cell micro structure of the cerebral cortex.

This suggests that the image-interpreting function of language is a "hard-wired" feature of the brain's biological development that all humans share in common.

According to the hypothesis promoted by Harry Jerison, (Intelligence and Evolutionary Biology, 1988), expanding language capacity was the causal agent in for the three-fold increase in brain size beginning about 2.5 million years ago.

The greater language skills resulted from the evolutionary selection process, wherein the environment that the organism resides selects a function based upon survival success.

According to Professor Jerison's hypothesis, the greater language skills resulted from an individual's need to build mental models, not primarily as a means of promoting speech communication.

Leakey and Lewin (Origins Reconsidered: In Search of What Makes Us Human, 1992) suggest that it was the social environment of early primates that was the driving causal force in creating the need for greater mental imaging power in the brain.

"Working out the complex rules for primate life, and understanding where in the picture one fits, demands a lot of brain power," they state.

Individuals with greater imaging brain power had a slight edge in making social alliances and monitoring the social alliances of other individuals.

According to this idea promoted by Leakey and Lewin, the greater social skills led, in the early primate social structure, to greater reproductive success.

Following this hypothesis, the five million year evolutionary path of the brain's development included many different possible functions, many of which are associated with hunting and gathering food.

These hunting and gathering functions were refined by the natural selection process, and contributed to the human brain's acquisition of superior technical skills in planning, coordination of resources, and use of technology.

On top of, and in addition to, these superior technical brain skills, the evolutionary path selected the activity of brain imaging and prediction of behavior.

The survival success of cooperation in hunting, gathering, and building alliances, rewarded the variations in brain development of these imaging functions.

The imagination functions of the brain required some type of mental interpretation function, which modern humans now call "language skills."

However, the social behavior of cooperation was a random variation in many different types of behavior possibilities that could have been the pathway selected in nature.

The social imperative of cooperation slowly evolved into a set of cultural rules of conduct, of morals, and of ethical rules regarding the treatment of others in transactions and exchanges.

However, to re-emphasize the point made by Leakey and Lewin, nothing about this relationship between social cooperation and cultural rules is preordained or certain.

Eccles and Popper describe the cultural social effects on the brains' evolution.

Cooperation may provide better adaptation and greater survival success but as a behavior trait it is contingent upon cultural values that could easily turn out to be, and has on many occasions, turned out to be, something else in human history.

Popper and Eccles refer to "our civilization," as a specific set of cultural rules and moral values that inform the decisions of the brain, primarily in individualistic societies that are characterized as free will societies.

The social alliances in early hominid groups were not permanent, nor were the cultural rules of conduct and morals.

According to Eccles, in the most recent periods of evolution, both biological processes, consistent with Darwin's theory of selection, and cultural processes, after the development of language, were both influencing the future evolution of the brain.

As Eccles writes,

"It is the story of the cultural evolution of man, and I think it has to be put in perspective that way - that man developed as a result of two interacting but quite different evolutions. One is the biological evolution by the ordinary chance and necessity with mutations and survival on the terms of natural selection; and the second way is with his development of the thought processes leading to creativity in a wide range of cultural performance; artistic, literary, critical, scientific, technological and so on" (Evolution of the Brain: Creation of the Self, 1989).

Eccles emphasizes the cultural influences on the brain's ability to solve decisions in the presence of new, unexpected events.

Eccles writes,

"New ideas have a striking similarity to genetic mutations. In the operations of the creative imagination, when something original is conceived that has never before been expressed in any way…This is the operation of the creative imagination. It is the highest level of the human performance… is the self -conscious mind exploring into its own resources, the immense potentialities that are available to it."

In the evolutionary period, after the development of language, social collaboration and cooperation became stronger evolutionary forces than the earlier survival processes of the brain.

The earlier biological forces were limited by the materialistic-deterministic laws of science, while the cultural forces were unlimited in the brain's ability to imagine different futures.

As Eccles notes,

"On the other hand, with cultural evolution there is no such biological limitation. Its future [of cultural evolution] is tied to human creativity…Cultural evolution then takes over from biological evolution and soon becomes crucial in natural selection, not only because of the wealth of technological innovations, but also because of the creation and development of the values [social cultural values].

According to Leakey and Lewin, individual hominids were,

"...always looking to their own best interests, and to the interests of their closest relatives, individuals sometimes find it advantageous to break existing alliances and form new ones, perhaps even with previous rivals."

The dilemma of survival success in early hominid social groups was knowing when to obey existing social rules, and when to ignore them to gain individual advantage.

Knowing when to obey social rules involved the mental evolution of values, the two most important for social survival are trustworthiness and honesty

In their research on how cultural values affect the brain decision-making, Camerer, et al,. write,

"Another important piece of the (brain's neuronal) framework is the existence of multiple valuation systems, which are sometimes in agreement, but often in conflict. Based on a sizable body of animal nnd human behavioral evidence several groups have proposed the existence of three different types of valuation systems: a Pavlovian, a habitual, and a goal-directed (valuation system). (A Framework for Studying the Neurobiology of Value-based Decision Making Systems, Nature Reviews Neuroscience, 2008).

In the application of moral and cultural values to the theory of Beneficial Economics, the moral and cultural values that influence the brain are different in collectivist, totalitarian systems, than the cultural values in an individualistic civilization.

As pointed out by Douglas Sloan, the philosophical emergence of individualistic values is a very recent historical development, primarily arising in the period called the Enlightenment, the same era when deterministic scientific laws of empirical science were developed.

Sloan writes,

"The emerging sense of individual selfhood in the West during the past four hundred years must be taken into account in any adequate conception of wholeness, or any effort to recover wholeness. (of the brain's functions).The emergence of individuality has been closely associated with the rise of science, indeed the two seem to have emerged hand in hand, each reinforcing the other. The modern experience of being a separate individual self, different from other selves and standing outside of 'nature, capable of looking at nature as an uninvolved observer, seems to be quite different from the experience of earlier ages. In contrast to a modern sense of individuality, humans of earlier periods seem to have felt themselves much more an integral part of their surroundings, immersed in the community, often finding their true identity not in themselves but in the tribe or the nation." (Insight-Imagination: The Emancipation of Thought and the Modern World, 1983).

Sloan characterizes the interplay and exchange between routine brain decisions and higher level cognitive decisions as imagination and insight.

Sloan writes,

"Imagination is recognized as insight. Imagination can only be regained, however, when the Imagination is recognized as that fundamental capacity for Insight that is the source of all cognition and of all new meaning and knowledge. The Imagination is that capacity for the grasp of reality which, in Phenix's phrase, constitutes "the faithful uses of reason." Imagination is that participation of the whole person—in logical thinking, feeling, and willing—in the act of cognition. The Imagination places the human being in a context of intelligibility that spans the cleavage between subject and object, a context of meaning that includes both."

Sloan writes,

"In coming to know our own inner being in imagination, we develop the capacity to know the inner being of another person: and of nature. In knowing (our self-conscious selves) and nature through imaginative participation, we come to know other people…. In dealing with other people we grasp quite readily how important an awareness of our own inner life is in coming to know and understand them. The more highly developed our understanding of ourselves—the greater our awareness of our own inner life, our feelings, fears, self-deceptions, foibles, ideals, needs, and so forth—the larger our capacity to understand and enter into the reality of the other. Here, inner knowledge is clearly part and parcel of our knowing another."

The brain's mental process of insight-imagination is relevant for all social, political and market exchange between humans. In other words, insight-imagination is significant for both its application to market decisions, and to broader social and political relationships.

But, at the moment of a market decision, the images that are gated through to the decision include the brain's anticipation of how the economic decision will affect the welfare of other humans.

Calvin describes a cultural value as the mental property of the "virtual environment" one has created inside one's head, a set of initial conditions that one applies to new situations."

Each individual has a unique value system which is peculiar to that individual's process of sorting and selecting images. This unique value system, in conjunction with the individual's unique imaging skills, are the defining biological characteristic of the term "individual."

The propensity of any individual to obey social rules in any given exchange is determined by how strongly that individual adheres to the cultural values of mutual obligation and mutual reciprocity.

Some early hominid groups developed the cultural values of obligation and reciprocity more extensively than others, and in those groups one would expect to find a high propensity of following social rules.

As Eccles notes in his book,

"...the brain is built with the propensity for performance according to value systems, and the value system initially learned is that of the ambient culture."

In other words, the propensity to obey social rules is a function of both the individual's own internal value system, which is further reinforced by the cultural and moral values in the ambient culture.

Whether an individual will obey social rules is contingent upon on how strongly the ambient culture emphasizes the values of obligation and reciprocity in exchanges

The brain's market decision-making capacities, especially around risk-taking and uncertainty, flourish when operating within stable constitutional rules that permit broad freedom of action and thought.

In other words. the emergence of spontaneous social order, in the brain's cognitive neuronal functioning, is based upon the existence of institutional and cultural rules which allow for human free will.

Evolution does not start over from scratch. Evolution builds upon what already existed, and the older brain's evolutionary changes continue to exchange neuronal activity with the more recent evolutionary changes.

In the brain's most recent evolution, the capacity for both language and social cooperation was added to the brain's older cognitive neurological functions.

Given these recent additions to the brain, under one set of fair institutional and cultural rules, the brain's ability to collaborate and cooperate with other humans leads to the emergence of spontaneous beneficial social order.

Under other sets of unfair institutional and cultural rules, such as feudalism or monarchy, the older evolutionary changes in the brain dominate decision-making to create neuronal images of future social conflict and war with other humans, primarily over the distribution of income and political rights.

When social and political institutions align with the modern brain, cognitive neurological processes for handling uncertain conditions, or the appearance of new, unforeseen events, social cooperation and collaboration occurs voluntarily.

Under other institutional frameworks, especially in the original creation of social contracts or constitutions, voluntary allegiance of citizens to obey the rule of law is replaced by a Leviathan, that operates without any barriers to the emergence of a permanent authoritarian tyranny.

The difference between the two forms of social organization is roughly the difference between a top-down centralized police-state control society, patterned on cognitive processes in the old brain, and a bottoms-up participatory democratic society, patterned on the new brain, when human brains are free to imagine how best to obtain the futures that their brains are imagining.

In the application to American social history, in the mid 1830's, what the French sociologist Alexis deTocqueville observed was the large scale bottom-up social experiment of American participatory democracy of how citizens were self-organizing a voluntary society that allowed for the emergence of spontaneous beneficial social order. (Democracy in America, 1836).

The social order that deTocqueville observed occurred in a specific cultural, historical and institutional framework of the early American society, which had recently emerged from the British ruling class top-down social order.

The brain can only optimize its own behavior within the specific cultural and constitutional configuration of rules, in the immediate time period of making a decision.

A human trapped in the social order of North Korea, or China, would process cognitive neurological images of the future differently from the future being imagined by the American citizens during the 1830s.

The brain essentially transforms external legal constraints into internal cognitive models of the most optimal course of behavior, given the legal and economic constraints on decision-making, at the time of decision.

One configuration of cultural and constitutional rules enables the free will voluntary compliance to social rules, through complex information processing.

In that type of free will constitutional framework, the brain integrates the rational evaluation of the best course of action, with emotional resonance of the possible consequences of that action, and experience gained in knowledge diffusion and social learning.

What may be considered rational decision-making in North Korea would not be the same rational decision-making in the early American society because humans in North Korea do not possess the free will to imagine their own future destiny.

The link between voluntary compliance with social rules and the brain's cognitive information processing involves several key neurological mechanisms that evolved over thousands of years of evolution.

Evolution of the brain's prefrontal cortex allowed for higher order decision-making, and rational evaluation of the long-term consequences of the decision. This evolutionary function allowed early humans to make tools.

Evolution of the brain's neuronal imaging circuits created almost instantaneous evaluation of the best course of action, given the structure of rewards and pain associated with a possible course of behavior.

The instantaneous evaluation of images of neuronal synapses occurs as the neurons line up, through electrical frequency synchronization, which leads to convergence in neuronal pathways about the behavior that optimizes benefits, at that moment of decision.

And, in the most recent evolutionary history of the brain, the mental models of external social structure allowed for the ability of social collaboration and cooperation with other humans on the best course of action, given the existing social and institutional structure of society.

The recent evolution of internal models of the external reality allowed the human brain to develop the capacity for language, which is the template for collaboration with other humans.

The application of the Eccles-Popper micro neuronal evolutionary functions of the brain conflict with an alternative view of the laws of science, which generally originated in the mid-1700s, in the era called the Enlightenment.

This more deterministic relativity theory of the brain suggests that all neurological cognitive functions can be represented by the empirical laws of physical material science, which occur within the brain's neuronal processes.

For example, in the determinist philosophy of the brain, Wilder Penfield suggests that humans have no free will.

In Wilder's paradigm of the brain, the physical-chemical-electrical functions of the brain always lead to a predictable, pre-determined set of responses, which can be explained and predicted by the application of empirical scientific rules. (The Mystery of the Mind: A Critical Study of Consciousness and the Human Brain, 2015).

This same idea about the absence of free will is shared by John Searle, who argues that self-conscious behavior is a biological response, explained by the scientific laws of biology.

Searle does not deny the empirical reality of self-consciousness, but argues, instead, that the brain's consciousness of its self is exclusively a biological phenomenon.

Searle suggests that human decisions are ultimately the product of prior causes (neurological, physical, chemical) rather than freely chosen. (Intentionality: An Essay in the Philosophy of Mind, 1983).

Under the philosophy of Searle's strict determinism, the human brain's ability to make conscious choices is merely an illusion because the scientific explanation of free will is not based in the laws of material empirical science.

The brain's decisions, according to Searle, are predetermined by biological processes, past experiences, and environmental factors.

The best way to think about the brain, according to Searle, is to imagine that the brain functions just like a computer.

Searle writes,

"The best way to study thinking, or as they [referring to Eccles and Popper] prefer to call it, 'cognition' is to study computational symbol-manipulating programs, whether they are in computers or in brains. On this view, then, the task of cognitive science is to characterise the brain, not at the level of nerve cells, nor at the level of conscious mental states, but rather at the level of its functioning as an information processing system." (Minds, Brains, and Science, 1984.).

For Searle, the idea of a human brain being able to see the world from the eyes of another human is not based in the laws of material science.

He writes,

"Reality is the subjectivity of mental states. This subjectivity is marked by such facts as that I can feel my pains, and you can't [feel my pain]. I see the world from my point of view; you see it from your point of view. I am aware of myself and my internal mental states, as quite distinct from the selves and mental states of other people."

Searle and Wilder's deterministic view of the brain is limited because it does not incorporate the brain's ability to visualize the effect, in the market decision-making process, on the welfare of other humans.

Therefore, Wilder and Searle's philosophy of mechanical determinism of the brain's imagination-insight function does not fit into Prigogine's macro theoretical principles of spontaneous order that emerge from complex adaptive systems.

Markets represent social systems where conscious deliberation and individual choice-making about the individual's best course of action are based upon the presence of individual free will, which only occurs under a specific institutional framework of cultural and moral rules.

Macro market behavior emerges from countless individual human decisions, at the micro economic level of a transaction.

When all the individual human decisions are aggregated into social patterns of behavior, the quantum coherence of external beneficial emergent social order may be one possible outcome

The emergence of macro economic social order is contingent upon the micro level cultural rules in place, at the moment of a brain's economic decision.

In the absence of cultural rules that allow for human free will, individual voluntary compliance with constitutional laws, and the unwritten rule of law, would not be possible.

In contrast to Searle and Wilder, Karl Popper and John Eccles propose that there are two parts of the brain, one physical, as the brain itself, and the other part mental cognitive processes, which are not based in the laws of material science.

According to Popper and Eccles, there are two functions of the human brain: the physical brain is like a physical computer, and the mind is like the computer programmer who directs the computer to perform its functions. (The Self and Its Brain, 1985).

The difference between the two philosophical interpretations of the evolution of the human brain is that the materialist deterministic philosophers (Wilder and Searle), deny that non-material, or non-biological events, can occur naturally in the decision-making functions of the neuronal synapses of the brain.

In the more recent evolution of the brain, the images of the future incorporate both the brain's self-conscious awareness of the external world, and the other-directed-consciousness of other humans.

All the neurons in the brain that are active in creating images, in the period of pre-decision chaos, contain a small electrical charge, that vibrates, known as the neuron's electrical frequency.

In the seconds before a decision, the brain functions at the "edge of chaos" characterized as neuronal image dissipation.

At the moment of decision, the internal chaos of multiple images gives way to an internal trajectory towards internal brain coherence about the best course of action.

The brain's attainment of internal coherence to gate through a decision is based upon the neural electrical frequency synchronization from a state of neural chaos to neural internal order, when the brain first confronts a risky, or uncertain event.

In his research on brain neuronal process, "Neuronal Processing," Faisal Mohammed describes that the brain is both gating through frequencies of neuronal images, leading to a decision, and at the same time, rejecting other frequencies of neuronal images that do not support the moment of decision. (University of Jordan, 2025).

Mohammed provides a graphic describing both the frequency convergence of images leading to a decision and the rejection of images, which are not gated through to the moment of decision.

The brain's frequency processing of neuronal images leading to neuronal convergence, at the micro level, represents the same thing as Prigogine's spontaneous emergent order, at the macro level, where energy dissipation leads to spontaneous order in the external natural world.

Chapter 3. Diagram 1. Neural Circuits, From Faisal Mohammed.

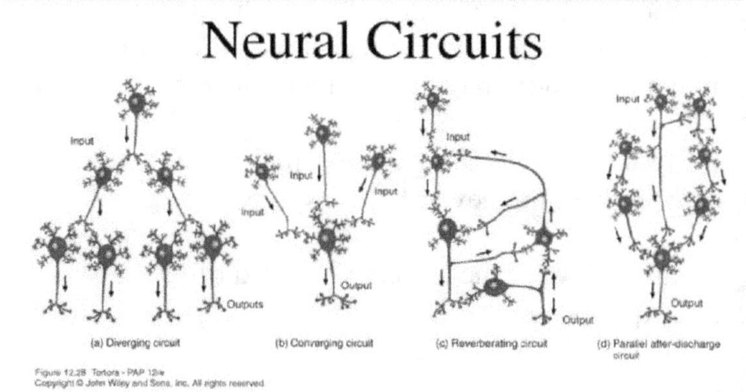

Image Credit: Faisal Mohammed, Power Point Presentation, 2025.

When making market decisions, particularly with visual information, the brain appears to transition from a state of chaos of multiple competing neural patterns, to a coherent, organized state representing the future outcome, as it may affect the decision maker, and the welfare of other humans affected by the decision.

The moment of a brain's market decision could be viewed as an electrical current phase transition, where neural activity shifts from exploring multiple options to focus on the best option, at the moment of decision.

This frequency phase transition can be interpreted as Prigogine's non-linear and sudden transition, similar to a bifurcation point in complex macro adaptive system.

Because evolution does not start from scratch, the older parts of the brain are communicating with the newer parts of the brain in processing hundreds of thousands of images, instantaneously.

At the moment of decision, in the most complex, risky, uncertain market decisions, the most recent evolutionary changes in the brain invoke the imagination and insight functions, which involve the self-conscious awareness of the effect of the decision on the brain, and an awareness of how that decision may affect other humans.

Mary Warnock, in Imagining (1978) also describes the interaction between the older brain and the newer brain as

"the mediating faculty between the 'objective' world of phenomena and our subjective experience."

Warnock writes,

"The [mental] images make possible our interpretations; for they are way in which we see and interpret the world and objects in world. The imagination, the image-making power of the mind therefore, shapes our everyday perception of the world, for it [the external world] is no perception separated from interpretation. The imagination lifts perceptions from raw, undifferentiated experience and gives them their shape, form, and significance. It is, therefore, imagination, that enables us [individual humans] to see the world as significant and as representing that which is not immediately present."

Norman Geschwind, (1965), suggests that the most recent evolutionary changes in the brain occurred in the middle space, between the lower brain and the pre-frontal cortex. Geschwind describes these areas as region 39 (also known as Brodmann's area 39), and 40, in the brain neurological terminology.

The diagram, below, indicates the mid-brain location of Area 39 and 40, just below area 4, which is consistent with how Warnock describes these areas as mediating the signals between the older brain and the newer evolutionary brain functions.

Chapter 3. Diagram 2. Location of Area 39 and Area 40 in Middle Part of Brain.

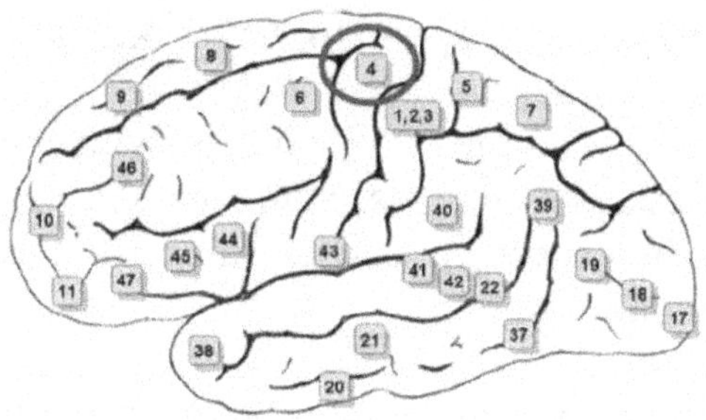

Image Credit: Anthony Wright, Higher Cortical Functions: Language, Neuro Science Onlline, 2025.

The role of Brodmann Area 39 and area 40 (the angular gyrus and supramarginal gyrus, respectively) enables human self-consciousness of a market decision, and the effect of the decision on other people's welfare.

This self-conscious awareness of a market decision are not the only functions Area 39 and 40 perform, but self-conscious awareness is significant in the context of market decision-making.

Brodmann Area 39 processes images related to language, spatial cognition of shapes and distance, and integrates external information from the five senses, into internal brain models.

Area 39 is important to market decision-making because it becomes active during self-conscious reflection and processing images of anticipating what other humans may do.

Area 40 interacts with the neuronal images of Area 39 in further processing sensations and imagining the consequences of future behavior.

The significance of Area 40 for market decision-making is the ability to interpret the beliefs and intentions of other humans, and to anticipate how other humans may respond to the market decision.

The neuronal interaction between the two regions is both convergent and divergent in the processing of images. Some market images are gated through for further processing, and some images are discarded, before the moment of decision.

This ability to interpret the intentions of other humans is critical in the brain's decision to extend the moral value of trust involving a market transaction.

The older brain regions process images involving immediate economic gratification and self-preservation, and in some decisions, those images from the older brain are processed through to the moment of decision.

The newer evolutionary parts of the brain enable the brain to imagine the consequences of longer-term planning, social cooperation, and the complex trust relationships that underpin functioning free markets.

In the application of Beneficial Economic theory, the older parts of the brain control behavior and image processing consistent with older forms of social control and hierarchical social class power relationships, such as those that exist in China, North Korea, or pre-revolutionary British America.

The more recent changes in Area 39 and 40, are more consistent with newer forms of participatory democratic societies because those areas are processing images that incorporate images for the free will social collaboration and cooperation, based upon voluntary obedience to the unwritten social rule of law.

Everyday market decision-making, like the decision to save money rather than spend, involve Area 39's abstract reasoning and Area 40's action planning of future scenarios.

At increasingly difficult, and risky economic decisions, like making an investment in a new technology venture, the image processing and interactions between the two brain areas intensifies.

Popper and Eccles propose 3 categories of the brain's image functions, based upon the evolutionary appearance of the brain's decision-making functions. (The Self and Its Brain, 1977).

Popper refers to the evolutionary appearance of the 3 categories as "worlds."

- World 1: Physical world of neurons, in the lower brain.
- World 2: Mental world of consciousness and subjective experience, in the pre-frontal cortex.
- World 3: Objective knowledge of cultural norms, and external institutional constraints on free will, in the mid-brain regions of Area 39 and 40.

Popper's 3 different levels of the brain's decision-making abilities reflect increasingly complex and abstract decisions.

These 3 levels are:

- Pavolvian decisions, based upon stimulus and response functions.
- Rule of thumb decisions based upon mental decision-making habits and memory of the consequences of past decisions.

- Future goal directed decisions which anticipate and imagine the future, and especially anticipation of the behavior of other humans.

Pavlovian decisions are formed in the lower areas of the brain, and are the most basic stimulus-response associations formed through classical conditioning.

Some observers of this part of the brain have called it the "fight or flight" response to emergency decisions about survival.

The rule-of-thumb/habit decisions in the pre-frontal cortex represent procedural learning where the brain develops shortcuts based on past experiences. These neuronal decision pathways become automated through repetition, but require more neuronal processing than less complex Pavlovian responses.

It is important to recall that all regions of the brain are in continuous communication with the other parts of the brain, just before the moment of decision.

The Pavlovian stimulus response is always present, as a neuronal process, even in rule-of-thumb decisions.

The spontaneous order that emerges in rule-of-thumb neuronal processing of every day market decisions are mental habits that reduce cognitive processing.

Buyers, for example, use visual signals, such as marketing brand images or radio brand jingles, that they have seen before, to gate through a rule of thumb market decision.

At the higher levels of World 3 abstract reasoning, the brain is confronted with a new, or unforeseen events, that cannot be resolved by recalling rule-of-thumb memory of past experience or past learning.

These World 3 high-level decisions involve complex brain simulations of future scenarios, to anticipate the consequences of the decision, and which incorporate anticipation of the behavior of other humans.

This World 3 neuronal processing requires integration across all the Pavlovian and pre-frontal cortex brain regions, which are primarily integrated and processed through to a decision in areas 39 and 40.

As described by Popper and Eccles, the higher levels of abstract complex decisions contain both feed-forward, and feed-back loops, that modify which neuronal images are gated through to neuronal convergence.

They write,

"We have to think of World 3 in two ways: that we are utilizing it in all of our civilized and skilled actions, the scientific, the artistic, the creative; and secondly we are also adding to it and therefore having a positive feedback to World 3, adding something to the great and wonderful storage of human creativity which we call World 3."

In the application of World 3 decision-making to the theory of Beneficial Economics, the sudden appearance of new, unexpected events, both in the minds of consumers, the first time they see a new product, or in the minds of technology entrepreneurs visualizing a new-to-the world product, the brain is constructing models of the future risk and reward s associated with the decision.

In the presence of an unexpected market event, World 2 is interacting with World 3 directly to perform the operation of creative imagination of the future.

The feed-forward images imagine the future, while the feed-back images are coded, or hard-wired, into the physical brain, as if the brain was a computer.

After the feed-back neuronal images of the future are hard-wired into the brain, the effects, following Prigogine, are irreversible. The prior shape of the brain has been changed, and decisions that were made in the prior period, will not be processed through as a rational decision, directed to a future goal.

According to Eccles, after the feed-back images of World 3 are hard-wired into the physical brain, the brain slightly changes it shape, due to neuronal plasticity.

Eccles' focus on the brain's neural plasticity supports dynamic decision-making processes consistent with Prigogine's systems of chaos that spontaneously emerge into order.

Eccles writes,

"It was as if the synapse [after a decision] 'remembered' its activation. Synapses at the lower level of the brain do not exhibit this long-term potentiation (LTP) as it was called…Learning is not just the remembrance of some initial intense stimulation. It is even more importantly the remembering of associated experiences." (Evolution of the Brain: Creation of the Self, 1989).

As Popper and Eccles conclude their 1977 book,

"Finally, we have come just now (circa mid 1970s) to recognize that, in the creative imagination, the self-conscious mind is actively engaged in the World 2-World 3 interchange in bringing about new, completely new, concepts or ideas or problems or proofs or theories. The creative imagination is being driven by the self-conscious mind into flights of imagination which of course are the greatest achievements of humanity. We can look back in the past and think of the great flights of imagination in all the creativeness of art and science and literature and philosophy and ethics, etc. That have made humanity what it is and given us our civilization."

Following the philosophy of Eccles, the evolution of the brain allows the mind to see the world from the perspective of the other person, which is the basis of social cooperation, in specific civilizations, primarily those based upon the moral values of trust and voluntary citizen compliance with the rule of law.

As David Eagleman writes, in The Brain: The Story of You,

"Our brains are primed for social interaction. After all, our survival depends on quick assessments of who is friend and who is foe. We navigate the social world by judging other people's intentions… The brain comes with inborn instincts to detect who's trustworthy, and who isn't." (2015).

Much of the mental cognitive ability to judge friend or foe is based upon the brain's visual interpretation of the messages emanating from the facial expressions of other people.

As Eagleman notes,

"From an evolutionary point of view, empathy, [interpreting the welfare of other humans] is a useful skill: by gaining a better grasp of what someone is feeling, it gives a better prediction about what they'll do next."

The implication of physical proximity, for the theory of Beneficial Economics, is that the moral value of trust and honesty in market exchange is based upon close proximity of the humans engaged in the exchange.

Neurologists and philosophers of knowledge describe this close proximity as the exchange of tacit knowledge, which is contrasted with the exchange of codified, or written knowledge.

Area 39 and 40, as applied to market decisions, are primarily based upon tacit knowledge exchange in interpreting the presence of trust and honesty involved with making a market decision.

For example, Karen Kreutz, a former marketing executive at Proctor and Gamble, describes how tacit knowledge exchange is used at Proctor and Gamble to create break-through-new-to-the world products. (Knowledge Creation For Breakthrough Innovation, Power Point Presentation, 2013).

Kreutz begins by contrasting tacit knowledge with codified knowledge, which she describes as "explicit" knowledge.
All knowledge, according to Kreutz, is based upon the brain's mental imaging processes.

She writes,

"Knowledge is information combined with experience, context and [mental] reflections that may be used to make decisions and take actions. its [knowledge] creation is a human act and for an individual it is the interpretation of the information based on their mental models." [areas 39 and 40].

Her emphasis on tacit knowledge exchange, at Proctor and Gamble, is based upon the brain's insight-imagination image processing of imagining the future.

She explains that, at Proctor and Gamble, breakthrough innovation requires tacit knowledge exchange at the highest level of cognitive neuronal image processing, in what would be described by Popper's World 3.

She writes,

"Tacit knowledge: lies beneath the surface of conscious thought and is derived from a lifetime of experience, practice, perception and learning, It is context specific, personal, hard to formalize and stored semi-consciously and consciously in peoples' heads. "

As she notes, the social collaboration and cooperation at Proctor and Gamble is "context specific."

She explains that Proctor and Gamble tries to create the internal corporate environment to allow employees to meet and exchange face-to-face tacit knowledge, in order to solve complex marketing issues.

She writes,

"The sharing of tacit knowledge is an extremely fragile process. The speed of tacit knowledge exchange depends on the degree to which the corporate social environment is collaborative."

The same mental process of tacit knowledge exchange at Proctor and Gamble's marketing departments applies to how a person's brain naturally creates social order through their everyday market decisions in the context of moral and cultural rules in the broader society.

In social and political environments where market exchanges are based upon the moral value of trust and honesty, beneficial social order may emerge from the brain's mental process of imagining the future.

The type of political and social environment required for beneficial social order to emerge means that insight-imagination must arise in what Joel Mokyr describes as a "sympathetic environment." (The Lever of Riches: Technological Creativity and Economic Progress, 1992).

Social cooperation arises between individuals when there is compatibility between the brain's natural biological search for truth, and society's emphasis on the values of mutual obligation and reciprocity in exchanges.

The brain's search for truth between the internal mental images it is sorting, and external images, is linked to the biological urge to control an individual's environment and destiny.

Social and cultural values can either reward or punish the individual's pursuit of sovereignty. Unlike genetic selection in Darwin's theory, the evolution of cultural and social cooperation is very much dependent and contingent upon human choice and human direction.

That mental value system is influenced by the ambient cultural value system, which can either support or deny the brain's quest for control over individual sovereignty.

J. L. Mackie, in his book, Ethics: Inventing Right and Wrong, suggests that the ambient culture influences ethical decisions made every day by individuals. Individuals are continually engaged, throughout their lives, in trying to answer the question: "What sort of person is it in my interest to be?"

According to Mackie, the answer is influenced by the ambient culture because the culture provides the context of the social good, or the public purpose. It is in one's interest, suggests Mackie, for individual behavior to be consistent with the social good.

In his book, Nature's Mind, Michael Gazzaniga, (1994), explores the connection between social values and the biological functions of the brain. He notes that the human need to control and influence the environment is one of the great motivations explaining human behavior.

He writes that,

"...the brain mechanism that allows for the "feeling of control" is one that has considerable survival power...Society must examine the social programs, policies and institutions that, although established to provide and care for us, actually minimize our influence over our environment."

For example, the type of social-political environment in North Korea would not be sympathetic to the emergence of beneficial social order because the humans in North Korea cannot answer Mackie's question of "What sort of person is it in my interest to be?".

A brain in North Korea processes cognitive neuronal images differently because: that society has:

- Different cultural symbols that hold different meanings and emotional associations,
- Different political systems that create different threat perceptions and reward benefits.
- Different social norms that establish different parameters for acceptable behavior.
- Different educational systems that prioritize different cognitive strategies and value frameworks.

However, if the ambient culture emphasizes the values of individual freedom and individual control over one's destiny, then what sort of person it is in one's interest to be is answered differently.

The emergent beneficial social order of Prigogine's theory are co-created through the interaction between the individual brain's neural mechanisms and social/cultural context of free will.

Prigogine's ideas about the emergence of spontaneous order in natural systems are consistent with Buchanan's constitutional economics and Adam Smith's market theory of the invisible hand leading to a stable social order.

When social and political institutions align with the modern brain's cognitive neurological processes for handling uncertain conditions, a person's everyday market decisions naturally create future beneficial social order.

The term "consent" also implies an on-going two-way agreement between those giving their consent, and the other party to the contract, those who agree to discharge obligations, in accordance with the initial grant of consent.

In other words, “consent of the governed” appears in the Declaration as expressing mutual obligations and duties to both parties to the contract.

We defined this mutual obligation as allegiance to obey the unwritten rule of law.

The way that Jefferson used the concept implies a certain type of social reciprocity based upon the duty to reciprocate equal liberty. Jefferson emphasized this reciprocity in his writings about the civil foundations of the new nation.

Jefferson wrote,

“What is here a right towards men, is a duty towards the Creator. It is the duty of every man to render to the Creator such homage and such only as he believes to be acceptable to him. This duty is precedent, both in order of time and in degree of obligation, to the claims of Civil Society.”

Rational individuals continue to obey social rules when they have mutual dependency on sharing benefits with other citizens.

Self-government, according to Jefferson, meant allowing citizens a sphere of sovereignty that could not be disrupted by the central government. Jefferson’s main principle of consent is that those bound most tightly by collective rules must be given the greatest say in the making and enforcing of the rules.

Jefferson stated this idea by writing,

“That which governs the best, governs the least.”

Chapter 4: Replacing Madison's Constitution of 1787 With A Better Economic Constitution.

The human brain naturally creates stable social order through everyday market choices when operating within institutional frameworks that are based upon the exercise of human free will.

The brain's decision-making neuronal functions operate in a specific moral or cultural environment and are profoundly influenced by external institutional structures and the ambient culture.

Technological innovation and the emergence of beneficial future markets only occur when the brain is free to imagine how best to obtain the future that the brain is imagining.

Traditional economic theory has a major flaw because the theory ignores the social and cultural rules of trust and honesty that govern how the human brain makes economic decisions.

Cultural and moral values, such as trust, honesty, and the legal frameworks for business contracts establish the basis for the brain's neurological cognitive decision making in anticipating the behavior of other humans, in a specific society.

Traditional economic theory begins by defining economics as a scarcity problem, which addresses the issue of how scarce resources are allocated among competing uses.

This initial definition about economics allows economists to use differential equations to solve the most efficient allocation of resources, when the second derivatives of their math equations all reach zero, at the same time.

In contrast to traditional economic theory, beneficial economic theory begins with the assumption that economics is about how the human brain makes market decisions in order to formulate strategies for maximizing an individual's welfare, in an uncertain future

The uncertain future is defined by uncertain economic conditions, as the economy evolves, and uncertain political and legal environments concerning whether other humans will obey the unwritten rule of law in honoring market transactions.

Traditional equilibrium theory does not address the fundamental uncertainty of the future because the variable of future uncertainty cannot be defined by linear math equations.

In other words, traditional theory cannot accommodate the institutional changes in the market that arise in uncertain future market environments, which means that traditional economics has a built-in bias towards maintaining the economic status quo.

The bias of traditional economic theory to the status quo extends to the status quo distribution of economic and political power in a given cultural setting.

For example, traditional equilibrium economic theory cannot explain the macro instability of the U. S. economy because the theory cannot incorporate a political/economic criticism of the social class status quo bias of Madison's unfair constitutional rules.

The economic professors and economic advisors who rely on traditional theory like to say that their science is "value-free," meaning that the conclusions of their math equations are value-neutral, and do not contain cultural value bias in favor of the American nobility status quo.

An important scholarly effort to address the defects in equilibrium theory occurred in the mid-1980s, with the creation of the Sante Fe Institute, in New Mexico.

In 1987, John Reed, then chairman of Citicorp and the New York Stock Exchange, funded the Santa Fe Institute think tank after becoming dissatisfied with the bank's conventional equilibrium

economic advisors who failed to predict the mid-1980's collapse, that damaged Citicorp's investments.
Reed funded the Institute's first seminar, "The Economy as an Evolving Adaptive System," led by Nobel laureates Phil Anderson and Kenneth Arrow.

Kenneth Arrow realized that traditional economic theory was defective because it was based upon an imaginary concept of a Keynesian grand social welfare function that economists attempt to maximize in making social and political decisions. (Social Choice and Individual Values, 1963).

Reed's seminar initiative was aimed at developing a new economic theory that could better explain and predict periodic economic collapse that was not based upon this concept of a grand social welfare function.

Queen Elizabeth asked this same question of her economic advisors, after the collapse of 2008,

"Why can't economists predict economic collapse?" asked the Queen. (W. Bryan Arthur, Complexity Economics: Why Does Economics Need This Different Approach? 2019).

Arthur hints at the hidden defect of equilibrium theory in his answer. "The reason [for the defect], I think is subtle," writes Arthur.

Arthur continues,

"If you assume equilibrium, which economists do, then by definition cascades of collapse cannot happen…Therefore, exploitive behavior can't happen. [under the value-neutral assumptions of economic equilibrium]. A subtle, muted, unconscious bias precludes ideas of exploitation or collapse."

In the example of Madison's constitutional rules, the periodic instability is caused by the unfair rules, which elevate the interests of a natural aristocracy over the financial interests of common citizens, in a system based upon social class control over the agencies of government and financial institutions.

The macro economic instability causes micro economic instability in the decision-making of citizens because their brains cannot predict how to accommodate the risk and uncertainty of the future economic path.

With a periodic economic collapse every ten years, the common citizens can never quite make progress on attaining economic prosperity.

Every time, they start saving up a little cash, the economy crashes again.

The social consequences of micro economic instability, in the brain's cognitive functions, decrease the citizen's level of allegiance to obey the unwritten American rule of law because the citizens can see that the rules do not apply equally to the ruling class, which insulates itself from the ensuing return to chaos.

A better, more realistic economic theory would include the concepts of social class exploitation and cultural rules, involving trust and honesty, as the framework for explaining how different market economies function under different constitutional rules.

While the Santa Fe Institute's new complex adaptive systems approach represents theoretical progress beyond static equilibrium models, it fails to address the institutional moral and cultural value framework of Madison's constitutional rules within which the U. S. market economy operates.

But, Arthur's application of Prigogine's complex adaptive theory has a gap in logic because under Madison's unfair constitutional rules, the natural organizing forces that Prigogine discovered for open systems are constantly disrupted in Madison's closed political system.

The U. S. economy can never reach the beneficial stability that Prigogine's complex systems theory predicts because Madison's rules are the cause of periodic economic chaos.

Every time the U. S. economic system tries to self-organize toward fairness, Madison's elite-protecting mechanisms kick in to prevent the emergence of stable social order.

Arthur's application of complex adaptive theory can describe the mechanics of complex economic systems, but cannot describe why the U. S. economy returns to chaos, every ten years.

A better economic theory, and a better economic constitution, would explain the future direction of the economy towards beneficial outcomes based upon fair moral and cultural rules that apply to all citizens.

Under fair constitutional rules, Prigogine's principles would allow individual brain decisions to naturally create the stable, beneficial economic order that serves everyone's interests.

We allege that economic theories do not cause economic collapse, the people who control the rules of the economy cause the collapse, and then those people use the "value-free rhetoric" to justify their exploitive behavior.

Explaining this periodic macro economic instability is not merely a failure of economic theory, but a direct consequence of Madison's constitutional rules that systematically channel wealth and opportunity towards established social class interests, through control over monetary policy, tax policy and national debt.

As Arthur notes above, "exploitive behavior can't happen," under equilibrium theory, and it cannot be explained in his new complex adaptive theory, either.

This oversight of the Sante Fe Institute mirrors a deeper historical issue embedded in Madison's 1787 document, which is not evident in Jefferson's document of 1776.

The two historical events, the one in 1776, and the one in 1787, are two distinct and separate events that have been conflated and combined by professional historians who write the history of the Nation, into a misleading term called, "the Founding."

The term "the Founding" is applied to another misleading historical term "the Founding Fathers," to convey the false impression that the people who wrote the Declaration, in 1776, and the people who wrote the constitution of 1787, are the same people, with the same cultural and moral values.

Rather than interpreting the two events as a consolidated single "founding," we agree with Michael Klarman, in his book. The Framers Coup, (2016), that the 39 elites who met in secret, in Philadelphia, to hammer out Madison's rules, constituted a Ruling Class coup to replace the Articles of Confederation.

Klarman wrote,

"Madison objected to the injustice of state legislation on creating paper money and debtor relief laws … Madison viewed society as two classes: creditors or debtors, rich or poor… Madison declared that the Senate ought to come from and represent the wealth of the nation. The Senate should serve as a bastion of privilege. Dickinson wanted the Senate to bear the likeness of the British House of Lords. Pinckney argued that, "only the wealthy would be able to afford to serve."…As Butler put it, "the great object of government was to protect property...the Senate would block any populist economic measures that might emanate from the House."

Madison said that the Senate needed to be a "check on the democracy. It cannot be made too strong."

As Sean Wilentz wrote about Madison's unfair rules, in The Rise of American Democracy: Jefferson to Lincoln, (2006),

"The people had no formal voice of their own in government. And, that was exactly how it was supposed to be – for once the electors [common citizens] had chosen their representatives, they ceded power, reserving none for themselves until the next election… [We]The people, as a political entity, existed only on election day."

Merrill Peterson, in The Jefferson Image in the American Mind, (1999), cited Madison's failure to establish individual liberty as the mission, or purpose of government, in his Preamble.

Peterson wrote:

"that Madison's division of powers,…became the chief means of checking the exaggeration of the democratic principle, and thus of securing an equilibrium of majority power and constitutional guarantees…"

Hamilton, in his 1780 letter to James Duane, [September 3, 1780], explains that the new government would obtain revenue from confiscating the land of farmers when the farmers failed to pay their taxes in gold or silver.

Hamilton writes:

"There are instances without number, where acts necessary for the general good, and which rise out of the powers given to Congress must interfere with the internal police of the states, and there are as many instances in which the particular states by arrangements of internal police can effectually though indirectly counteract the arrangements of Congress… The confederation too gives the power of the purse too intirely to the state legislatures. It should provide perpetual funds in the disposal of Congress—by a land tax, poll tax, or the like. All imposts upon commerce ought to be laid by Congress and appropriated to their use, for without certain revenues, a government can have no power; that power, which holds the purse strings absolutely, must rule. This seems to be a medium, which without making Congress altogether independent will tend to give reality to its authority… As to a tax in kind, the necessity of it results from this principle—that the money in circulation is not a sufficient representative of the productions of the country, and consequently no revenues raised from it as a medium can be a competent representative of that part of the products of the country, which it is bound to contribute to the support of the public. The public therefore to obtain its due or satisfy its just demands and its wants must call for a part of those products themselves."

In other words, what Hamilton means is that the police power of the state should be used to either confiscate the crops [the products themselves] or the land of the farmers, in order to provide perpetual funds to the government.

This type of unfair land confiscation of farmers was the cause of Shays Rebellion, in 1787, which led to Madison's phrase in the Preamble "to insure domestic tranquility."

This technique of elites obtaining farmer's land explains the huge accumulations of land by the natural aristocracy during the period of time after 1789, and the ensuing rampant asset speculation that continues to plague the operation of the U. S. financial system.

The same legal technique of confiscation of common farmer's lands worked well after the Civil War in the debt-lien system of debt peonage, when the plantation elite consolidated their holdings of land owned by the common farmers in the South.

Madison's rules of civil procedure were supplemented by Hamilton's banking and monetary system, based upon elite plunder and corruption.

During his dinner with Jefferson, in 1792, to discuss the chartering of the First National Bank, Hamilton candidly told Jefferson that Madison's system of government would not work without the essential ingredient of corruption and special interest plunder provided by Hamilton's banking system, modeled on the Bank of England.

Gordon Wood, in The Creation of the American Republic, cited Hamilton in Federalist # 35 on the logical justification of elite rule.

"What justified elite rule, together with the notion of virtual representation," [in the unelected Senate and Supreme Court] noted Wood,

"was Hamilton's sense that all parts of the society were of a piece, that all ranks and degrees were organically connected...the state was a cohesive organic entity with a single homogeneous interest in a chain in such a way that those on the top were necessarily involved in the welfare of those below them."

Madison's Constitution of 1787, for all its celebrated innovations, was modeled on the British social class conflict model of government, which elevated the power of the British nobility over the interests of the common British subjects.

Madison, in the Federalist Paper #10, says,

"The first object of government is the protection of "the diversity in the faculties of men, from which the rights of property originate." The chief business of government, from which, perforce, its essential nature must be derived, consists in the control and adjustment of conflicting economic interests. The regulation of these various and interfering interests forms the principal task of modern legislation, and involves the spirit of party and faction in the ordinary operations of the government."

Madison's term "diversity of faculties," means that a small set of virtuous elites should make collective decisions for all citizens because their brains are superior to common citizens in making social and political decisions.

Madison stated that his representative republic was based upon “the delegation of the government...to a small numbers of citizens, elected by the rest.”

Madison wrote that his system would work well, if,

“there was unequal access by those without power to adjudicate justice by making claims against those who had institutional power (natural aristocracy).

Madison over-weighted the authority of the natural aristocracy in his constitutional arrangement so that the elite could make collective decisions for the benefit of the entire society.

Madison provides his analysis of the cause of conflict between the two social classes.

Madison writes,

“The most common and durable source of factions [class interests] has been the various and unequal distribution of property. Those who hold [property] and those who are without property have ever formed distinct interests in society. Those who are creditors, and those who are debtors, fall under a like discrimination. A landed interest, a manufacturing interest, a mercantile interest, a moneyed interest, with many lesser interests grow up of necessity in civilized nations, and divide them into different classes actuated by different sentiments and views."

The difference between the two social class interests in America, at the time Madison was writing, was that the natural aristocracy had a coherent social class ideology, or as Marx would have described, a social class consciousness, that united them in writing their rules.

Madison’s logic in replacing the Articles of Confederation with the centralized authority of the new nation was based upon the obvious fact that state legislatures reflected the social class interests of farmers and common citizens.

Madison writes about the state legislatures,

"State Legislatures reflect these [common citizen] interests...What are the different classes of legislators but advocates and parties to the causes which they determine. There is no help for it. The causes of faction cannot be removed, [at the State level] and we well know that neither moral nor religious motives can be relied on as an adequate control."

Consequently, Madison concluded that the only way to remove the authority of the State legislatures was to eliminate their authority with a centralized, supreme authority.

The common citizens posed a potential danger to the ideological unified power of the natural aristocracy if the common citizens ever formed a coherent social class awareness of their own financial interests.

The potential threat of the majority of common citizens was well understood by the 39 elites at the Convention.

[From Madison's notes]

Charles Pinckney, [a slaveowner from South Carolina], did not oppose those wealthy [northern] merchants and professional men, many of whom were delegates to the Convention. His goal was to build a state in which these codependent class interests could be balanced toward a common, general interest and build a government "best suited" to this class structure.

Max Farrand explains that Pinckney also assumed that the as-yet-created American common citizen ideology would eventually replicate the social class structure of England, which would threaten the existing social class ideology of the ruling class especially the slaveocracy of the South. (The Records of the Federal Convention of 1787).

Pinckney is quoted, during the Convention,

“The United States is divided into three different classes: (1) professional men, (2) commercial: men, and (3) farmers, The landed interest, the [property] owners and cultivators [slave-owners], are the, and ought ever to be the governing spring in the system over the commercial class.

Pinckney said:

"If that commercial policy [favoring the landed interests] is pursued, conceive it to be the true one, the merchants of this Country [common citizens] will not for a considerable time have much weight in the political scale.”

Pierce Butler [a second delegate slaveowner from South Carolina] argued that basing representation on population size alone was faulty, and “He contended strenuously that property was the only just measure of representation. This was the great object of Govern't: the great cause of war, the great means of carrying it on.”

In other words, what Pinckney and Butler sought at the convention was a coalition of the American nobility, from both the South and North, to defeat the potential of a social class consciousness of common citizens.

According to Michael Klarman, in his book. The Framers Coup, (2016), paraphrasing Madison:

“they [the common citizens] will have their separate principles and "sentiments"; but the supreme danger will arise from the fusion of certain [social class] interests into an overbearing majority, which Madison, in another place, prophesied would be the landless proletariat, an overbearing majority which will make its "rights" [common citizen social class] paramount, and sacrifice the "rights" of the minority. [the American nobility]… The machinery for doing this is created by the new Constitution.”

George Mason, the delegate from Virginia, stated that the delegates were,

"appointed for the special purpose of revising and amending the federal constitution, so as to obtain and preserve the important objects [state sovereignty] for which it was instituted."
After Mason discovered the intent of Madison to overthrow the Articles, he refused to sign the finished document.

Rather than follow the constitutional process of amending the Articles, the federalists adopted a resolution for separate ratifying conventions to be held in each state.

The Federalist strategy for over throwing the Articles of Confederation consisted of 3 inter-related acts that the federalists implemented in re-creating the British social class conflict model of society.

- Strategy 1. Delegates to the convention exceeding authority of their instructions to amend the Articles of Confederation.
- Strategy 2. Adopting an illegitimate ratification process to "hurry the ratification through."
- Strategy 3. Disconnecting the constitution from the founding documents of 1776 and the Articles

Strategy 1. The delegates appointed to the Convention from each state exceeded their authority granted to them by their state legislatures to "fix" the Articles.

The delegates from Massachusetts were instructed by their legislature to "solely" amend the Articles of Confederation to "render the federal constitution adequate to the exigencies of government and the preservation of the union."

The Empire State's delegates were under the same instructions as those from Massachusetts. Several weeks into the Philadelphia convention, two of the New York delegates realized Madison's intent and left, leaving only Alexander Hamilton.

Hamilton was prohibited, by the instructions of his legislature, from casting any votes, without the other two delegates being present.

Instead of following his instructions, Hamilton signed the new constitution, on behalf of New York.

Hamilton later argued that he had not exceeded his authority, knowing in advance that he was lying.

In Federalist #78, Hamilton explained that the goal of creating a new constitution overrode his legislative authority to act without the presence of the other 2 New York delegates.

Hamilton's logic is that the urgent goals of overriding the Articles justified his means of signing Madison's document.

In other words, Hamilton argues in #78 that his signing of the finished document, on behalf of New York, according to Hamilton, would have been "void," under other less extreme goals.

Strategy 2. The 39 elites in Philadelphia adopted an illegitimate process to ratify the new constitution. Even though the delegates acted under the authority of the states, they never asked either Congress or the state legislatures to approve the proposed Constitution.

The contents of Articles XXII and XXIII were passed, in secret deliberations, as a separate formal act adopted unanimously as an official act of the Convention.

The resolutions stated,

"The ratification of the Conventions of nine States shall be sufficient for the establishment of this Constitution between the States so ratifying the same."

Their resolutions for ratification were placed in a separate document that was not attached to the main finished document submitted to Congress.

Congress subsequently sent those partial documents to each state, with no recommendations on how each state could proceed with calling the extra-legal ratifying conventions.

The resolutions did not contain safeguards on how the delegates in each state would be selected, resulting in special interest manipulation by the federalists to stack the conventions with supporters of Madison's arrangement.

In other words, the ratifying conventions did not derive their authority from "the consent of the governed."

As noted by Federal Farmer, who opposed Madison's constitution,

"Pennsylvania appointed principally those men who are esteemed aristocratical…Ten other states appointed men principally connected with commerce and the judicial department. In the nature of things, nine times in ten, men of elevated classes in the community only can be chosen—Connecticut, for instance, will have five representatives —not one man in a hundred of those who form the democratic branch in the state legislature, will on a fair computation, be one of the five—The people of this country, in one sense, may all be democratic; but if we make the proper distinction between the few men of wealth and abilities, and consider them, as we ought, as the natural aristocracy of the country, and the great body of the people, the middle and lower classes, as the democracy; this federal representative branch will have but very little democracy in it, even this small representation is not secured on proper principles. . ." (John, Kaminsky and Richard, Leffler, ed., Federalists and Antifederalists: The Debate Over the Ratification of the Constitution, 1998.).

Convention Delegate Morris disclosed that Madison's entire ratification process was designed to gain illegitimate approval in a procedure under the control of the elites, who appointed the delegates to the ratification conventions.

Madison argued that ratification by 13 state legislatures, as in the ratification of the Articles, was flawed because the Articles represented the authority of states over the constitution, while his ratification by conventions would be seen as ratification "over the whole body of the people."

Delegate King responded to Madison that the amendment not to seek ratification by state legislative approval was equivalent to giving up on a legitimate ratification process.

Delegate Martin responded to King by asserting that the ratification process would fail, unless common citizens were, "hurried into it by surprise."

[From Madison's notes]

Mr. L. MARTIN believed Mr. MORRIS to be right, that after a while the people would be against it; but for a different reason from that alleged. [government control by the elites]. He believed they would not ratify it, unless hurried into it by surprise.

[From Madison's notes, August 31].

Article 21, as amended, was then agreed to by all the States, Maryland excepted, and Mr. JENIFER being aye.

Article 22 was then taken up, to wit:

"This Constitution shall be laid before the United States in Congress assembled, for their approbation; and it is the opinion of this Convention that it should be afterwards submitted to a Convention chosen in each State, under the recommendation of its Legislature, in order to receive the ratification of such Convention."

Mr. GOUVERNEUR MORRIS and Mr. PINCKNEY moved to strike out the words, “for their approbation.” [removing the approval by Congress].

In the only actual vote of citizens in any state on the new constitution, the citizens of Rhode Island rejected the Constitution by a vote of 2,714 to 238.

In Pennsylvania, when the delegates to the ratifying convention learned of the fraud for ratification, they refused to attend, causing a lack of quorum.

The federalists in Pennsylvania sent out the secret police to restrain two delegates, against their will, and held them against their will at the convention, in order to preserve the subterfuge of a legitimate quorum.

The state’s rights leaders, like George Mason, called the ratification fraud of Madison’s nationalists exactly what it was.

Mason wrote,

“this outrageous violation employed all the arts of insinuation, and influence, to betray the people of the United States."

The citizens of North Carolina's, at their 1788 convention, refused to adopt the Constitution because it did not contain a citizen’s Bill of Rights.

While Madison and Hamilton argued in their Federalist Papers that no state was bound to obey the Constitution until its people gave their consent, the federalists coerced and subjugated the citizens of North Carolina, over a period of three years, to force the state to submit to the illegal authority of Madison’s constitution.

In the Virginia ratification convention, James Monroe cited the differences between the authentic British mixed social class system and the truncated American version of Madison's checks and balances.

Monroe wrote:

"The English constitution is based upon social orders which have a repellent quality which enabled it to preserve itself from being destroyed by the other. [social class]. The American division of power had no such basis and, indeed, no such intention. There are no real checks in the Constitution that would prevent a coalition of the branches of government and encroachments on the rights of the people."

As Madison admitted, in his 1792 essay, A Candid State of Parties,

"...some of the supporters of the Constitution openly or secretly attached to monarchy and aristocracy."

The Federalists had, according to Madison,

"debauched themselves into a persuasion that mankind are incapable of governing themselves, and believed that government can only be carried on by the pageantry of rank, the influence of money and emoluments, and the terror of military force."

Terry Bouton writes of the exchange during the Virginia ratification convention between James McHenry and Edmund Randolph, where McHenry describes the dangers of citizen democracy., (Taming Democracy: "The People," the Founders, and the Troubled Ending of the American Revolution, 2009),

"James McHenry noted about Randolph's message, that,

"our chief danger arises from the democratic parts of our [state's] constitutions. None of the [state] constitutions have provided sufficient checks against the democracy."

Bouton explains that in the period between the end of the Seven Years' War [1763] and the American Revolution, Pennsylvania farmers —those independent household and petty commodity producers —lived in a state of crisis. They owed taxes to the government and to private merchants, linked to the Atlantic trade system, that they could not afford to pay, especially given the scarcity of paper money, made worse by Britain's Currency Act, which prevented more colonial paper money from being printed."

The delegates to the state ratifying conventions derived their authority to ratify the new constitution from a grant of authority that they gave to themselves.

Strategy 3. Madison's intent to overthrow the Articles is evident in the way Madison disconnected the text of his new constitution from both the nation's founding document, The Declaration of Independence, and from the Articles of Confederation.

The American Declaration established the clear legal supremacy of the states. The States created the Union. The States created the Articles of Confederation. The States appointed the first members of Congress.

Madison knew when he left the Annapolis Convention in 1786, that he did not have legal constitutional authority to create a new constitution.

The five states that attended the Annapolis Convention had agreed to discuss fishing rights in rivers adjacent to their state borders.

Rather than discussing fishing rights, the delegates decided to call second convention to discuss modifications to the Articles of Confederation, which was the motive for Madison to attend the Annapolis Convention.

Madison began the work of drafting the Virginia Plan for the new constitution when he arrived home from the Annapolis Convention.

Madison was unwilling to admit that the Convention had broken with its instructions and performed a revolutionary act.

Madison drafted his legal and moral justification for overthrowing the Articles because the end goal justified the means of his strategy.

Charles Beard, wrote in, An Economic Interpretation of The Constitution of The United States, 1962),

“That Madison argued that the delegates were bound to make such revisions in the Articles as would render them adequate to the exigencies of the union; but an adequate government, he pleads, could not be made by revising the Articles, and the Convention was either compelled to sacrifice the greater [the creation of a new constitution] for the less [retaining the Articles] by strictly obeying its instructions or to do its whole duty by sacrificing the letter of the law.

Then, Madison clinches the argument:

"Let them [the opponents] declare whether it was of most importance to the happiness of the people of America that the Articles of Confederation should be disregarded and an adequate government be provided and the Union preserved; or that an adequate government should be omitted and the Articles of Confederation preserved."

In Madison’s logic, the elected representatives in state legislatures were engaged in an oppressive tyranny against the natural aristocracy by arbitrarily passing laws that allowed common citizens to pay their taxes in state-issued paper money, not in gold and silver, the preferred currency of the elites.

In Madison’s mind, the tyranny of the majority of common citizens in the states was so severe that the end goal of eliminating the Articles justified the means of creating his new constitution.

Madison correctly determined that the early American nobility's wealth and privilege, prior to 1775, had been a result of their social connections to the British nobility and to their relationship with the Bank of London to issue loans and issue money, to the nascent American nobility.

Charles Beard writes

"The state of society in England is much more favourable to such a scheme of government than that of America. There they have a powerful hereditary nobility, and real distinctions of rank and interests; but even there, for want of that perfect equality of power and distinction of interests in the three orders of government, they exist but in name; the only operative and efficient check upon the conduct of administration is the sense of the people at large. ...If the administrators of every government are actuated by views of private interest and ambition, how is the welfare and happiness of the community to be the result or such jarring adverse interests?" (An Economic Interpretation of The Constitution of The United States, 1962),

Madison's concept of the rules of government for the United States were designed to protect and perpetuate the interests of the American natural aristocracy, and to limit the political participation of the vast majority of the population, whom Alexander Hamilton called "the howling masses."

Madison wrote:

"The three principle classes. into which our citizens are divisible, were the landed, the commercial, & the manufacturing. The 3rd, class bears as yet a small proportion to the first. Their number however will daily increase. We see in the populous Countries in Europe what we shall be hereafter…in process of time, when we approximate to the kingdoms of Europe; when the number of landholders shall be comparatively small, through the various means of trade and manufactures, and not the landed interest be

overbalanced in future elections, and unless provided against, what will become of your government?
In England, if elections were open to all classes of people, the property of the landed proprietors would be insecure. An agrarian law would soon take place. If these observations be just, our government ought to secure the permanent threats of the country against innovation. [common citizens]. Landholders ought to have a share of the government to support these invaluable interests and to balance and check the other. They ought to be so constituted as to protect the minority of the population against the majority. The senate, therefore, ought to be this body; In order to answer these purposes, they ought to have permanency and stability. Those have been the propositions; but my opinion is, the longer they continue in in office, the better will these views be answered." (From Farrand Records, vol. 1, pp. 421-423.Italized text added).

The liberty Madison refers to is the liberty of the natural aristocracy not to have property rights infringed by the majority vote of common citizens in the new government.

The liberty of the American nobility that Madison sought to protect was the same social class liberty that the English nobility sought to protect in the Magna Carta, of 1215.

That earlier liberty was not extended to British subjects, but only extended to the English nobility.

"In order to lay a due foundation for that separate and distinct exercise of the different powers of government," wrote Madison,

"The (geographical) extent of the country and number of people comprehended under the same government so that the society itself will be broken into so many parts interests and classes of citizens that the rights of the individuals or of the minority will be in little danger from interested combinations or the majority."

The vaunted and much discussed “extended republic,” was not designed to bring more common citizens into the government. It was designed by Madison to prevent common citizens from ever forming a social class ideology, like the common citizens in England, by breaking up those interests from forming a combination of the majority of voters.

Madison’s goal was to prevent the "tyrannical concentration of all the powers of government” in the elected hands in the House of Representatives.

In Federalist #68, Madison writes,

“unless these departments be so far connected and blended, as to give to each a constitutional control over the others, the degree of separation...essential to a free government can never in practice be duly maintained.”

As Madison wrote in Federalist #48,

“It is agreed on all sides, [federalists and anti-federalists] that the powers properly belonging to one of the departments, ought not to be directly and compleatly administered by either of the other departments. It is equally evident, that neither of them ought to possess directly or indirectly, an overruling influence over the others in the administration of their respective powers."

As Madison wrote in Federalist #51,

"the great security against a gradual concentration of the several powers in the same department, consists in giving to those who administer each department, [the elites] the necessary constitutional means, and personal motives, to resist encroachments of the others… which to a certain extent is admitted on all hands to be essential to the preservation of liberty. It is evident that each department should have a will of its own...”

Delegate John Dickinson, for example, stated at the Constitutional Convention, that he,

“wished the Senate to consist of the most distinguished characters, distinguished for their rank in life and their weight of property, and bearing as strong a likeness to the British House of Lords as possible; and he thought such characters more likely to be selected by the State Legislatures, than in any other mode.” (James Parisot, Capitalism and the Creation of the U.S. Constitution, 2023).

Thomas Paine stated,

“The US Constitution of 1787 is an ill-advised attempt to replicate the British form of mixed constitution...their basis for justice becomes the balancing of particular class interests….they make it difficult for citizens to participate.”

When Nathan Dane, the representative from Massachusetts departed from the Convention, he stated,

"Madison’s constitution appears to be intended as an entire system in itself, and not as any part of, or alteration in the Articles of Confederation" the Congress was powerless to take any action thereon.”

Elbridge Gerry, from Massachusetts, speaking about Madison’s Virginia resolution to establish a new centralized national government stated,

"The commission from Massachusetts empowers the deputies to proceed agreeably to the recommendation of Congress. This is the foundation of the convention. If we have a right to pass this resolution we have a right to annihilate the confederation.”

Shlomo Slonim quotes Gouverneur Morris, an aristocrat delegate from New York, who strangely represented Pennsylvania, as almost giddy at the thought of the natural aristocracy oppressing the common citizens.

“The Rich will strive to establish their dominion and enslave the rest. They always did. They always will. The proper security agst. them is to form them into a separate interest. The two forces will then controul each other. Let the rich mix with the poor and in a Commercial Country, they will establish an Oligarchy.. . By thus combining & setting, apart, the aristocratic interest, the popular interest will be combined agst. it. There will be a mutual check and mutual security [for the ruling class]. (Shlomo Slonim, Framers' Construction/Beardian Deconstruction: Essays on the Constitutional Design of 1787, 2001).

As described by Robert Horwitz, in The Moral Foundations of the American Republic, (1986), Madison thought that, if the farmers and working class had the same moral values, which Madison called “virtue,” that the rigid separation of powers in the constitution would not be necessary.

Horowitz wrote that Madison thought that,

“If all citizens (working class) have the same impulse of passion and interest (of plundering the system) they would not divide into oppressive and dangerous factions... if (working class) Americans can be made to divide themselves according to their narrow economic interests they will avoid the fatal factionalism.”

As Madison noted,

“the central function of the legal system is to protect autonomous individuals (elites) from the "tyranny of the majority" (working class).”

The 38 Framers who signed the document, (one of the 39 delegates was sick that day so his friend, Elbridge Gerry, signed for him), were predominantly wealthy landowners, slaveholders, merchants, and creditors, who crafted a constitutional system that institutionalized economic advantages for their social class.

Just prior to the vote to approve Madison's Constitution, on September 15, 1787, Madison inserted the language and sanctions against free states that refused to return escaped slaves to their owners.

There was no discussion and no debate about the fugitive slave clause, before the final vote was taken. The other delegates had never seen this text.

From Madison's notes, September 15.

Took up Article IV, Section 2 (Fugitive Slave clause): Struck out "no person legally held to service or labor in one state escaping into another" and replaced it with "no person held to service or labor in one state, under the laws thereof, escaping."

On the issue of the authority of the President, Madison slipped in the final text just before the final vote on September 17, 1787.

The entire body of delegates had not reached agreement on the powers of the Presidency, or what title to give to the office of the President.

The Committee on Style, appointed 3 days before the Convention ended, never released the final clauses of Article II, on the Presidency to the delegates, before they voted on them, on September 17, 1787.

On the last day of the Convention, George Mason wrote,

"We are not indeed constituting a British Government, but a more dangerous monarchy, an elective one."

The misrepresentation of Madison's intent of creating a new constitution is obvious in the opening text of the Preamble, that declares that it was crafted by "We, the people," presenting it as a universal framework for liberty, as if it was written by "We, the people."

Madison argued that the Articles of Confederation had been created by the 13 states, while this new constitution was created by the collective will of "We, the People."

Madison wrote,

"Should all the states adopt it, it will be then a government established by the thirteen states of America, not through the intervention of the legislatures, but by the people at large. In this particular respect the distinction between the existing [Articles of Confederation] and the [Madison's] proposed governments is very material. The existing system (The Articles), has been derived from the dependent derivative authority of the legislatures of the states; whereas, this is derived from the superior power of the people."

As Madison had done with slipping the Fugitive Slave Clause into the document the night before the vote, on September 17, 1787, Madison also replaced the earlier version of the Preamble with his own version of the Preamble about "We, the people."

Prior to the night of September 16, 1787, the delegates had imagined that the rules they would be voting on the next day would contain the previous Preamble amending the Articles' constitutional rules for 13 independent states.

The Preamble text that they had seen before, in August of 1787, referenced the people of each state, which would have been consistent with King George's transfer of sovereignty, to the 13 states, in The Treaty of Paris, of 1783.

King George recognized the Thirteen Colonies, which had been part of colonial British America, to be 13 free, sovereign and independent states.

According to the analysis of James Parisot, Madison's deception in replacing the prior Preamble, based upon rules for 13 states, with rules to govern all citizens was, because,

"The interests of the [American] elite [in the Preamble] would be presented as the universal interests of all social classes, under which consent for class domination could be forged, backed by military force and violence, if necessary…As the [1787] Convention proceeded, then, the question underlying some of the issues at hand was how to build a state that would support the interests of merchants, speculators, and capitalists in a way that brought the lower and middling classes into the system but limited their power as so they could not challenge the power of the financial and merchant elite." (Capitalism and the Creation of the U.S. Constitution, 2023).

Thomas Paine accurately described Madison's Preamble as a "nominal nothing," because it did not state the ultimate purpose or goal of the constitution, but only described rules of civil procedure, as if the ultimate goals had already been set.

Paine explained that when Madison and Hamilton said in their Federalist Papers, that the central government needed more energy, "what they want is energy over the citizens."

Madison's defect of not explicitly stating the ultimate goal of the constitution has continued to plague the purpose, or mission, of the government, as pointed out above, by Kenneth Arrow, in his "impossibility theorem." (Social Choice and Individual Values, 1963).

Arrow denies the existence of a grand social welfare function that government elites attempt to maximize through their manipulation of interest rates and national debt.

According to Arrow, the reason for the periodic cycle of boom-bust economic behavior of the U. S. economy is, that in the absence of an explicit ultimate constitutional goal, the economy continually recycles or repeats the chaos of the earlier period.

Arrow's "impossibility theorem" of endless cycles of economic chaos is consistent with the macro economic analysis of Prigogine's theory of complex adaptive systems.

In Prigogine's theory, a natural chemical or material state will not emerge into a natural order under the conditions of entropy, a measure of the disorder or randomness, in a closed system.

Applied to Madison's constitution, the rules of the American government constituted a "closed political system," where only the American nobility made collective decisions.

In other words, Madison's Preamble sets the foundation for the re-establishment of economic chaos, from which the beneficial market economy can never emerge, through individual voluntary market decisions.

In today's American judicial context, the absence of a goal statement in the Preamble makes the strict construction judicial interpretation of the Constitution "impossible."

Peter H. Aranson, of the Cato Institute, explains that there are two valid interpretations of the Constitution in every Supreme Court decision. (Procedural and Substantive Constitutional Protection of Economic Liberties, 1987).

One interpretation was favored by Justice Scalia, as strict construction of what the writers meant, at the time they wrote the Constitution.

The second interpretation, as described by Aranson, is "noninterpretive."

Aronson writes,

"Noninterpretivists, by contrast, regard the Constitution's "open texture" as an invitation to discover "fundamental values" emanating from the document. They take this perspective not merely to fill in the interstices that its [constitution] passages leave empty, but to go beyond the text's plain meaning, sometimes extending to "penumbras formed by emanations from" the "specific guarantees in the Bill of Rights."

The two interpretations of the Constitution are both valid because Madison failed to state the goal of the Constitution in his Preamble.

Therefore, there is no single best interpretation of the rule of law in American jurisprudence. The law is whatever 5 justices agree that the law is, on the day they make their decisions.

In other words, Madison's rules became an effective instrument of control over common citizens precisely because the rules, once adopted, grant the Supreme Court arbitrary power to decide what the rules are, given the ideological bias of the Justices.

The arbitrary decisions of the Supreme Court create cognitive dissonance in the minds of common citizens in making market decisions because the citizens can never be certain what the rule of law may mean in the future.

Charles Beard explains that the wealthy citizens, in 1787, saw a way to use the supremacy of the Supreme Court to use government debt in an investment scheme still in practice today.

"But by creating a national legal system essentially standing above all, presented as unbiased or legitimate, the extent to which the entire legal structure would be structurally designed to support certain powerful class interests above others would not be questioned."

What Beard meant by his phrase, "would not be questioned," was explained by Delegate James Wilson, who noted that after the Supreme Court became the supreme law of the land, it would not matter if the laws were unfair or unjust.

Wilson stated,

"Laws may be unjust, may be unwise, may be dangerous, may be destructive; and yet not be so unconstitutional as to justify the Judges in refusing to give them effect. But with regard to every law, however unjust, oppressive or pernicious, which did not come plainly under this description, they would be under the necessity as judges to give it a free course."

Beard continues in his analysis of the social class conflict model of government in Madison's constitution.

"The concept of the Constitution as a piece of abstract legislation reflecting no group interests and recognizing no economic antagonisms is entirely false. It was an economic document drawn with superb skill by men whose property interests were immediately at stake; and as such it appealed directly and unerringly to identical interests in the country at large. It supports the conclusion that in the main the men who favoured the Constitution were affiliated with certain types of property and economic interest, and the men who opposed it were affiliated with other types."

In a letter to Jefferson, written in October, 1787, after the convention had ended, Madison elaborates the principle of federal judicial control over state legislation, and explains the importance of the U. S. Supreme Court, in connection with the restrictions laid down in the Constitution on laws affecting property rights.

"The mutability of the laws of the States," Madison states,

"is found to be a serious evil. The injustice of them [on the American nobility] has been so frequent and so flagrant as to alarm the most steadfast friends of Republicanism. I am persuaded I do not err in saying that the evils issuing from these sources [state courts] contributed more to that uneasiness [Shays' Rebellion] which produced the Convention, and prepared the public mind for a general reform, than those which accrued to our national character and interest from the inadequacy of the Confederation to its immediate objects. A reform, therefore, which does not make provision for private rights [at the federal judicial level] must be materially defective."

In other words, according to Madison, it was not exclusively the defects of the Articles of Confederation that precipitated the need for a new constitution, but the power of state courts and state legislatures to grant debt relief to farmers and common citizens who owed money to the American nobility.

Having dealt with the ratification method, on the last day of the Convention, the delegates then addressed the issue of how to handle the evidence of the notes taken by Madison, and other official minutes of their deliberations.

Madison had taken notes throughout the convention, and the delegates were concerned that Madison's notes not be made public, or else the citizens may not approve of the constitution.

[From Madison's notes, September 17, the last day of the Convention].

Mr. KING suggested that the Journals of the Convention should be either destroyed, or deposited in the custody of the President. He thought, if suffered to be made public, [the secret deliberations] a bad use would be made of them by those who would wish to prevent the adoption of the Constitution.

Mr. WILSON preferred the second expedient. He had at one time liked the first best; but as false suggestions may be propagated, it should not be made impossible to contradict them.

A question was then put on depositing the Journals, and other papers of the Convention, in the hands of the President; [George Washington] on which, — New Hampshire, Massachusetts, Connecticut, New Jersey, Pennsylvania, Delaware, Virginia, North Carolina, South Carolina, Georgia, aye, — 10; Maryland, 4 no, — 1.

As a historical aside on the treatment of Madison's convention notes, Madison kept the notes secret under his personal control, until he died in 1836.

His notes were released, by his estate, in a limited public offering, in 1839.

Max Farrand, in The Records of the Federal Convention of 1787, pieced together the private records of the delegates, and published his 3 volumes, in 1911.

In other words, common citizens in the U. S. were not aware of the proceedings of the convention for 125 years.

By that time, the myth of the goodness and benefits of Madison's constitutional rules had been well established by the professional historians and economists who write the history of the Nation. (James Madison and Marvin Meyers, The Mind of the Founder: Sources of the Political Thought of James Madison, 1981).

As Thorstein Veblen observed, Madison's constitutional rules created financial and market institutions that foster "conspicuous consumption" and "pecuniary emulation" among the leisure class. (The Theory of the Leisure Class,1899).

In addition to limiting political participation of common citizens in government, Madison's unfair rules established barriers to upward social mobility for the majority of working and middle class citizens.

The periodic economic collapse serves two related functions for the elite.

First, the elite are able to buy up assets at a cheap price when the market crashes, and hold on to sell at a higher price, when the economy regains strength.

For example, in February, 1788, Franklin wrote concerning the public indebtedness:

"Such Certificates are low in Value at present, but we hope and believe they will mend, when our new Constitution of Government is established. I lent the old Congress £3000 hard money in Value, and took Certificates promising interest at 6 per cent, but I have received no Interest for several years, and if I were now to sell the principal, I could not get more than 3s 4d for the Pound which is but a sixth part."

The investment scheme described by Franklin was to buy for pennies on the dollar, the government certificates from the American Revolutionary soldiers who had been paid in government notes, and after the new government was established, have the government redeem the certificates at full face value, including the 6% interest."

In other words, Franklin described the first government bailout of wealthy citizens, which is why Hamilton called the national debt a "blessing" because it would bind the allegiance of the elite to preserving the new government to conduct future bailouts.

George Mason, a delegate from Virginia, saw right through this government bailout scheme during the convention. (George Mason's America, 2023).

Mason made his arguments against the Constitution in the context of the interest and principle repayments of the Revolutionary War debt.

"Will it not be the duty of the Federal Court to say," said Mason, "that such state laws [against debt relief] are prohibited? This goes to the destruction and annihilation of all the citizens of the United States, to enrich a few."

Mason correctly perceived that Madison' rules on separation of power really were not a separation of power because it elevated the Federal judges above the Executive and Legislative branches.

Second, the periodic collapse serves to discipline the common wage earners, who never quite obtain financial stability before the next crash occurs. By spreading the factions across the national geography, the common citizens were never able to form a social class consciousness of their common financial interests.

For common citizens, the next crash is equivalent to a return to the state of chaos, from which the wage earners can never escape.

When citizens do not have freedom to pursue the future that their brain is imagining, the citizens no longer have voluntary allegiance to obey the rule of law, under an unfair constitution.

Many opponents of Madison's constitution attempted to explain to the public the dangers of placing centralized authority into the hands of the American nobility during the illegitimate and truncated ratification process.

The convention ended on September 17, 1787.

By December 18, 1787, 3 states out of the required 9 states had already ratified the document. Six months later, in June 1788, 6 other states had rushed through the ratification process.

Centinel, an opponent, explained how the ruling class elite had engaged in secret manipulation of the ratification process to rig the vote.

Kaminsky and Leffler (1998), cite the article by Centinel about the secret political work by the natural aristocracy to overthrow the Articles of Confederation.

Centinel writes,

"In many of the states, particularly in this and the northern states, there are aristocratic junto's of the well-born few, who had been zealously endeavouring since the establishment of their [state] constitutions, to humble that offensive upstart, equal liberty; but all their efforts were un-availing, the ill-bred churl [common citizens] obstinately kept his assumed station… A comparison of the authority under which the convention acted, and their form of government will show that they have despised their delegated power, [to amend the Articles of Confederation] and assumed sovereignty; that they have entirely annihilated the old confederation, and the particular governments of the several states, and instead thereof have established one general government that is to pervade the union; constituted on the most unequal principles, destitute of accountability to its constituents, and as despotic in its nature, as the Venetian aristocracy; a government that will give full scope to the magnificent designs of the well-born; a government where tyranny May glut its vengeance on the low-born, unchecked by an odious bill of rights: as has been fully illustrated in my two preceding numbers… The wealthy and ambitious, who in every community think they have a right to lord it over their fellow creatures have availed themselves very successfully of this favourable disposition; for the people thus unsettled in their sentiments have been prepared to accede to any extreme of government. All the distresses and difficulties they experience, proceeding from various causes, have been ascribed to the impotency of the present confederation, and thence they have been led to expect full relief from the adoption of the proposed system of government ; and in the other event immediately ruin and annihilation as a nation."

In one of his letters, Centinel asks how the opinions of common citizens are translated into government policy in the proposed natural aristocracy.

"If the people are sovereign how does the opinion of citizens direct the policies of government? There is nothing in the Federalist constitution, like the detailed definition of consent in the various state constitutions."

In his book, The Articles of Confederation, Merrill Jensen answers Centinel's question.

"The Federalists adopted a theory of the sovereignty of the people in the name of the people, erected a nationalistic government whose purpose was to thwart the will of the people in whose name they act."

George Mason steadfastly refused to sign the document, which ruptured his personal relationship with George Washington. (Laurie Thomas Vass, George Mason's America: The State Sovereignty Alternative to Madison's Centralized American Ruling Class Aristocracy, 2023).

In The Antifederalists: Men of Great Faith and Forbearance, David J. Siemers, summarizes Mason's arguments against ratification.

Siemers noted that on September 15, 1787, the last day of formal debate at the convention, Mason stated,

"The plan of amendments is exceptionable and dangerous. As the proposing of amendments in both modes to depend in the first immediately and in the second ultimately on Congress, no amendments of the proper kind would ever be obtained by the people, if the Government should become oppressive, as he verily believed would be the case."

Mason wrote,

"Inherent rights" to which all men are born include the enjoyment of life and liberty, with the means of acquiring and possessing property, and pursuing and obtaining happiness and safety."

Mason correctly perceived that Madison' rules on separation of power really were not a separation of power because it elevated the Federal judges above the Executive and Legislative branches.

Mason repeatedly warned the other delegates that Madison's rules would lead to centralized elite tyranny.

As described from Madison's notes:

Mr. RANDOLPH. We have in some revolutions of this plan made a bold stroke for Monarchy. We are now doing the same for an aristocracy. He dwelt on the tendency of such an influence in the Senate over the election of the President in addition to its other powers, to convert that body into a real & dangerous Aristocracy.

Col: MASON. As the mode of appointment is now regulated, he could not forbear expressing his opinion that it is utterly inadmissible. He would prefer the Government of Prussia to one which will put all power into the hands of seven or eight men, and fix an Aristocracy worse than absolute monarchy. The words "and of their giving their votes" being inserted on motion for that purpose, after the words "The Legislature may determine the time of chusing and assembling the electors."

Philanthropos, another opponent of Madison's document, argued that there was nothing seriously wrong with the Articles of Confederation that Madison could not have easily fixed at the convention in Philadelphia.

"Our present constitution, (the Articles), with a few additional powers to Congress, seems better calculated to preserve the rights and defend the liberties of our citizens, than the one proposed, (by Madison), without proper amendments. Let us therefore, for once, show our judgment and solidity by continuing it, (the Articles), and prove the opinion to be erroneous, that levity and fickleness are not only the foibles of our tempers, but the reigning principles in these states."

Philanthropos correctly predicted that Madison's compromises on slavery would cause a civil war.

He wrote that Madison's constitution would allow,

"the people to be fleeced, and the public business neglected. From despotism and tyranny good Lord deliver us."

Federal Farmer's insights into the coherent social class ideology of the natural aristocracy documents Madison's intent to overthrow the Articles.

Federal Farmer wrote,

"In my idea of our natural aristocracy in the United States, I include about four or five thousand men; and among these I reckon those who have been placed in the offices of governors, of members of Congress, and state senators generally, in the principal officers of Congress, of the army and militia, the superior judges, the most eminent professional men, &c. and men of large property*—the other. persons and orders in the community form the natural democracy; this includes in general the yeomanry, the subordinate officers, civil and military, the fishermen, mechanics and traders, many of the merchants and professional men. It is easy to perceive that men of these two classes, the aristocratical, and democratical, with views equally honest, have sentiments widely different, especially respecting public and private expences, salaries, taxes, &c. Men of the first class associate more extensively, have a high sense of honor, possess abilities, ambition, and general knowledge: men of the second class are not so much used to combining great objects; they possess less ambition, and a larger share of honesty: their dependence is principally on middling and small estates, industrious pursuits, and hard labour, while that of the former is principally on the emoluments of large estates, and of the chief offices of government. Not only the efforts of these two great parties are to be balanced, but other interests and parties also, which do not always oppress each other merely for want of power, and for fear of the consequences; though they, in fact, mutually depend on each other; yet such are their general views, that the merchants alone would never fail to make laws favourable to themselves and oppressive to the farmers, &c. the farmers alone would act on like principles; the former would tax the land, the latter, the trade. The manufacturers are often disposed to contend for monopolies, buyers make every exertion to lower prices, and sellers to raise them; men who live by fees and salaries endeavour to raise them, and the part of the people who pay them, endeavour to lower them; the public creditors to augment the taxes, and the people at large to lessen them."

Melancton Smith, another natural rights delegate to the convention, wrote that,

"The Constitution is radically defective. It vests in Congress "great and uncountroulable powers" that it will use "to annihilate all the state governments, and reduce this country to one single government."

Smith warned that instead of creating a balance of power, Madison's constitution would combine legislative power with judicial power that would eventually destroy the local governments.

He stated that the Supreme Court would interpret the Constitution according to the justices', "spirit and reason, and they would mold the government into any shape they please."

As noted by Brutus, a natural rights proponent, during the ratification debates,

"The framers of this constitution appear to have followed that of the British, in rendering the judges independent, by granting them their offices during good behaviour, without following the constitution of England, in instituting a tribunal in which their errors may be corrected; [by the King] and without adverting to this, that the judicial under this system have a power which is above the legislative, and which indeed transcends any power before given to a judicial by any free government under heaven."

Brutus reiterated this sentiment. He wrote,

"The costs of [legal representation] in the supreme court will be so great, as to put it out of the reach of the poor and middling class of citizens to contest a suit in it."

Madison's constitutional framework established economic rules that benefit what Veblen would call the "vested interests," or what James Buchanan calls crony capitalism. (James Buchanan and Gordon Tullock, The Calculus of Consent,1999).

The crony capitalist fusion of corporate and state power, under Madison's framework, allows the American nobility the unchecked political and financial power to:

1. Manipulate prices outside of market forces.
2. Extract wealth through financial manipulation of money supply and interest rates and through crony political mechanisms.
3. Use the regulatory police state powers to capture agencies in order to maintain their privileged positions.
4. Leverage technology and data control as new forms of unchecked power in the emerging world of artificial intelligence and human-like robots.

A better, more fair, constitutional system would limit the government's authority to what Buchanan calls the "protective and productive" state. (James Buchanan, The Limits of Liberty, 1975). Under Buchanan's fair constitutional rules, a better economic constitution would:

1. Protect property rights and enforce contracts (protective).
2. Provide necessary public goods for the most efficient operation of the government to support economic markets. (productive).
3. Avoid the "welfare-plunder" of the current crony capitalist redistributive functions that distort market price incentives for innovation and tacit knowledge sharing.

We apply the same logic for a complete replacement of Madison's document with the same logic used by Madison for replacing the Articles of Confederation.

Madison's British social class conflict model is based upon a collectivist philosophy that rights inure to social classes, not to individuals.

As Forrest McDonald explains,

"In the English system each branch of government represented people whose status was inherited…In the United States, there was no hereditary status…therefore [Madison's] the English model was inappropriate…[The British] constitution separated the people from government in two ways: some officials were chosen directly [by the aristocracy]; there was also the time barrier…there was no way for the people could express their will directly and immediately." (McDonald. Forrest, A Constitutional History of the United States. Franklin Watts, 1982.).

Madison's primary defect of social class collectivism cannot be resolved by amendments.

Madison's constitution must be replaced with a constitution based upon individualism.

In the rare historical circumstance, of 1776, a unique culture emerged that defined individual freedom as the jointly-held goal of society.

Patriots called this idea "the Spirit of '76."

The initial condition for creating the constitutional contract, in 1776. was the equal natural rights of all individuals, as parties to the contract.

If the purpose of the constitution is to provide rules to coordinate actions of individuals in the pursuit of jointly-held goals of society, and if rights inure to individuals, then the mutual interdependency of all individuals in rule adherence creates the social conditions for pro-social behavior.

Rights are claims that citizens have against transgressions, and social justice is achieved through fair rules of adjudicating conflict and promoting social cooperation.

Once American civil society had been created, in 1776, a fair constitution would establish a mechanism to continually evaluate the justice of rights claims in the civil society. (Richard Tuck, Natural Rights Theories: Their Origin and Development, 1981).

Alternatively, if the constitution exists to provide rules of civil procedure for institutional sharing of power between social classes in their capacity of special financial interests, and if rights inure to social groups, then, pro-social rule adherence depends on the application of institutional power, or as Hamilton suggests in his 1780 letter, the application of the police power of the state.

Madison's constitution is devoid of reference to the moral values of Jefferson's Declaration, or the moral obligations that citizens have to each in preserving liberty for all citizens.

Madison only provides civil rules of procedure, or what Michael Zuckert calls "institutional instrumentalism." This description means that Madison deals with the institutional rules that are instrumental in effecting the distribution of power in the republic. (The Natural Rights Republic, 1997),

Madison's rules were the instruments to balance and check factional political power in order to insure that social elites, the natural leaders, who made important decisions on behalf of all society, were insulated from the tyranny that could be imposed by the people.

As Stuart Hill notes in Democratic Values and Technological Choice, (1992), Madison's main concern was "...how one faction would use political power to oppress another group."

As the case of debt peonage in North Carolina, after the Civil War, it is quite possible to have legal institutional instruments, in a nominally democratic constitution, wherein the civil rules of procedure are followed perfectly, but whose outcomes result in the confiscation of farmer's lands.

A better, more fair, constitution than Madison's version of the British model would begin by identifying that natural rights inure, exclusively, to individuals.

Madison's view that rights inure to social classes can be contrasted with Jefferson's view of individual rights.

Jefferson wrote,

"We come to respect those rights in others that we value in ourselves."

That rights inured to individuals, and that they were natural in origin, seemed self-evident to Jefferson.

He saw rights as claims in civil society that contained reciprocal duties of citizens towards each other.

The purpose of government, from Jefferson's perspective of rights, is to provide the institutional instruments through which rights could be equally recognized and exchanged.

Jefferson promoted the idea that certain forms of government were

"...better calculated than others to protect the individual in the free exercise of their rights."

The idea that Jefferson is expressing is that the moral and cultural values vary from society to society, and that the citizen obedience to the rule of law did not require Leviathan to enforce the rules in the specific historical context of 1776.

In their explanation of how constitutions can create citizen voluntary allegiance to the rule of law, Markus Böckenförde et al., describe the close relationship between "the constitution and the shared values that underlie the moral basis of the society." (Rule of Law: A Practical Guide to Constitution Building, 2011).

The difficulty in creating the fair constitution, according to them, is to codify voluntary citizen agreements, prior to the constitution, into a legal text that courts will enforce as the purpose of the government, after the constitution has been created.

The essential components of the fair constitution are that the application of the law is predicable, accessible and universally applicable.

As codified in the American Bill of Rights, a fair constitution requires the accused the right to a fair hearing and fair, equal access to the judicial system.

When Jefferson's set of cultural values and institutional arrangements are placed into the constitution, obedience to the rule of law, does not require a King, or a Church, or Leviathan.

Individuals are connected to each other through these external moral values because the values influence the way each individual's brain processes the truth.

The point is that a just social democracy depends on a unique set of moral values to insure the emergence of social stability, after the constitution has been ratified..

Whether this unique constellation of cultural values is widespread and commonly-held throughout the society, before the constitution is ratified, is contingent upon the open, transparent, process of social consensus about the shared moral values.

To re-apply the evolutionary theory of the brain, from Eccles and Popper, the brain's sorting of images about other humans incorporates the moral value of trust when they are involved in a political exchange of constitutional rights.

The brain's evaluation of the trust to extend to another in political exchange is the same neuronal image processing that occurs in market exchanges, and is a result of the functions of Brodmann Area 39, and area 40.

Daniel Dennett, in his recent book Consciousness Explained, describes this image processing to extend trust to another human as a "conscious point of view," similar to Popper's level 3 of neuronal processing. (Daniel C. Dennett, Consciousness Explained, 1992).

Dennett writes.

"Wherever there is a conscious mind, there is a point of view. This is one of the most fundamental ideas we have about minds – or about consciousness. A conscious mind is an observer, who takes in a limited subset of all information there is."

In contrast to Madison's collectivist interpretation of common citizens as an appendage to the superior elite social class, Jefferson's individualist perspective contains the idea that the individual has a unique mental "point of view."

J. L. Mackie, in Ethics: Inventing Right and Wrong, outlines the idea that society and cultural values, such as the idea of ethical values and trust, are creations of society. (1991).

Mackie's suggestion about the invention of ethical social rules means that there is a unique constellation of ethical values and institutional arrangements in politics and economics that define the pursuit of the public purpose from an individualist value orientation.

As Mackie points out, societies are capable of creating values, but the adoption of one set of values versus some competing set of values depends on who controls the flow of information in society.

There are no formal rules of civil procedure, such as majority voting in an election, that determines which set of ambient cultural values becomes dominant in a specific society.

For an individualistic society, the way that one set of values becomes dominant over another set of values in society involves individuals making decisions about their own life's mission, and linking those decisions to an awareness of this same mental process occurring in the brain of another individual.

The set of values that supports an individualistic society depend upon an individual making the connection between his own welfare and the welfare of others,

Under the unique American set of cultural values, in 1776, regarding individual sovereignty, the public purpose is related to how and why the brain performs the insight/imagination function of anticipating the welfare of another human.

In the case of market exchange, the human brain is evaluating the level of trust and honesty to extend to the other human.

In the case of political exchange, the brain is evaluating the level of trust to extend on the other human's allegiance to obey the unwritten rule of law because commonly held values of liberty depend on fair rules being applied equally to all citizens..

The logic of replacing Madison's constitution with a better constitution, in other words, is that the biological function of the individual brain provides the rationale for why and how the future American society should define the public purpose in terms of improving individual welfare.

The role of society should be to extend and enhance the individual's own biologically designed pursuit of sovereignty. The linkage between an individual's brain sorting images and the public purpose arises in the context of exchanges with another individual.

In this context of exchange, the internal mental world of one individual is related to the internal mental world of another individual through shared external values created and perpetuated by the ambient culture.

A shared set of values about trust within a culture strengthens the degree of social cooperation. The shared values makes it more likely that individual brains will be sorting and selecting images based upon the coherence between internal models and external images during the course of an exchange.

Both individual and social cooperation occur when individual brains see the same external truths related to the value of trust. The image being sorted in one brain rely on the ambient values to inform the decision that trust extended to the other individual will be reciprocated.

In other words, the extension of trust is an act of faith in the sense that the individual assumes, during the course of the exchange, that the other brain is seeing the same external values, and is being influenced by those values.

In political exchanges involving individual freedom, the institutions of society provide the mechanism, over generations, through which the act of faith is reciprocated.

Madison and the elites who wrote the constitution of 1787, deluded themselves into thinking that only a certain special few have the mental ability to spin out images of what's good for themselves and what's good for society.

Their biologically superior brains, they think, provide the constitutional logic of making all collective social decisions, in what Prigogine would describe as a closed system.

Madison's centralized collectivist rules are transitioning the American society towards totalitarianism.

In this American collectivist elitist variant of totalitarianism, the ruling class elites provide a total vision of what is politically correct behavior and politically correct values.

In the individualist society, the role of government is to reduce the chance situations that other individuals, or the police power of the state, will be used to override the individual's freedoms of choice in pursuing their sovereign life mission.

The government serves this function by administering a framework of collective decision making whose goal is to secure just outcomes to the laws that individuals give to themselves.

The constitution provides rules, after the ratification of the constitution, as a fair process, not a fair outcome, as determined by the American nobility.

The exclusive focus of the public purpose in this better constitutional framework of decision making is the individual's control over the life's mission.

The public purpose is not the wealth of nations, the welfare of groups, or the equal distribution of incomes that conform to a collectivist vision of fairness.

The essential, primary function of government in an individualistic society is to enforce a constant system of justice derived from rules that citizens give to themselves, before the constitution is created.

The goal of the new constitutional system of justice is to reduce the arbitrary and capricious application of the rules of justice.

The greater level of constitutional certainty means that the individual spends less time, energy and resources dedicated to short-term survival, and more time in Popper's level 3, devoted to imagining the future path of sovereignty.

It is much easier for America's nobility to maintain political power over common citizens under Madison's collectivist conception of society than it would be for elites, under a new Jeffersonian individualistic conception of society.

Madison's rules have transitioned from the more benign British social class conflict model of ruling class dominance into a more vicious economic predatory capitalism that operates beyond the consent of the governed, and beyond their power to change the system.

The centralized power of Madison's government, initially reserved to the American nobility, has been seized by a predatory capitalist class that uses the agencies of government to reward themselves.

That recent corporate seizure of power cannot be modified or amended under Madison's existing constitution, which continues to be based upon the philosophy of collectivism

Madison's constitution as defective, beyond repair, for confronting the emerging technological totalitarian future of American society.

A better, more fair constitution, would aim at rules that align the human brain's most recent evolutionary image processing with cultural and moral rules that would allow a beneficial social order to emerge, naturally.

Unlike the example of general equilibrium theory, based upon material scarcity, under the theory of beneficial economic theory, human ingenuity is an unlimited natural resource, which functions in the constitutional moral value system of human free will.

That concept of human free will is threatened by the recent emergence of the modern predatory capitalist state and corporate globalism, whose goal is eliminating American national sovereignty.

Chapter 5. The American Economic Transition to Predatory State Capitalism

Madison created the constitutional machinery that replaced the Articles of Confederation state sovereignty model with a centralized supreme national power,

The centralized power of Madison's British social class conflict model of government, initially reserved to the American nobility, has been seized by a predatory capitalist class that uses the agencies of government to direct global income and profits to themselves.

Madison's 1787 amoral rules of civil procedure replaced the moral values of Jefferson's 1776 Declaration that all men are created equal, and disrupted the ability of common citizen's ordinary market decision making in the beneficial social system that DeTocqueville had observed in the 1830s.

While the first 70 years of Madison's British social class conflict model were already experiencing the boom-bust economy of Hamilton's First Bank, it was not until after Lincoln centralized Federal power to conduct the Civil War that the transition to a society dominated by large corporations and private banks gained precedence. (Laurie Thomas Vass, Reclaiming The American Democratic Impulse, 2023).

Madison's checks and balances were designed to check the ambition of powerful ruling class elites, and did not have any checks and balances against the concentration of corporate and financial power.

This transition to a more corporate-dominated American political system occurred over 4 historical eras:

1. From around 1875 to 1913, the era commonly called the "Gilded Age," Madison's rules facilitated the emergence of giant corporations, who used the centralized machinery of government to create monopolies in important industrial sectors like steel, oil and railroads. Madison's amoral constitution allowed the monopolist to exploit common

citizens in an early version of crony capitalist alliance between government and corporations because Madison's rules were silent on how competitive free markets create beneficial social outcomes.

2. From around 1913 to 1945, at the end of World War II, progressive era legislation combined with the centralized power of the Federal government to conduct the War, to facilitate the alliance of corporate power with government power, unfettered by consent of the citizens. In this era of crony state capitalism, Big Government combined with Big corporations, to set the economic agenda of the Nation.
3. From around 1945 to 1985, the Bretton Woods global agreement, between allies at the end of the War, ushered in a new type of global financial system, dominated by the military and financial power of the U. S to enforce global compliance with the agreement. The alliance of power between Big corporations and Big government added a new partner of Big Labor. The 3 party power alliance is immortalized in the 1953 U. S. Senate confirmations hearing on the appointment of Charles Wilson, President of General Motors, to be Secretary of Defense.

From Library of Congress Blogs:

"Senator Hendrickson. Well now, I am interested to know whether if a situation did arise where you had to make a decision which was extremely adverse to the interests of your stock and General Motors Corp. or any of these other companies, or extremely adverse to the company, in the interests of the United States Government, could you make that decision?

Mr. Wilson. Yes, sir; I could. I cannot conceive of one because for years I thought what was good for our country was good for General Motors, and vice versa. The difference [between the government's interests and private corporate financial interests] did not exist. Our company is too big. It goes with the welfare of the country. Our contribution to the Nation is quite considerable."

4. From around 1992, with the first enactment of NAFTA, and subsequently, the Chinese entrance to the World Trade Organization, in 2001, the emergence of a "rules-based" global trading order, began the replacement of the concept of national sovereignty with the concept of a global corporate New World Order. The "rules-based-order" eventually morphed into the current American Predatory Capitalist State.

At each historical era, the centralized government power became more insulated from the consent of the citizens, and the boom-bust economy became more erratic.

In the early era, as Sean Wilentz noted in The Rise of American Democracy: Jefferson to Lincoln, (2006),

"The people had no formal voice of their own in government. And, that was exactly how it was supposed to be – for once the electors [common citizens] had chosen their representatives, they ceded power, reserving none for themselves until the next election… [We]The people, as a political entity, existed only on election day."

In the later, most recent era of Predatory State Capitalism, computerized vote counting machines rig the election day outcomes to fit the agenda of global corporatism.

We, the people no longer exist, even on election day.

The most recent era of Predatory State Capitalism occurs at the same time in history as the appearance of artificial intelligence, and human-like robots, which tends to enhance the corporation's technological control over the behavior of common middle and working class American citizens, unhindered by any constitutional concept of the "consent of the governed."

The intent of Madison's centralized machinery was to insulate the will of the citizens from participating in the operation of the agencies of government.

After the transition to the Predatory Capitalist State, the common citizens are left without mechanisms and procedures to regain their consent of the governed that Jefferson wrote in the Declaration.

If the voting machines are rigged, then the question of how the opinions of common citizens are translated into government policy, raised by Centinel, in 1788, is relevant again.

“If the people are sovereign how does the opinion of citizens direct the policies of government? There is nothing in the Federalist constitution, like the detailed definition of consent in the various state constitutions.”

In other words, Madison’s centralized machinery has transitioned from the more benign British social class conflict model of ruling class dominance into a more vicious technological, predatory capitalism that operates beyond the recourse of common citizens to change the global system.

There are no provisions in Madison’s rules to eliminate this emerging technological threat to individual liberty because

Madison’s document is based upon a contract between ruling class elites that protects the property rights of the American nobility, not on rules to protect the liberty of common citizens.

We noted in Chapter 3 that the spontaneous order that emerges in the brain's every day decision-making processes is fundamentally shaped and constrained by the cultural, political, and social systems in which the brain develops and operates.

Madison overturned and disrupted the decentralized US constitution, favored by Jefferson, which would have been more aligned with the human brain’s natural capacity for market decisions which would lead to the emergence of a beneficial economic social system.

The immediate threat of global corporate technological tyranny makes Jefferson’s alternate vision, built on an entrepreneurial economy in a decentralized state sovereignty framework, superior to Madison's British social class conflict model in defeating the forces of global corporate tyranny.

Josh Stylman explains that global corporate elites believe that the world has too many humans for the future New World Order technological age, and one goal of the technocratic global state is to reduce the world's population through war or engineered pandemics. (The Technocratic Blueprint, The Brownstone Institute, 2025).

Stylman writes,

"As artificial intelligence eliminates the need for human labor, the focus [of the global corporate elite] shifts from creating compliant workers to managing population reduction – not through overt force, but through sophisticated social engineering…BlackRock CEO Larry Fink recently made this shift explicit, explaining how AI and automation will reshape population dynamics: In developed countries with shrinking populations…these countries will rapidly develop robotics and AI technology…the social problems that one will have in substituting humans for machines will be far easier in those countries that have declining populations." His candid assessment reveals how technological capability drives elite agendas

Madison's constitution served to centralize power, unchecked by social or institutional power, and that earlier form of centralized power is now being consolidated in the hands of a very small group of global elites.

Stylman continues,

"Today's Globalism 2.0 operates through corporate and financial institutions, steering power toward centralized global governance without the need for formal empire [national sovereignty]. Organizations like the Bilderberg Group, Council on Foreign Relations, Trilateral Commission, and Tavistock Institute have spent 50 to 100 years guiding global programs and policies, gradually centralizing power, influence, and resources among an increasingly concentrated elite. The Bilderberg Group, in particular, has facilitated private discussions among influential political and business leaders, shaping high-level decision-making behind closed doors."

After 1860, Lincoln had to increase the power of the central government, to the point where Noah Feldman states, that he broke Madison's constitution. (The Broken Constitution: Lincoln, Slavery, and the Refounding of America, 2021).

In Feldman's analysis, the breaking of the constitution constituted a second founding, [more accurately a third founding] which laid the foundation for the transition for a powerful central government, without the minimal guardrails established by the Bill of Rights, in Madison's British social class model.

Feldman suggests that Madison's constitution lacked moral values because it was a legal contract based upon negotiated compromises between ruling class elites, and was not a moral compact, like the Mayflower Compact, of 1620.

Feldman explains the difference between a negotiated contract, between ruling class factions and a moral compact, as denoted by Locke, when American citizens left the state of nature, in 1775, to form a new nation.

A compact is based upon shared moral and cultural values that citizens agree to, before the compact is enacted.

The compact defines a set of social and moral rules that citizens agree to follow, after the compact has been ratified. Generally citizens voluntarily agree to follow the rules, without government coercion, which is commonly called "allegiance to the rule of law."

The compact defines the mission of the Nation, such as the moral values expressed by Jefferson, in the Declaration, and in American history, the rules were codified in the Articles of Confederation, as a "league of friendship" among 13 independent states.

According to Feldman, Madison's constitution was "not a higher law in the moral sense," but a legal contract, or as we argue, the rules of civil procedure to adjust and adjudicate financial conflict among ruling class elites.

The Early Historical Transition to A Centralized Predatory State 1860 – 1913.

The economic flaws of Madison's British social class model were evident, as early as 1835, beginning with President Jackson's veto of the re-chartering of Hamilton's Second Bank.

Joseph Fishkin writes,

"The mass of ordinary white farmers and those Jackson called "the laboring classes of society" were fearful of the new "paper- money system"; the new boom- and- bust business cycle; and the growing inequalities of wealth, opportunity, and political power between the poor many and the rich few. The new "paper- money system places "all power in the hands of the few . . . to govern by corruption or force…the money system is essentially an aristocratic institution" that "bands the wealthy together" and tends "to give exclusive political, as well as exclusive money privileges to the rich." (Joseph Fishkin, TheAnti-oligarchy Constitution : Reconstructing the Economic Foundations of American Democracy, 2022).

Fishkin quotes Congressman John Bell, of Tennessee, a political ally of President Jackson, who summarizes the defects of Madison's amoral rules of civil procedure.

Bell states,

"True constitutional principles would not aim for the "European" goal of maximizing national wealth "without regard to the manner of its distribution"…The accumulation of great wealth in the hands of individual citizens subverts the natural "equality of rank and influence" that is "the very end and aim of all our political institutions."

While the social class boom-bust economy was already evident in the 1830s, it was not until the period after the Civil War, that the economic instability of Madison's rules became more pronounced.

A series of U. S. Supreme Court rulings began the process of defining corporate rights as the same type of legal civil rights as citizens.

Joshua Stylman characterizes this era as a type of "corporate takeover," of the government, but without public relations press releases.

It is important to recall, that at this time in American history, Madison's convention notes and the deliberations of the Constitutional Convention were still unknown to American citizens, who continued to labor under the myth that Madison had created a fair republic, written by selfless, virtuous people.

Stylman writes,

"After the devastating Civil War left America financially desperate. Over the next few decades, a series of legal and financial changes gradually transformed how our country functions – from natural rights to commercial codes, from elected officials to administrative experts, from gold-backed currency to digital debt entries. Think of it as the world's longest corporate takeover – just without the press release… With the addition of digital surveillance and now, artificial intelligence, we're witnessing the activation of this long-prepared system. [of corporate control] What started as a subtle governance shift [after the Civil War] has evolved into an all-encompassing digital control grid that's being switched on before our eyes. The corporate transformation was step one; I believe the [corporate] technocratic takeover is the endgame."
(America, LLC: The Corporate Takeover We Were Never Taught, 2024).

Richard White writes of the odd Supreme Court interpretations of the 3 Reconstruction amendments [13th, 14th, and 15th] that were used to transition the Constitution from the intent of freedom for former slaves to legal protections for Big Business. (The Republic for Which It Stands: The United States during Reconstruction and the Gilded Age, 1865-1896, 2017).

The Thirteenth Amendment (proposed in 1864 and ratified in 1865) abolished slavery and involuntary servitude, except for those duly convicted of a crime.

The Fourteenth Amendment (proposed in 1866 and ratified in 1868) addresses citizenship rights and equal protection of the laws for all persons.

The Fifteenth Amendment (proposed in 1869 and ratified in 1870) prohibits discrimination in voting rights of citizens on the basis of "race, color, or previous condition of servitude."

White writes,

"Cruickshank, in 1875, and Slaughterhouse 1873, were part of a parade of disastrous decisions that ruled the Reconstruction amendments did not protect freedmen from actions of one citizen against another or from actions by the states."

Eric Foner, in The Second Founding, explains the strange path of the 14th Amendment, from protection of slaves to protection of corporations.

He writes,

"Increasingly, the Court construed the 14th Amendment as a vehicle for protecting corporate rights…The Court employed a state-centered approach in citizenship matters and a nation-centered approach in affairs of business." (The Second Founding: How the Civil War and Reconstruction Remade the Constitution, 2019).

In The Burden of Southern History, (2008), C. Vann Woodward, writes,

"By a series of opinions beginning in 1873, the Supreme Court constricted the 14th Amendment by a narrow interpretation which proclaimed that privileges and immunities [for citizens] that we call civil rights were not placed under federal protection at all…the commitment to equality had never really been made."

As Supreme Court Justice Oliver Wendell Holmes lamented in 1903, after the series of prior decisions on the 14th Amendment, there was nothing the Courts could do to correct the decisions, because precedent in civil rights cases had elevated the rights of corporations over the rights of citizens.

Justice Holmes, in Giles v Harris, 1903, wrote:

"If the great mass of the white population intends to keep blacks from voting there was nothing the justices could do…relief from a great political wrong could only come from the people of a state."

In the context of strict construction of the intent of the "Founders," what Justice Holmes means is that former decisions of the Court hold priority, no matter how unfair or unjust the former decision may be.

Precedence becomes the most important basis of a decision because Madison's Constitution fails to state a national mission or purpose, in the Preamble, that Supreme Court Justices could use to define the intent of the "Founders."

Alex Park, in his article, "Supreme Court Rulings That Turned Corporations Into People, (2014), noted that,

"Justice John Paul Stevens argued in his dissent to Citizens United (2010) that,

"Corporations…are not themselves members of 'We the People' by whom and for whom our Constitution was established."

But, Justice Stevens was outvoted by the majority, who ruled on the 130 year precedence of cases that defined corporations as the same a "We, the people."

As we noted, in Chapter 4, "We, the people," did not write the Constitution. It was written in secret, behind closed doors and drawn shades, signed by 38 ruling class elites and ratified in a fraudulent corrupt process.

After the precedence of rulings regarding the 14th Amendment, corporations sought many of the same constitutional rights guaranteed to individual citizens, including the rights to own property, enter into contracts, and to sue and be sued, in Federal Courts, just like individual citizens.

The judicial transition of corporations having the same civil rights as natural persons gained precedence in 1882.

According to Adam Winkler, in his article Corporations Are People' Is Built on an Incredible 19th-Century Lie: How a farcical series of events in the 1880s produced an enduring and controversial legal precedent. (The Atlantic, 2018.).

The judicial farce began in 1882, and, according to Winkler.

"The farce involved three parties: a lawyer who lied to the Supreme Court, an ethically challenged justice, and a corrupt court recorder who modified the text of the opinion in a case involving one of the most powerful corporations of the day." [a railroad].

The corrupt attorney, Roscoe Conkling, who lied to the Supreme Court, represented the Southern Pacific Railroad, and had been a member of Congress, during the Civil War.

While in Congress, Conkling served on the committee that drafted the text of the 14th Amendment [in 1868].

Conkling both represented the railroad in the case before the Supreme Court, and also provided direct testimony, and introduced evidence, based upon his work in Congress, drafting the 14th Amendment.

According to Winkler,

"The head lawyer representing Southern Pacific was a man named Roscoe Conkling. Conkling told the justices that the drafters had changed the wording of the amendment, replacing "citizens" with "persons" in order to cover corporations too.
Laws referring to "persons," he said, have "by long and constant acceptance ... been held to embrace artificial persons as well as natural persons."

Conkling buttressed his account of the 14th Amendment with a surprising piece of evidence: a musty old journal he claimed was a previously unpublished record of the deliberations of the drafting committee.

The direct testimony and evidence of the unpublished records persuaded the Supreme Court to embrace Conkling's interpretation of the Fourteenth Amendment that the amendment intended to cover both natural persons and corporations.

The corrupt court reporter modified the text of the opinion, and added his revised rendition at the top title of the Court's ruling.

The Court reporter, J. C. Bancroft Davis, was also an attorney and also had represented railroads, before he became a Supreme Court recorder.

According to Winkler,

"By tradition, the court reporter writes up a summary of the Court's opinion and includes it at the beginning of the opinion. The reporter's wildly inaccurate summary of the Southern Pacific case stated that the Court had ruled that "corporations are persons within … the Fourteenth Amendment."

The corrupt Supreme Court Justice was Stephen Johnson Field.

According to Winkler, Field used the fraudulent document, prepared by the Court recorder, as legal precedent to be followed by subsequent Courts.

"A few years later, in an opinion in an unrelated case, Field wrote that "corporations are persons within the meaning" of the Fourteenth Amendment. "It was so held in Santa Clara County v. Southern Pacific Railroad," explained Field, who knew very well that the Court had done no such thing."

Justice Field had prior knowledge of Conkling's strategy and knew at the time, in 1882, that Conkling was lying to the Court.

In the 1886 case, Chief Justice Morrison Waite, wrote an opinion in support of Field.

Waite stated,

"The Court does not wish to hear an argument on the question whether the provision in the Fourteenth Amendment to the Constitution which forbids a state to deny to any person within its jurisdiction the equal protection of the laws applies to these corporations. We are all of opinion that it does…The defendant Corporations are persons within the intent of the clause in section 1 of the Fourteenth Amendment to the Constitution of the United States, which forbids a state to deny to any person within its jurisdiction the equal protection of the laws."

Winkler concludes his article by noting that the 14th Amendment, purportedly passed to protect the civil rights of Black people, had instead been turned into a political weapon to protect the civil rights of corporations.

He writes,

"Between 1868, when the 14th amendment was ratified, and 1912, the Supreme Court would rule on 28 cases involving the rights of African Americans and an astonishing 312 cases [affirming] the rights of corporations as persons."

In the crony capitalism of the Gilded Age, corporations were in a partnership with the government to build railroads, and sell worthless bonds to unsuspecting investors.

In the American context of 1875 to 1913, corporations bought and sold elected representatives and lobbyists, like Conkling, gave instructions to the Supreme Court on the type of decisions that would benefit corporate financial interests.

In the earlier era of Supreme Court rulings, before 1875, corporations were not natural persons.

For example, in Bank of the United States v. Deveaux (1809), the Court ruled,

"The jurisdiction of this court being limited, so far as respects the character of the parties in this particular case, "to controversies between citizens of different states," both parties must be citizens, to come within the description…A corporation aggregate, is certainly not a citizen; and, consequently, cannot sue or be sued in the courts of the United States, unless the rights of the members, in this respect, can be exercised in their corporate name."

According to Alex Park, in his article, "Supreme Court Rulings That Turned Corporations Into People,"

“Deveaux argued that, because corporations weren't people, [citizens], they couldn't sue in federal court. Chief Justice John Marshall agreed. This meant businesses could only sue or be sued in federal court if all the shareholders, and at least one member of the opposing party, lived in the same state.”

Park continues,

“Thirty-five years later, after hearing the Louisville, Cincinnati, and Charleston Railroad case, the Supreme Court reversed course, ruling that corporations were "citizens" of the states where they incorporated.”

In 1853, according to Park,

“In Marshall v. Baltimore and Ohio Railroad, the Supreme Court upheld the notion that corporations were citizens, but only for the purposes of court jurisdiction; [standing], they did not have the same constitutional rights as actual people. [citizens].The court also ruled that, for litigation purposes, shareholders would be considered citizens of their company's home state.”

According to Park,

“In 1898, (Smyth v. Ames): Building on the Santa Clara decision, (Santa Clara County v. Southern Pacific Rail Road), the court voided a Nebraska railroad tax, ruling that it [the tax], was akin to the government taking a corporation's property without due process —a violation of its 14th Amendment rights.”

Park continues,

“In 1906, (Hale v. Henkel): Having blocked unlawful seizures of corporate property, [taxes], the court went on to shield companies from other kinds of intrusion. Writing for the majority, Justice Henry Billings Brown found that corporations, like people, [citizens], are protected from unreasonable searches and seizures under the Fourth Amendment.” [in the Bill of Rights for “citizens” not persons].”

As referenced above, the precedence that the civil rights of corporations are the same as "We, the people," culminated in the 2010 Citizens United case.

In Citizens United v. Federal Election Commission, the Supreme Court ruled that corporations and unions cannot be prohibited from making independent political expenditures, citing First Amendment protections of free speech, for persons.

This 2010 ruling is important in tracing the historical trajectory to the American Corporate Predatory State because it forever changed campaign finance laws in the United States by cementing the crony capitalist connection between elected representatives and the special financial interests of banks and corporations.

Something changed in American politics and economics after the Civil War, and that change was the cause of the emergence of a new type of corporate domination of American society.

During the early period of the Gilded Age, before corporations became "persons," the Ruling Class business elites had allegiance to the domestic economy, because most of their investments were in physical capital, like railroads and steel mills, located in the geographic territory of the United States.

What changed, during the corporation's transition to a global imperial power, after they gained the legal rights of persons, was that monopoly capitalism shifted its allegiance from the U. S. markets to becoming an imperial power in the global market.

That connection between the political power of corporations and the election of representatives cannot be undone by Madison's rules, and is beyond the consent of the citizens to repeal the damage to the concept of the rule of law.

The Modern Historical Transition to An American Imperial Power.

1913 – 1945.

From around 1913 to 1945, at the end of World War II, progressive era legislation combined with the centralized power of the Federal government to conduct the War, to cement the alliance of corporate power with government power, unfettered by consent of the citizens.

In this era of crony state capitalism, Big Government combined with Big Corporations to set the economic agenda of the Nation.

Three related events, in 1913, set the stage of further structural modification of Madison's checks and balances in the direction of greater centralized power over citizens.

First, in Madison's conception of the British social conflict model, the U. S. Senate was intended to be comprised of unelected representatives, appointed by the state legislatures to represent the interests of the states, as a replica of the British House of Lords.

Madison's intent for a Federalist government was overturned by the Seventeenth Amendment to the Constitution, which enacted popular elections of two senators from each state.

Second, the 17th Amendment was passed as a part of a logrolling political deal in Congress to pass the 16th Amendment, enacting a Federal income tax.

Both amendments were part of a coordinated corporate political strategy to make the United States a formidable global economic power, which required a Congressional Act to establish the Third National Bank, chartered as the Federal Reserve Bank, as a replica of the Bank of England.

The three major events were supplemented by a series of social welfare programs that were designed to cushion the devastating financial effects of corporatism on the daily lives of ordinary common citizens, as experienced during the Gilded Age. (Laurie

Thomas Vass, Equal Rights For All. Special Privileges for None: Re-Examining the Agrarian Arguments Against a Centralized American Government, 2012).

Rather than a balanced political system between the central government and the states, the 17th Amendment disrupted, forever, Madison's checks and balances framework of government.

Todd Zywicki writes. in "Senators and Special Interests : A Public Choice Analysis of the Seventeenth Amendment, (1994),

"The Seventeenth Amendment eliminated [Madison's] institutional arrangements which restrained special-interest groups' use of the federal government as a tool for wealth redistribution. In so doing, the Seventeenth Amendment made possible the explosion in the size of the federal government in the twentieth century. Without the Seventeenth Amendment, most major political initiatives of the twentieth century likely would have failed, as had occurred in previous centuries."

The enactment of the 17th Amendment had the political effect of transitioning the government from the pursuit of a general public interest, as stated in the "General Welfare Clause," [The Congress shall have Power To lay and collect Taxes, Duties, Imposts and Excises, to pay the Debts and provide for the common Defence and general Welfare of the United States; but all Duties, Imposts and Excises shall be uniform throughout the United States;"] to a special interest purpose, consistent with Hamilton's interpretation in his advocacy of the First National Bank.

Any proposed piece of special legislation that could possibly be interpreted by the Supreme Court as serving Madison's undefined mission of government, could be used to justify special interest legislation.

As Zywicki notes,

“The direct election of U.S. senators, undermined the twin structural pillars of the Constitution: federalism and the separation of powers… Senators could now convert special-interest support into reelection assets. While senators’ new independence raised the costs of influencing them, this increase was dwarfed by the de crease in costs resulting from their ability to contract with [other senators] directly, rather than work through the state legislatures. Rent-seeking expenses could be equalized across the House and the Senate, rather than through the less efficient process of having to spread [lobbying costs] resources across the House and the various state legislatures.”

In other words, the costs of crony capitalism, for corporations, came down for special interest legislation, and the benefits, for elected representatives, in supporting special interests, went up.

In that version of the American special interest crony capitalist framework, there is no political interest that promotes the citizen’s public interest in protecting liberty, because Madison’s rules did not define liberty as a component of the negotiated contract between elites.

The passage of the 16th and 17th Amendments, in conjunction with the passage of the Federal Reserve Act, in 1913, was part of a carefully executed global political strategy of corporations, and the U. S. Treasury, beginning with secret meetings on Jekyll Island in Georgia.

Zywicki explains,

“It appears that the Seventeenth Amendment was part of a logrolling deal with the Sixteenth Amendment (making income tax constitutional). The two were passed within approximately one month of each other. Although the Sixteenth Amendment was introduced first, its passage was suspended until the Seventeenth Amendment was ratified.”

As described by James Livingston, in Origins of the Federal Reserve System, Money, Class, and Corporate Capitalism, 1890-1913.,

(1986.), the desired corporate transition to a global imperial power required a new, and different type of banking system, than the "free banking" system that existed during the Gilded Age.

The type of banking system required by corporations to be a global imperial power looked exactly like Hamilton's First Bank, and the subsequent Second Bank, that was killed by President Jackson, in 1832.

Livingston writes,

"The federal reserve system was a product of the crisis of the 1890s…the market investment [banking] system was reorganized and stabilized…The banking and monetary reform movement of 1894 must be understood as the context in which a corporate business elite began to work on [creating] a world view and a program appropriate to its control over an emergent modern industrial society."

As we noted above, Madison's more benign British social class conflict system was replaced by a more vicious predatory capitalism, beginning in 1913, that targeted small business and entrepreneurs as enemies to the globalist quest for power.

Livingston explains,

"The movement to a global imperial power was accomplished with political propaganda that viewed small business and entrepreneurial capitalism as the main economic problem that was acting as a barrier to global greatness."

The corporation's line of political attack on entrepreneurial capitalism, according to Livingston, was that unlimited capital investments in small businesses was unproductive, and lead to "over production in the economy, which caused prices to decline because there was a glut of too many products in the market."

The same political propaganda message of Big Business, for the Federal Reserve Bank, in 1912, was also used in the political campaigns to enact the 16th and 17th Amendments, with the additional provisos that the new imperialist power of the Nation would benefit common citizens by the direct election of senators, and the new source of government revenue from income taxes.

As a historical aside, this same language of propaganda by Big Business was used effectively again, in 1992, in the enactment of the global trade agreements, which promised greater economic prosperity for the average American citizen.

Livingston notes, that the faux public purpose of the corporation's propaganda was to,

"prevent "unproductive" investments [by small business] …They [the corporations] did not want to give small entrepreneurs the opportunity to convert redundant currency [i.e. small business profits] into capital, [investments] to undertake "unproductive" enterprises and thus [create] chronic overproduction.…The creators and proponents of the new corporate order based their defense of industrial consolidation on a critique of the competitive-entrepreneurial regime….because it produced chronic overproduction…."

The logical solution to eliminating the economic problem of small business for the Big corporations, according to Livingston was,

"centralization of financial responsibility," whose power over the money supply would eliminate capital investments by small businesses.

Livingston explains, that from the perspective of corporations,

“If individual banks were granted the power of note issuance on their general assets, [duringthe free banking era after the Civil War] small or regional entrepreneurs would be able to convert currency [profits] into capital…a central bank that had a monopoly on the right of note issuance was critical to the restriction of unproductive capital investments [by entrepreneurs]… the overthrow of the competitive entrepreneurial regime could not be completed unless the banking system, which converted the savings of society into investments was managed by the large corporations.” [the Third National Bank].

The third bank was created in secrecy, at a remote island, off the coast of Georgia, appropriately called “Jekyll Island.” (Laurie Thomas Vass America’s Final Revolution: Reconstructing Jefferson’s American Dream of An Entrepreneurial Capitalist Society, 2022).

The participants in the secret meetings were bank owners of the four biggest banks in the nation, a powerful Ruling Class U. S. Senator, and a senior officer of the U. S. Treasury Department.

The historical pretext of the creation of the Federal Reserve Bank was the continuing boom-bust collapse of the U. S. economy.

The economy collapsed in 1893, and the depression, called “one of the worst” in U. S. economic history, lasted about 4 years.

The economy collapsed again, in 1897.

Then, about 10 years later, in 1907, the economy collapsed again, and the depression lasted about 7 years, to around 1914.

The panic of 1907 started when the credit issued by Knickerbocker Trust to commercial businesses turned out to be worthless. Knickerbocker’s bank debt assets were secured by worthless business assets.

Knickerbocker owners needed a government bailout, and approached the New York Clearing House for a loan, which was denied.

This bailout denial created a big financial problem for the owners of Knickerbocker because, under free banking, shareholders of the bank faced double liability.

If a bank failed, the shareholders could be forced to pay an additional assessment in order to compensate depositors and other creditors.

In other words, the owners lost both the value of their initial capital investment in the bank, and also faced double liability to compensate depositors, who lost their savings when the bank went bust.

The intent of the banking reform, beginning with the Aldrich-Vreeland Act, aimed at eliminating this double liability of bank shareholders, but the creation of the FDIC required another economic collapse, in 1929, to be implemented.

After the Fed was created, the Federal Reserve subsequently eliminated the double liability of bank collapse by shifting the bank's liability to an independent government agency, in 1933, called The Federal Deposit Insurance Corporation,

The two banking reform acts, the Fed, in 1913, in conjunction with the FDIC, in 1933, created a new type of banking authority that was much more conducive to corporate global imperialism because U. S. banks gained freedom of liability from wrongful acts committed against the depositors.

A quasi-government agency absorbed the market risk of bank default, allowing corporations and banks to engage in risk-free global investment opportunities.

The risk for banks and corporations was greatly reduced because of the government's promise to bail them out, during the next economic collapse.

Senator Aldrich, the convener of the Jekyll Island meeting, was not an ordinary, middle-class citizen. He was a powerful member of the

Northeastern ruling class. He was referred to by the press and public alike as the "general manager of the Nation."

Part of the secrecy of the group was an early agreement to call the new bank the "Federal Reserve," and not "The Third National Bank," or the "American Central Bank."

Another part of their secrecy was to only call themselves by their first names in meetings and in public.

To this end, members of the Jekyll Island group traveled to Jekyll Island by first name only, on Senator Aldrich's personal railroad car.

Attending the Jekyll Island meeting with Aldrich were:

• Prominent European banker and Kuhn, Loeb, & Co. partner Paul Warburg, who would later serve on the Federal Reserve's first Board of Governors, and whose knowledge of European central banking was crucial to the meeting's success. [because the model of the U. S. central bank looked just like the Bank of England.]
• J.P. Morgan & Co. senior partner Henry Davison.
• National City Bank of New York president Frank Vanderlip.
• Banker's Trust of New York vice president Benjamin Strong, who would later head the Federal Reserve Bank of New York.
• A. Piatt Andrew, Assistant Secretary of the Treasury.

Attendee Frank Vanderlip later wrote in his autobiography,

"None of us who participated [in the secret meeting] felt we were conspirators; on the contrary we felt we were engaged in patriotic work… Yet, who was there in Congress [elected representatives] who might have drafted a sound piece of legislation dealing with the purely banking [Ruling Class] problem with which we were concerned?"

In other words, like the 39 delegates to Madison's Convention, who possessed virtue, the only people with enough patriotic virtue to write the new banking legislation were the members of the group that met on Jekyll Island, in secret, to hammer out the details of the new bank.

At the meeting on Jekyll Island, Paul Warburg introduced a plan that was modeled on European central banks. The European banks were privately owned, and operated in secret and independent [beyond the consent of citizens] of the national governments of Europe. (Michael Bordo and William Roberds, A Return to Jekyll Island. The Origins, History, and Future of the Federal Reserve, 2013).

The primary function of the European banks was to act as a "reserve" bank to provide regional banks with reserves to meet economic emergencies, and to rapidly increase the money supply to provide liquidity to avoid a run on the bank's deposits.

Thus, the origin of the term "Federal Reserve."

This concept of a reserve of money to fund market transactions by the Bank, was also used in the Bretton Woods agreement after World War II, to establish the Fed as banker for the world, using U. S. dollars as the world's reserve currency to fund global corporate transactions.

Warburg's proposal aimed at granting power to the Federal Reserve to deny credit to small businesses, based upon the Fed's rules of the credit worthiness of small business loans.

According to Livingston,

"Warburg proposed to separate the money and capital markets by using the central bank to redefine acceptable bank assets, making it virtually impossible for small entrepreneurs to obtain capital to make investments in "unproductive" enterprises."

In other words, under Warburg's logic, bank loans to small business created over production, while bank loans and investments in Big Business created national economic growth.

Livingston notes the prevailing Ruling Class animosity to small business entrepreneurs by citing an editorial in the leading Business Magazine, in 1907:

"From the standpoint of the corporate-industrial business community, the magazine defined as a benefit [of a central bank] was precisely the problem with assets currency [providing small business with capital]… it would apparently benefit mainly small or marginal producers. Asset currency would not meet the requirements of an investment system dominated by large industrial corporations." [global imperial corporations]."

Warburg explained that his reason for creating the central bank was to control loans of the regional Federal Reserve banks to small business, by noting that,

"If individual banks were granted the power of note issuance on their general assets, small or regional entrepreneurs would be able to convert currency [small business profits] into capital. [to make investments]. A central bank that had a monopoly on the right of note issuance was critical to the restriction of unproductive capital investment." [by small entrepreneurial businesses].

Upon their return to Washington, the Jekyll Island group began a public relations campaign headed by Warburg, and funded by Big Banks, to promote the "Aldrich Plan."

At the time, Senator Carter Glass, a Democrat of Virginia, opposed the Aldrich Plan.

Glass stated:

"We object to the Aldrich Bill on the following points:

- Its entire lack of adequate government or public control of the banking mechanism it sets up.
- Its tendency to throw voting control into the hands of the large banks of the system.
- The extreme danger of inflation of currency inherent in the system.
- The insincerity of the bond-funding plan provided for by the measure, there being a barefaced pretense that this system was to cost the government nothing.
- The dangerous monopolistic aspects of the bill."

At the same time that Senator Glass was making his case against the Aldrich Plan, another committee, in the House, released its findings on the existence of a "Money Trust," that existed during the Gilded Age, in the American economy.

The Pujo Committee, a subcommittee of the House Banking Committee, found that:

"If by a 'money trust' is meant an established and well-defined identity and community of interest between a few leaders of finance ... which has resulted in a vast and growing concentration of control of money and credit in the hands of a comparatively few men ... the condition thus described exists in this country today ... To us the peril is manifest ... When we find ... the same man a director in a half dozen or more banks and trust companies all located in the same section of the same city, doing the same class of business and with a like set of associates similarly situated all belonging to the same group and representing the same class of interests, all further pretense of competition is useless."

The pattern of national economic collapse, after the creation of the Fed, follows a historically observable path.

According to Carmen M. Reinhart and Kenneth S. Rogoff, in their article, "International Aspects of Financial-Market Imperfections: The Aftermath of Financial Crises." (American Economic Review,

2009.), the observable sequence of events includes a pattern of money creation, speculation, and economic collapse.

They state,

"Severe financial crises share three characteristics:
First, asset market collapses are deep and prolonged. Real housing prices decline an average of 35 percent over six years, while equity prices collapse an average of 55 percent over a downturn of about three and a half years.

Second, the aftermath of banking crises is associated with profound declines in output and employment. The unemployment rate rises an average of 7 percentage points over the down phase of the cycle, which lasts, on average, over four years. In addition, output falls, from peak to trough, an average of over 9 percent, although the duration of the downturn, averaging roughly two years, is considerably shorter than for unemployment.

Third, the real value of government debt tends to explode, rising an average of 86 percent in the major post–World War II episodes…the main cause of debt explosions is not the costs of bailing out and recapitalizing the banking system. The main cause of debt increases are the inevitable collapse in tax revenues that governments incur as a result of deep and prolonged output contractions, and the countercyclical fiscal policies in advanced economies aimed at counteracting the downturn."

Reinhart and Rogoff cite the relationship between the economic collapse and the downturn in government tax revenues, as the culprit for causing the collapse, in something like the "infinite regress," described by Kenneth Arrow, as the impossibility theorem."

In their telling, the government needs more money, after the collapse, in order to engage in more Fed manipulation of the money supply aimed at "countercyclical fiscal policies aimed at counteracting the downturn."

In other words, the culprit of collapse is Keynesian General Equilibrium theory, which directs the government agents to increase government debt, taxes, and spending, to prop up economic growth so that the economy can return to the prior equilibrium, which occurred ten years earlier, in the boom part of the collapse.

The era of loose credit allows elected representatives and corporate crony agencies to plunder national financial resources, and make worthless investments that do not create "real" economic growth.

The era of loose credit allows the crony capitalists and corrupt elected representatives to rack up incredible profits during the bubble part of the era of plunder for the assets that they bought during the previous collapse, for pennies on the dollar.

The era of plunder, and investment speculation ends in economic collapse, where the Ruling Class escapes unharmed, because crony capitalism allows the government to bail them out, and make them "whole" again from their losses.

The period of economic collapse is preceded by a sharp contraction of economic aggregate demand caused by both credit restrictions on small business and decreased money supply, which causes commodity prices of farmers to collapse, and the income of small business owners to decline.

The three events of 1913, (the Fed creation, the 16th and 17th Amendments), were coordinated with a series of social welfare acts, intended to cushion the economic effects of the transition of the American economy to a global imperial power.

The legislation to promote the transition to a global imperial power was based upon a continuation of Madison's ideology that only a certain small set of elites should control the agencies of government.

In the earlier version of this ideology, the belief was based upon the idea that the natural aristocracy possessed the moral value of virtue that would allow the elites to make selfless decisions that would benefit all social classes.

In the later version of this ideology, beginning with President Wilson, the ideology shifted to the logic that government should be run by experts, whose brains were more advanced than the brains of common citizens.

Joshua Stylman writes,

"In his 1887 essay "The Study of Administration," Wilson explicitly advocated for a government run by 'experts' insulated from public opinion: 'The field of administration is a field of business. It is removed from the hurry and strife of politics... Administrative questions are not political questions.' He argued directly that 'The many have no business with the selection of technical administrators any more than they have with the selection of scientists.' ...Wilson's vision was deeply intertwined with both class and racial prejudices. Historical records document his belief that only people of a certain education, social class, and background possessed the capacity for wise governance of everyone else. In the name of democracy, he effectively advocated for a class oligarchy as the ruling paradigm."

In the Progressive Era legislation, following the 1913 events, the new version of the ideology promoted the idea that the government should become the welfare protector of common citizens, and act as a counter-force to the power of global Big Business.

According to Randall Holcombe and Donald Lacombe,

"Trusts were oppressing factory workers as well as farmers, and big banking interests were as hard on small businesses as they were on small farms. The solution, both Populists and Progressives agreed, was more government control of economic activity, and as already noted, the Progressive agenda was advanced substantially in the first two decades of the 20th century." (Interests Versus Ideology In the Ratification of the 16th and 17th Amendments, 1998).

In the boom period, after the economic collapse of 1914, corporate profits increased by 76%, leading up to the next economic collapse in 1929.

Using the precedent that Big Corporations are persons, the U. S. Supreme Court issued a series of rulings that favored corporations on conflicts over union organizing, minimum wage laws, child labor laws.

Secretary of the Treasury Andrew W. Mellon, of the Mellon banking empire, convinced Congress to cut income taxes from 50% to 20%, which was partly the cause of the boom era of the 1920s.

In October 1929, the stock market and the economy crashed, again.

By 1933 at least a quarter of the U. S. work force was unemployed. Adjusted for deflation, salaries had fallen by 40 percent and industrial wages by 60 percent, over four years.

During the time leading up to World War II, the U. S. Government sent a half billion dollars to states for emergency welfare relief.

By 1935, about 6 million American workers were employed by various government work force projects.

President Roosevelt's work projects were a part of the earlier ideology of President Wilson that the government experts could manage the U. S. economy, as if it were a gigantic corporation, similar in concept to how the Soviets believed that communist experts could manage a planned economy.

The economy crashed again, in 1937, demonstrating the fallacy of Keynesian economic theory that increased government spending could cause economic growth.

Following the advice of his economic experts, Roosevelt cut government spending dramatically, in 1936, further prolonging the economic recovery, which did not materialize until after the increased war production, in 1942.

Roosevelt's new social security plan removed an additional $2,000,000,000 from private sector aggregate demand,

Between August 1937 and May 1938 the index of production fell from 117 to 76 (on a 1929 base of 100), and unemployment increased by perhaps 4,000,000 persons.

From 1941 to the end of World War II, in 1945, about 60% of the entire cost of the War was financed by debt. The same investment technique mentioned by Benjamin Franklin, during the Revolutionary War, worked again after 1945, for wealthy investors who had enough income to buy the debt at a cheap price, and sell at the much higher price, in the boom of 1951.

The Transition to Monopoly Capitalism.
1945 – 1985.

From around 1945 to 1985, the Bretton Woods global agreement, between allies at the end of the War, ushered in a new type of global financial system, dominated by the military and financial power of the U. S to enforce global compliance with the agreement.

The alliance of power between Big Corporations and Big Government added a new partner of Big Labor, whose union membership increased from around 15% of the U. S. labor force, in 1940, to around 25% in 1950.

The Bretton Woods Agreement established the U. S. dollar as the global reserve currency, meaning that global economic transactions would have to be paid in U. S. dollars.

The "reserve" being mentioned is a reserve of dollars, held in foreign central banks, that could be used by those other nations, to convert their local currency into U. S. dollars.

This type of reserve in central banks required sophisticated coordination among banks to keep the payment settlement process running smoothly, which required the creation of a new bank in Switzerland called the "Bank for International Settlement,"

In addition to the new Swiss bank, the Bretton Woods agreement established a new International Monetary Fund (IMF) and the new World Bank, to manage and administer loans between Western developed nations and third world, underdeveloped nations.

The creation of these new global institutions was a part of the gradual shift of the American monopoly capitalist system to a more global predatory corporate system because corporations domiciled in the U. S. began to see themselves as citizens of the world, not linked to the sovereignty of the United States.

The 1951 Fed-Treasury Accord and the subsequent "Lean Against the Wind" policy period was a crucial turning point in the Fed history of managed corporate globalism.

The 1951 Accord freed the Fed from its obligation to maintain fixed rates on government debt (which had been in place since WWII), marking the beginning of the Fed's more independent monetary policy.

The "Lean Against the Wind" approach, primarily associated with Chairman William McChesney Martin (1951-1970), aimed to preemptively tighten monetary policy during economic expansions and ease during contractions.

The fundamental idea was to use Keynesian theory to moderate economic cycles rather than react to economic collapse after the fact.

In the Fed's application of "Lean Against the Wind," whatever the direction the economic winds were blowing, the Fed would lean against the wind, in the other direction.

This policy guarantees future economic collapse, in another example of Kenneth Arrow's idea of infinite regress, that the boom-bust business cycle will continue to repeat itself, caused by the Fed's policy.

The New York Federal Open Market Committee (FOMC), operates without Congressional oversight, entirely disconnected from the consent of the governed, and makes interest rate decisions based upon their Ruling Class social backgrounds, not on behalf of the interests of common citizens.

The Federal Reserve Bank, as a private corporation, also makes a guaranteed profit from the interest paid from owning U.S. Treasury notes it acquires as part of open market operations.

The New York Regional Federal Bank acts as a broker to buy and sell U. S. Treasury notes through its Open Market Window. The New York Regional Bank makes commissions and fees from acting as the broker for the U. S. Treasury.

A great portion of the U. S. Treasury bonds are bought and held by the Federal Reserve Bank.

Currently, of the entire $36 trillion in U. S. debt, the Federal Reserve Banks owns about 20%, on which it receives a guaranteed rate of interest, paid by the U. S. Treasury.

The left hand of the government, the Treasury, issues bonds, and the right hand of the Fed buys the bonds, and makes a guaranteed profit.

In the language of the Fed, this transaction of buying government debt is called "quantitative easing."

The economic effect of quantitative easing is to inject imaginary, non-physical dollars into the economy, in a computerized accounting system, where commercial bank assets are credited with the new imaginary money, created by the Fed.

The Fed also receives interest and profits on its foreign currency investments, when the New York Regional Bank engages in foreign currency exchange markets.

Because the U. S. dollar serves as the global reserve currency, the New York FRB is in a perfect position to forecast the movement of the U. S. dollar against other currencies, because the Fed controls the rate of money expansion and money contraction.

In other words, the Fed has a very beneficial insider insight to profit on the currency exchange market because foreign currency reserves are denominated in U. S. dollars, as a result of the Bretton Woods Agreement.

The Fed uses its guaranteed profits to pay all of its fixed operational costs, including the lavish salaries of the Directors, professional staff, and Presidents of the Fed and regional banks.

After the Fed pays all of its fixed operational costs, it returns the left-over profits to the U. S. Treasury.

This business model is called "Win-Win," for the Fed and U. S. Treasury.

In 2020, the Fed earned $90.5 billion in profits. Of this, $1.6 billion was paid out in dividends on stock owned by the member commercial banks of the regional Fed banks.

After the payment of corporate operating costs of managing and administering the Fed and the regional banks, the Fed sends the rest of the profits back to the U. S. Treasury.

The right hand of the Fed makes guaranteed profits, and the left hand of the U. S. Treasury obtains the profits from the Fed at the end of each year.

The annual remittance of profits from the Fed back to the U. S. Treasury provides the ideological justification for the Fed's statement that its mission is to serve the public.

We agree with George Selgin, William D. Lastrapes, and Lawrence H. White, in their article, "Has the Fed Been a Failure?" (SSRN, 2012.).

They cite a consistent pattern of monetary policy mistakes made by the Fed, over a long period of time.

They write,

"Our model also shows no clear improvement after World War II in the dynamic response [Lean Against the Wind] of output to aggregate demand shocks. Whereas one might expect the Fed, in its role as output stabilizer, to tighten the money supply in the face of positive IS (investment-spending) shocks and to expand it in response to positive shocks to money demand, [LM, liquidity money], the response functions we estimate indicate instead that the Fed has tended to expand the money stock in response to IS shocks, causing larger and more persistent deviations of output from its natural level than would have occurred in response to similar shocks during the pre-Fed period. At the same time, the Fed was less effective than the classical gold standard had been in expanding the money supply in response to unpredictable reductions in money‘s velocity."

We disagree with the conclusion of Selgin that the Fed's management of the economy has been a failure.

From the perspective of traditional economic theory, what first appears to be a policy failure is actually systematic wealth extraction, based upon the Fed's economic objective to manage the economy to benefit the American nobility class.

From the perspective of the American nobility, the Fed's management of the boom-bust economy has been a huge success, and is operating according to the initial negotiated agreement at Jekyl Island, in 1913.

The Federal Reserve Bank of St. Louis publishes the GDP-Based Recession Indicator Index, which looks back in history at past economic data and measures the probability that the U.S. economy was in a recession during the indicated quarter.

The statistical hindsight of the St. Louis Fed is better than real-time estimates of the beginning of a recession, based upon contemporaneous subjective data, which are usually not released to the public for several years.

The Fed Index describes a perfectly symmetrical, recurring five year cycle of Fed induced economic chaos. The great benefit of this index is that its construction is entirely mechanical, and is based solely on real, not subjective, GDP data.

The Fed's data indicates that after 1970, the frequency of economic collapse increased, from the historical average of one every 10 years, to one economic collapse every five years.

Chapter 5. Diagram 1. St. Louis Federal Reserve Bank GDP-Based Recession Indicator Index. 1967 – 2020.

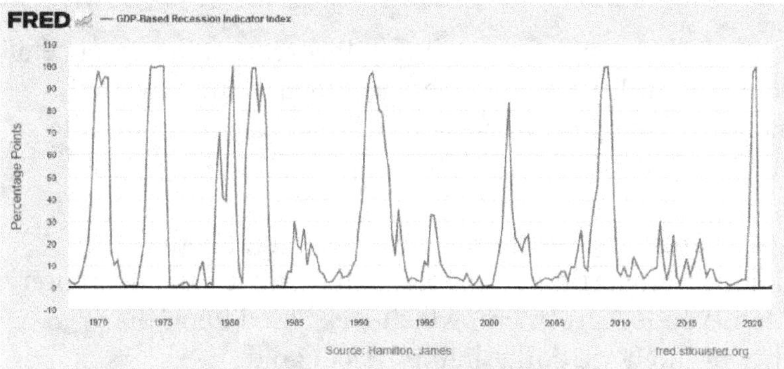

A better, new U. S. constitution would eliminate the Fed's discretionary authority to manipulate money supply and interest rates, in order to allow the U. S. economy to emerge into a beneficial economy.

The Fed does not have a valid economic model of the U. S. economy that informs the Fed of the projection of the macro economy, even though the Fed often refers to the "evolution" of the U. S. macro economy.

The "Lean Against the Wind idea is simply an intellectual fraud, perpetrated on an unsuspecting American public that the Fed Board of Governors knows what is good for the American economy, and is managing the economy with precision.

John Taylor, in his article, "Systemic Risk and the Role of Government." Speech given at the Conference on Financial Innovation and Crises, Federal Reserve Bank of Atlanta, Jekyll Island, Georgia, May 12th, (2009), stated,

"In short, the Federal Reserve System, as presently constituted, is no more worthy of being regarded as the last word in monetary management than the National Currency System it replaced almost a century ago…More generally, government should set clear rules of the game, stop changing them during the game, and enforce them. The rules do not have to be perfect, but the rule of law is essential."

Following Kenneth Arrow's impossibility theorem, in the absence of a economic grand utility national welfare function, that the Fed seeks to maximize, the policy decisions of the Fed lead to infinite regress to the next economic collapse.

Beginning in August 15, 1971, President Nixon unilaterally terminated dollar convertibility to gold, and disrupted the operation of the Bretton Woods Agreement, which was based upon the convertibility of the U. S. dollar into physical gold.

After the elimination of the gold standard, the value of the U. S. dollar was entirely a mirage based upon the strength of the U. S. economy, and the military power of the U. S. to enforce the terms of the Bretton Woods Agreement.

The sudden elimination of the gold standard disrupted the operation of the global central banker's ability to predict the value of their own currencies against the value of the U. S. dollar.

The western alliance bankers met in New York, in 1985, to craft a new agreement on how to determine the value of the U. S. dollar. Robert Brenner, in The Boom and the Bubble: The U. S. in the World Economy, (2002), writes,

"The Plaza Accord was a joint agreement signed on September 22, 1985, at the Plaza Hotel in New York City, between France, West Germany, Japan, the United Kingdom, and the United States, to depreciate the U.S. dollar in relation to the French franc, the German Deutsche Mark, the Japanese yen and the British pound sterling by intervening in currency markets. The U.S. dollar depreciated significantly from the time of the agreement until it was replaced by the Louvre Accord in 1987."

According to Brenner,

"They all agreed that they would intervene in the currency markets whenever necessary to push down the US dollar."

In other words, in the absence of the gold standard, the value of the U. S. dollar was artificially too high, and a reduction in value, called "devaluation," by the other central bankers, was required to maintain the Bretton Woods global trade agreements.

The reason, or cause of the U. S. dollar's inflated value, was the increased issuance of long term debt, by the U. S. Treasury, to finance the current consumption of the Welfare State, and increased military expenditures, related to the U. S. enforcement of the Bretton Woods Agreement.

The Transition From Monopoly Capitalism to American Predatory State Capitalism.
1992 – 2025.

From around 1992, with the first enactment of NAFTA, and subsequently, the Chinese entrance to the World Trade Organization, in 2001, the emergence of a "rules-based" global trading order, began the replacement of the concept of national sovereignty with the concept of a global market government.

During this economic era, large corporations moved their production and supply facilities to China and Mexico.

This is why small communities and large metro regions lost middle and working class jobs.

For example, in North Carolina, manufacturing employment dropped from around 800,000 jobs, in 1985 to around 150,000 jobs in 2000, leaving towns and counties economically devastated, 25 years later. (Laurie Thomas Vass, Industrial recruitment and the path of North Carolina's economic development to the year 2000 : a public discussion paper for North Carolina's Project 2000, N. C. Department of Labor, 1982).

This final step towards Corporate Predatory Capitalism cemented a global financial architecture in which the three central bank power centers [London, Berlin, D. C.] operated through interlocking directorates and financial relationships independent of constitutional constraints.

Soon after the transition to the American Predatory State began, the U. S. economy collapsed again, in 2008.

The cause of the 2008 collapse was the Fed's manipulation of credit and money supply, on behalf of the American nobility class, which caused real estate assets to skyrocket, in the boom phase of the business cycle, leading up to the crash in asset values at the end of 2008.

According to Brenner (2002), the Fed increased the M2 money supply by over 8% per year, from 1995, to the entrance of China, to the WTO, in 2001.

The manipulation of the money supply was the fuel that ignited the asset boom before the 2008 crash.

In his 2013 comments about the Fed's bailout of Big Banks, after the 2008 economic collapse, Richard Fisher, former President and CEO of the Federal Reserve Bank of Dallas, stated,

"I will argue that the big banks represent not only a threat to financial stability (of the U. S. economy), but to fair and open competition, that they are the practitioners of crony capitalism and not the agents of democratic capitalism that makes our country great."

Prior to the 2008 collapse, the biggest 5 banks owned about 41% of all domestic financial assets.

After 2008, the 5 banks owned 49% of all U. S. domestic assets. The increase in assets of the 5 banks is entirely due to the Fed's policy decisions to eliminate small banks, in order to consolidate power in the 5 big banks.

The chairmen of the Fed, and the Secretary of the Treasury, during the time of the 2008 crisis were former employees of the 5 big banks.

Fisher noted that there were 10 big banks, primarily located in New York, who obtained special banking privileges [for buying and selling U. S. bonds], at the Fed's New York Federal Open Market window.

As a result of their privileged status at the Fed's Open Market Window, the big banks obtained a type of insurance policy from the Fed that insulated them from credit risk, and the economic chaos inflicted on ordinary American citizens, by the Fed's boom-bust policies.

Fisher explained,

"A dozen megabanks today control almost 70 percent of the assets in the U.S. banking industry. The concentration of assets has been ongoing, but it intensified during the 2008-09 financial crisis, when several failing giants were absorbed by larger, presumably healthier ones. [crony capitalism]. Today, these megabanks—a mere 0.2 percent of banks, deemed candidates to be considered "too big to fail"—are treated differently from the other 99.8 percent and differently from other businesses... Without fear of failure, these banks and their counterparties can take excessive risks."

George Selgin, et. al., also cite the rule of law in their analysis of the Fed's persistent failure to manage the U. S. economy, on behalf of the common American citizen.. (Has the Fed Been a Failure? Cato Institute Working Paper, 2013).

They write,

"At the most philosophical or jurisprudential level, the case for a constitutional constraint on monetary policy-makers derives from the general case for —the rule of law rather than rule by authorities. The rule of law means constraints against arbitrary governance so that citizens can know what to expect from their government."

Brenner, in the Boom and the Bust (2002), explains that in the transition to American Predatory Capitalism, the Fed is trapped in a failure do-loop because U. S. economic growth is the mirage that foreign banks use to calculate the value of their own currencies, but the data on economic growth is related to increased government spending, not on increased private domestic investment.

Increased government spending, and increased government debt, do not generate real economic growth, and the service sector does not possess the income and employment multipliers for distributing economic growth to the broader society.

As a result of the transition to Predatory Capitalism, the U. S. economy does not possess the capacity to generate future economic growth because private consumption now constitutes about 80% of all GDP, and service sector jobs constitute about 70% of all jobs.

The key factor in future real economic growth is private domestic investment, primarily into 9 high technology industries.

After the transition to Predatory Capitalism, the rate of private domestic capital investment in the domestic U. S. economy has not been great enough to bring the U. S. economy out of the Nash equilibrium, after the 2008 economic collapse.

A Nash Equilibrium is an example of a stalled economy, where no economic force is great enough to move the economy out of the period of stagnation, where it can rest for decades at a time.

The increased government spending, and increased debt, in conjunction with the structural economic change related to moving industrial manufacturing to China, is not great enough to generate sustained economic growth.

The Fed's management of the economy, after 2008, has led to vastly increased concentration of wealth and profits in the top 1% of the U. S. society.

Brenner writes,

"The ownership of equities, and thus gains from speculative appreciation, is highly concentrated. The top 20 per cent owners of all equities thus possesses between 96 and 98 per cent of all assets in the form of stocks. Researchers at the Federal Reserve Board have now, however, demonstrated: first, that those in the top 20 per cent by income accounted for 79 per cent of the aggregate increase of the ratio of net in personal disposal income that took place in the 1990s." George G. Kaufman, a professor of economics, and consultant to the Chicago Regional Federal Reserve Bank, explained in his 2000 article, "Banking and currency crises and systemic risk: Lessons from recent events (Federal Reserve Bank of Chicago, 2000),

"It is a common misconception to think that imposing losses on [bank] management and shareholders, while shielding counterparties and creditors, is enough to contain moral hazard. [plunder]. So long as bank creditors can expect high returns on the upside, with implicit government guarantees against losses on the downside, they will lend too cheaply to risky poorly diversified banks, making overly high leverage (thin capital) [worthless investments] an attractive strategy. Normal market discipline against risk-taking is thus significantly undermined."

James K. Galbraith, in The Predator State (2008), describes predatory state capitalism as

"A system wherein the rich have come to feast on decaying systems built for the middle class, characterized by a finance-led, corporate-dominated economy that prioritizes elite interests through deregulation, privatization, and exploitation of public resources."

In the transition from the earlier era of monopoly capitalism, Big Corporations moved their production facilities from the U. S. to China and Mexico in order to exploit the slave labor in those nations.

As a result of the lower labor costs, U. S. domiciled companies doing manufacturing in China were able to increase U. S. prices on their goods by about 70% over the marginal cost of production, when those goods were eventually sold in the U. S.. (David Autor, H., Dorn, David, Hanson, Gordon H., The China Syndrome: Local Labor Market Effects Of Import Competition In The United States, NBER Working Paper 18054, 2012.)

Autor et al., describe this increase of price over marginal cost as "pure profit."

Instead of the promised reduction in U. S. domestic inflation, after 2001, the rates of inflation increased, caused by the money and interest rate manipulation by the Fed, which continues to cause asset bubbles in real estate and hard assets, which serves to benefit bankers and wealthy citizens.

The component of GDP comprised of pure profits, which was previously earned by middle class citizens in domestic. U. S. production, prior to 1992, has been shifted from the middle and working classes to the executives and owners of the large U. S. corporations.

The share of U. S. GDP composed of pure profits increased from 3% of GDP, in 1985, to 17% of GDP, in 2015. (Gauti B Eggertsson,. et al., quoting Kaldor And Piketty's Facts: The Rise Of Monopoly Power In The United States, NBER Working Paper 24287, 2018.).

In the absence of the former profits and income flows in the U. S. domestic economy from domestic production, the domestic economy does not have the levels of aggregate demand to cause domestic economic growth.

Into this gap in aggregate demand caused by global trade with China, steps the Fed, with increased government spending, increased issuance of debt, and vastly increased military spending, intended to enforce the Bretton Woods Agreement.

Paul M. Sweezy and Harry Magdoff explain that the U. S. economy has become dependent on U. S. government spending on both welfare and the military to keep the U. S economy from enduring another Great Depression.

They write,

"The more than $55 billion spent (1972 figures) annually on what the government agencies classify "national defense" has a chain-reaction effect, called the "multiplier" effect. It is estimated that for every $1 spent on "national defense" another $1 to $1.40 of economic output is stimulated in other supply chain industries... approximately 7 million people are employed in some phase of "national defense," and another 6 to 9 million are employed due to the economic stimulus of defense ending." (The Dynamics of U. S. Capitalism, 1972).

We agree with the economic analysis of Baran and Sweezy that, after the transition from monopoly capitalism to predatory capitalism, the U. S. domestic economy is too weak to generate economic growth because all the income and employment multiplier supply chains moved to China.

The purported Keynesian economic income and employment multiplier effects of increased government spending no longer occur in the domestic U. S. economy because those intermediate supply chains were moved to China.

They explain,

"There is no way to avoid the conclusion that monopoly capitalism is a self-contradictory economic system. It tends to generate ever more surplus, [pure profits] yet it fails to provide the consumption and investment outlets [in the domestic U. S. economy] required for the absorption of a rising surplus…it follows that the normal state of the monopoly capitalist economy is stagnation." (Paul Baran and Paul Sweezy, Monopoly Capital: An Essay on the American Economic and Social Order, 1966).

We slightly disagree with their conclusion that the cause of U. S. economic dysfunction is exclusively the power of the ruling class to set the national economic agenda.

Rather, we allege that the cause of the economic dysfunction in American economic history is the unfair rules in Madison's constitution, which placed the monetary power in the hands of the Fed to perpetuate the boom-bust economy.

Baran and Sweezy were, however, correct in identifying the moral value of Jefferson's egalitarianism in the Declaration as the social glue that holds American society together in citizen allegiance to obey the rule of law.

They write,

"The egalitarianism of capitalist ideology is one of its strengths, not to be lightly discarded. People are taught from earliest childhood and by all conceivable means that everyone has an equal opportunity, and that the inequalities which stare them in the face are the result not of unjust institutions but of their own superior or inferior natural endowments. It would contradict this teaching to set up, in the manner of European class—divided societies, two distinct educational systems, one for the oligarchy and one for the masses."

If Madison's constitution had been written as a compact between citizens, that citizens had agreed to, before the compact was ratified, then citizens would continue, today, to have a reason to obey the unwritten rule of law.

However, Madison's constitution is not a compact between citizens, but an amoral legal contract between ruling class elites, to ameliorate financial conflict by establishing rules of the game.

The modern incarnation of those ruling class elites betrayed the American middle and working classes when they moved their production facilities to China.

After China's WTO entry in 2001, large U. S. global corporations increasingly operated through internal import-export value chains that were insulated from traditional price mechanisms that operate in a competitive market.

Traditional Fed monetary policy assumes price transmission mechanisms where interest rate changes affect domestic prices and economic behavior. That initial assumption of Keynesian theory is no longer valid in the era of Predatory State Capitalism.

The only real economic effect of the Fed's monetary policy is to guarantee the start of the next boom-bust cycle.

Domestic U. S. global corporations, with internalized value chains are relatively immune to domestic monetary conditions caused by the Fed.

The income and employment multiplier effects of Keynesian theory occur in foreign value chains, not in the domestic U. S. economy.

As a condition of production in China, the CCP requires U. S. corporations to share U. S. product and production technology with the CCP, which replicates the technology in communist production plants.

The current build-up of Chinese military strength has largely been financed by the shared profits with U. S. domestic corporations.

(Laurie Thomas Vass, Ending The Predatory Corporate Capitalist War on the American Middle Class: The American Entrepreneurial Alternative to Totalitarian Corporate Globalism, 2024).

In its more general application, Arrow's impossibility theorem explains that the concept of a grand social welfare function that ruling class elites attempt to maximize in making beneficial collective decisions is a myth.

Both Madison and Arrow were concerned about the tyranny of the majority oppressing the rights of the minority.

Madison's unfair rules created the exact opposite form of tyranny, where a self-selected elite, insulated from the consent of the governed, make decisions to direct global income to themselves.

In the transition to Predatory State Capitalism, the global ruling class has essentially created a system that transcends both market capitalism and state control, and deploys AI to enhance censorship control over citizens, and uses human-like robots to eliminate jobs for American workers.

The key for continued corporate control over American society is control over the direction and pace of technological innovation because technology commercialization causes economic growth.

In the context of confronting the tyranny of AI and robotics, human creativity and ingenuity can continually generate new value through recombination, reimagining, and innovation.

AI and robotics could either amplify this unlimited human resource, by removing routine tasks and freeing human cognition or constrain the insight-imagination of the human brain, with increased government surveillance and social rule enforcement..

The theory of beneficial economics recognizes that the truly scarce resource in America isn't human ingenuity itself, but rather the specific social, institutional, and cultural conditions that allow the human brain to make natural everyday market decisions that lead to the emergence of a stable social order.

The brain's self-organization neuronal processes are open systems that exchange information with their environment. The emergent decisions are co-created through the interaction between neural mechanisms and social/cultural contexts.

This is why fair constitutional rules are the essential factors of production that transform potential American ingenuity into actual beneficial innovation.

A fair constitutional system would limit the functions of government to protection of equal civil rights and government activities that increase the rate of economic growth through increased rates of private domestic capital investment.

A better U. S. constitution would

1. Protect property rights and enforce contracts. Your home, your business, your privacy. (The protective state).
2. Provide necessary public goods. Public spending on infrastructure that helps all citizens prosper. (The productive state).
3. Eliminate the unfair rules that have allowed large corporation to prey upon a defenselss population (The citizen sovereignty state).
4. Guard against the loss of America's technology. (The entrepreneurial technology Innovation state).

Better constitutional rules that would best support human ingenuity as an unlimited resource in the AI era likely need to:

1. Address the potential for technological concentration of power.
2. Support regional metro technological diversity.
3. Protect the conditions for tacit knowledge creation and diffusion
4. Establish guardrails that prevent the Chinese Communist Party from capturing U. S. technological innovation.

The only American factor of production, after the transition to Corporate Predatory Capitalism, to globalism that is not controlled by the corporations and the government is the unlimited imagination of American entrepreneurs to dream up new products.

This factor of production was the initial national comparative advantage, in 1776, and now constitutes a threat to the corporate control over the pace and direction of technology evolution. (Laurie Thomas Vass, Ending The Predatory Corporate Capitalist War on the American Middle Class: The American Entrepreneurial Alternative to Totalitarian Corporate Globalism, 2024).

American middle and working class citizens must understand U. S. economic history, and its connection to Madison's unfair rules of the game, in order to begin their task of crafting a better economic constitution.

Chapter 6. How Modern American Crony Capitalism Prevents the Emergence of A Beneficial Social Order.

In its more general application, Kenneth Arrow's 1951 impossibility theorem predicts that majority tyranny over minority rights, will be the general social welfare outcome of democratic voting rules. (Kenneth Arrow, Social Choice and Individual Values, 1951).

In democratic political decision-making, Arrow concludes that there is no rational way, or coherent way, to aggregate individual voting preferences into a consistent social ordering of the end-state that citizens desire.

About 37 years later, Arrow worked with economists at the Sante Fe Institute to provide a new economic theory, focused on how complex adaptive systems can lead to the emergence of a stable beneficial society. (Philip W. Anderson, Kenneth J. Arrow, David Pines, The economy as an evolving complex system : the proceedings of the evolutionary paths of the global workshop, held September 1987, in Santa Fe, New Mexico, 1988).

The difference between democratic voting systems and market choice systems can be seen using the example of citizens in a metro region voting on the best restaurant in the city.

In the voting system, voters preferences are inconsistent in ranking the best restaurant. Some voters might prefer Italian over Chinese, Chinese over Mexican, but Mexican over Italian.

But in a market system, the best restaurants naturally emerge to serve different tastes, price points, and preferences without anyone voting on what should exist.

In Arrow's new economic theory, when people are free to make individual market choices, based upon attaining their personal, individual goals, a beneficial economic order emerges naturally.

The barrier to attaining a rational social welfare outcome from political voting does not affect the rational, beneficial social outcome from aggregating, or counting up, individual market choices to determine a preferred social ordering. (Brian Kogelmann, Buchanan and Arrow on Democracy, Impossibility, and Market, 2018).

In other words, majority voting to attain a desired society has theoretical defects that market choices do not have.

Arrow's solution to the defect in democratic voting systems is to allow the market, as a complex adaptive system, to create individual free choice to attain desired social welfare outcomes.

Arrow's concern over a democratic majority oppressing a political minority was the same concern Madison had about the majority of common citizens using their voting power to oppress the property rights of the American natural aristocracy, in 1787.

As we described in Chapter 3, Madison established an unfair set of constitutional rules that benefitted the natural aristocracy by limiting the participation of common citizens in the operation of the centralized government.

Under Madison's rules, "We, the people" only existed on the day of election.

As we described in Chapter 4, in the transition to American Predatory State Capitalism, (1992 – 2025), the global ruling class has essentially created a system that transcends elections, competitive market capitalism and state regulatory control, and deploys AI to enhance control over citizens.

The choice of American voters to vote on eliminating Predatory State Capitalism is not a choice on the ballot.

As a consequence, the range of market choices to pursue individual destiny, in the brains of individual citizens, is limited to the set of options offered by the Predatory Capitalist ruling class.

In the language and philosophy of Arrow, the translation of citizen preferences from voting, after the transition to Predatory Capitalism, would have the features of a social welfare preference ordering that violates his rule of non-dictatorship.

In Arrow's conception of dictatorship, one set of social preferences becomes the social welfare preference imposed by the dictator on all citizens.

In a dictatorship, the only social preference that matters for determining what the society will look like is the exclusive preference of the dictator.

In the case of modern American politics, the only preference that matters is the preference of the global corporate elite, who manage the global economy, independent of the will of the citizens, as if the corporate elite were a dictator.

The everyday market preferences of citizens, in their role as voters, are never considered in the decision-making process of the dictator, which means that in Predatory Capitalism, the beneficial social order that results from the individual brain's market choices can never emerge.

As an example of modern dictatorship, Angelo Codevilla, in "America's Ruling Class And the Perils of Revolution," (2010), explains how the elites used tax money to bail themselves out of the global financial crisis in the Fall of 2008.

Codevilla wrote,

"The leaders of the Republican and Democratic parties, agreed that spending $700 billion to buy the investors' "toxic assets" was the only alternative to the U.S. economy's "systemic collapse." In this, President George W. Bush and his would-be Republican successor John McCain agreed with the Democratic candidate, Barack Obama."

In other words, the only choice for managing the economic collapse was the exclusive social class political preferences of the ruling class to use tax dollars to bail out big banks and corporations. [The more accurate figure of the amount of bailout was $1.7 trillion, not $700 billion].

The decisions by the elites to bail themselves out were reached in secret, primarily by two former bankers, one in the Fed and one in the Treasury Department, whose banks were the biggest beneficiaries of the bailouts.

The same set of elites, at the Fed and the Treasury Department, who caused the collapse in 2008, were also the same set of people who made the social political decisions on what to do about the collapse.

The decision to bail out the banks and corporations was not on the ballot, and there were no alternatives presented to citizens, by the bankers, on what to do.

Like the top-down, one party political system in China, the American global corporate uni-party political system is a one party top down system, based in Washington, which functions entirely independent of the consent of the governed. (Laurie Thomas Vass, Ending The Predatory Corporate Capitalist War on the American Middle Class: The American Entrepreneurial Alternative to Totalitarian Corporate Globalism, 2024).

Sundance, writing at The Last Refuge, explains the crony capitalist system as the "uni-party" because the financial interests of Big Government, Big Business, and Big Labor, operate as one political organization. (The DC UniParty and the SSCI Have One Overarching Issue They Will Defend, Support for the Surveillance State, January 11, 2025).

The uni-party's power and control over the political system is being enhanced by the recent entrance of the use of artificial intelligence and control over the media propaganda, to create a permanent surveillance state to control citizens around the globe.

Sundance writes,

"The core of their creation [crony capitalist system] aligns and supports a fully comprehensive American surveillance state…As a result, the corrupt DC functionaries operate without any accountability, [rule of law] no corrective action ever takes place, no accountability is metered out..We [the people] are in an abusive relationship with our government. There really is no other way to look at it."

The operation of the uni-party surveillance system explains why the votes of American citizen don't matter, and why citizens are powerless to reform the Predatory Capitalist State.

As we described in Chapter 4, the transition to the American Predatory State occurred over 150 years, through 4 distinct economic eras, each with a progressively more powerful centralized government, and all of which were increasingly disconnected from the consent of the governed.

The collective economic decision making of the elites in the global Predatory system are not based upon written rules, or objective science, to determine the best course of action. The decisions reflect a common, unified social class ideology of how to use government to attain their social class financial goals.

Unlike the unified, coherent social class ideology of the American ruling class, the middle and working classes in America do not have a coherent ideology of their own class interests.

Instead of a social class ideology, the middle class has an imaginary grand social welfare function, proposed by Keynes, which purports to improve social welfare for all citizens by manipulating money supply and interest rates.

The public relations to promote the existence of an imaginary social welfare function is that the Fed's decisions are objective and scientific.

In the modern, Predatory dictatorship, the only social preference that matters is the social preference determined by the Fed. As James Buchanan has observed, the welfare the Fed attempts to maximize is their own.

As Arrow has demonstrated, the Keynesian grand social welfare function does not exist, in reality. Its existence is entirely an imaginary fiction in the minds of current liberal economists.

The Keynesian grand social welfare function is imaginary because it assumes that some external observer can weigh and compare the welfare of different people, or in the era of Democrat Party collectivism, of different social groups.

That decision by the mythical observer, who compares fair social justice outcomes, only occurs after market decisions have been made, and after income and profits from the market exchange have already been distributed in the form of wages and profits.

In other words, the Keynesian solution to obtain social justice is entirely based upon re-distribution of income and profits to attain the desired social welfare outcomes, after citizens have made their market decisions about the future life they want to attain by their market choices.

The mythical observer who implements the decisions about attaining social welfare outcomes is the Fed, by constantly changing the rate of money creation and interest rates.

But, it is not social welfare, or social justice, that is maximized by the Fed, it is social class welfare of the ruling class, based upon their ruling class ideology.

As we explained in Chapter 4, the Fed does not have a credible economic model to guide its decisions that would aim at beneficial social welfare outcomes.

As in the case of the 2008 bailouts, the Fed always does what is in the best financial interests of banks and corporations.

The Fed’s decisions, since 1913, have lead to permanent boom-bust economic cycle, that allows elites to benefit during the boom phase, and to avoid losses, in the collapse phase..

The Fed’s monetary policy acts as insurance to bail the elites out of the economic crisis that the elites create with their risky, speculative investments, during the boom phase.

The absence of a Keynesian social welfare function doesn't mean collective decisions stop getting made. It means that the collective decisions, both economic and political, get made according to the preferences and interests of those with the power to impose their will on society.

And, after the transition to the American Predatory State, that power to impose its will on society is the ruling class global corporate elites.

Madison's constitutional structure enables the Predatory State to impose its will on society because there are no constitutional rules that limit the monopoly power of banks and large corporations.

Madison's system of checks, balances, and minority veto rights in the Senate structure and Electoral College, institutionalized the impossibility of democratic vote aggregation into a stable social welfare outcome that reflects the will of the majority of common citizens.

Rather than improving the decentralized state sovereignty system of The Articles of Confederation, , Madison’s rules institutionalized a permanent minority ruling class tyranny over the majority of citizens.

That minority tyranny is now in the hands of the Predatory Capitalist State.

In contrast to Feldman, who writes that Lincoln broke the Constitution (The Broken Constitution: Lincoln, Slavery, and the Refounding of America, 2021), we argue that the Constitution is not broken, it's working exactly as designed, by Madison, to prevent the majority of voters from pursuing their natural rights.

In the recent historical transition from monopoly capitalism to the Predatory Capitalist State, the concentrated political and economic power combines into a new unfair political system, described by Todd Zywicki as the Crony Capitalist State. (Rent-seeking, Crony Capitalism, and the Crony Constitution, 2015).

Zywicki explains,

"In the United States, the term "crony capitalism" refers to a political/economic system that resembles traditional political "corporatism." As used here, it describes a system in which government, big business, and powerful interest groups (especially labor unions) work together to further their joint interests…under crony capitalism politicians and regulators use businesses to advance the interests of politicians and interest groups [plunder] in a symbiotic relationship: government creates rents and then distributes them to itself and favored interests. Many of the relationships that grew up during the financial crisis and its aftermath through legislation such as the Dodd-Frank financial reform legislation [after the 2008 collapse] illustrate the differences between crony capitalism and mere rent-seeking."

The era of "mere rent seeking" refers to the monopoly capitalist period, from about 1945 to 1985.

In this prior era, before the transition to global corporatism, an alliance of power between Big Corporations, Big Government and Big Labor used lobbyists and political influence over elections to bend government policy to their own financial interests.

In the earlier period, corporations were successful in capturing the regulatory agencies, and used their political power to shift taxes to the middle and working class.

The financial and economic interests of common middle and working class citizens were not represented in the rent-seeking power alliance, and common citizens did not have an organized political party to represent their interests in D. C.

Towards the end of this era, around 1985, Big Business had a type of collective "eureka moment," when the CEOs of big American corporations determined that a global market, which American corporations would control, did not require loyalty or allegiance, to the sovereign economic interests of the United States.

Richard D. Wolff, in his Salon article, "How racism became the essential tool for maintaining a capitalist order," explains how this collective "eureka" moment occurred. (Salon, June 26, 2020).

Wolff writes,

"So in this eureka moment, capitalists said, "What are we doing here in Western Europe, North America and Japan? [based upon the Bretton Woods Agreement]. It's much more profitable if we produce in China, India and Brazil." And there begins what we're still in the middle of: the [manufacturing plant] exodus, the abandonment of the places of origin of capitalism by the capitalists. If you go from high wages in the United States to low wages in China, the bottom line is that the people earning wages are earning a lot less than they used to. It's not just that they're not Americans; they're Chinese, but they can't buy back what you're building."

It was after this eureka moment, that U. S. monopoly capitalism transitioned to Global Predatory Corporate Cronyism, and began the betrayal of American citizens by moving production plants to Mexico and China.

As Leonard Lynn and Hal Salzman note in "Collaborative Advantage,"

"U. S. multinationals are weakening their national identities, becoming citizens of the countries in which they do business and providing no favors to their country of origin. This means that the goal advocated by some U.S. policymakers of having the United States regain its position of leadership in all key technologies is simply not feasible, nor is it clear how the United States would retain that advantage when its firms are only loosely tied to the country." (Issues In Science and Technology, Winter 2006).

In the prior monopoly capitalist rent-seeking era, the distribution of rents [plunder] did not require that the plunder be distributed to elected government agents or to foreign political interests.

After 1992, the plunder had to be shared with financial interests both in the American political system, and in foreign governments, in order for the global Predatory economy to function.

The police state global enforcement arm of the Predatory State, the CIA, also had to be paid by revenues from the plunder, to enforce the global rules.

The financial mechanism for sharing plunder is the modern American crony capitalist system, which operates outside of the rule of law and the rules of the Constitution, in the fictitious "rules-based" global government of the U. N., and a network of government-funded non-profit agencies

Marina Ottaway explains that the rules-based global control framework originated during a 1999 speech by United Nations Secretary-General Kofi Annan. (Corporatism Goes Global, Carnegie Endowment For International Peace, 2001).

Ottaway writes,

“In January 1999, speaking at the World Economic Forum in Davos, Switzerland, proposed a "global compact" between the UN, business, and civil society to tackle the crucial and contentious issues of environmental protection and human and workers' rights. The tripartite model-an international organization, civil society (NGOs and labor organizations) and business-was evident in this initiative as well. A year later, again during the meeting of the World Economic Forum, the first modest step to make the global compact a reality was taken, with the official launch of a website, dubbed as the world's most comprehensive resource center on global citizenship.”

The intent of the new global control framework was to replicate the emerging American Predatory Capitalist State on a global scale.

Ottaway continues,

“The global compact was an attempt to recreate at the global level the corporatist tripartite arrangements including government, business and labor unions familiar to many European and Latin American countries… the tripartite corporatist model of participation is being reinvented.

The most explicitly corporatist proposals call for the formation of tripartite councils that include business representatives alongside those of NGOs and international organizations. "Partnership" is hailed by its proponents as a bold innovation introducing an unprecedented element of democracy into the international system.”

The transition to the Predatory Capitalist State, over the past 150 years, did not lead to economic efficiency or increased rates of domestic economic growth, but toward ever-more sophisticated global mechanisms for wealth extraction from common citizens and a more effective system of corporate plunder.

With the more advanced crony capitalist political system, reform of the existing system is impossible because the crony capitalists have control over the financial system, the economy, the agencies of government, and the CIA.

In other words, the parties sitting at the global table are not elected representatives of American citizens, but self-appointed elites, with the power to impose their will on a global system.

In the monopoly capitalist era, "We, the people" only existed on the day of election.

After the transition to the global Predatory State, "We, the people" no longer exists. It is a fictitious, imaginary concept, which serves a public relations effort to disguise who rules America. (William Domhoff, Who Rules America? 1967).

As Zywicki explains, Predatory corporatism has the appearance of a legal contract, much like the legal constitutional contract of Madison.

"Crony capitalism thus rests on an implicit guarantee by the government, that it will protect certain politically-connected firms from the rigors of competition, thereby guaranteeing those firms and industries a certain flow of revenues. In (implicit unwritten) exchange for this guaranteed flow of revenues, [in the contract] the firm promises to share some of that surplus with politically-favored groups, such as labor unions or favored interest groups (such as environmental groups), and with the politicians themselves through campaign contributions and other means of support."

Michael Munger, a professor at Duke University, explains how this implicit legal contract operates.

Munger writes,

"Corporatism is a social system where the government intervenes aggressively into the economy, typically with political instruments that benefit large corporations and enterprises to the detriment of smaller businesses and private citizens. Such instruments include subsidies, tariffs, import quotas, exclusive production privileges such as licenses, antitrust laws, and compulsory cartelization designs. Rational companies cut back on hiring engineers and shift their focus to lawyers and lobbyists. The use of patents, lawsuits, professional licensing, and other regulatory barriers to competitive entry into "your" industry or product line can produce enormous revenues, even though it adds nothing to the value of the product and does nothing to benefit consumers." (Michael Munger and Mario Villarreal-Diaz, The Road to Crony Capitalism, 2019).

Munger correctly points out that, during the transition to the Predatory Capitalist State, there wasn't an organized political party that defended individual liberty or market-based solutions, because Madison's rules left that part out of his constitutional contract.

Munger explains,

"While everyone benefits from competitive markets, no one in particular makes huge profits from keeping the system competitive and the playing field level. [fair rules] Thus, nobody has a strong vested interest in promoting and defending free markets."

The enemies, or intended targets of the global corporatist system, today, are exactly the same small business components of American society that were targeted in the 1912 Jekyll Island meeting to create the Fed.

Munger concludes his analysis of American crony corporatism,

"We would argue that successful capitalism leads to an impulse on the part of economic powers and political agents to restrict and control the destructive power of entrepreneurship. This unholy partnership is "rational" in the sense that the participants [of cronyism] benefit, in some cases creating wealth and privilege far beyond any other mechanism that is available to them. Disruptive entrepreneurial capitalism is the real enemy of today's corporate behemoths, as shown by the earlier story of the transition of

Microsoft and other technology entrepreneurial firms to crony capitalist business practices."

The political strategy of the crony capitalist corporations was to use the power of the Fed to eliminate the source of capital for new venture creation, and to control the pace of technological innovation by eliminating the free flow of tacit technological knowledge of potential entrepreneurs, if they left the global unit to start a new venture.

If large corporations can control the direction of technological change, then the rate of economic growth can be controlled, restricting the upward occupational mobility of the working and middle classes.

If large corporations can control the creation and diffusion of tacit knowledge, then they can control what social classes benefit from technology innovation.

In the absence of economic growth, global corporatism can make citizens dependent upon government welfare, and eliminate the American cultural value of individual initiative for risk taking for starting a new venture.

After the "eureka moment," of corporate CEO,'s in the late 1980's, a new global partnership between U. S. corporations and the Chinese Communist Party emerged that required crony corporations to share profits with the Chinese, in exchange for using Chinese slave labor in the production plants that moved from the U. S. to China.

In his article, The Hidden Price of American Chinese Advocacy, Robert S. Spalding, cites the continuation of the collaboration between American corporations and both political parties, and the Chinese Communist Party (CCP).

Spalding cites the network of lobbyists and think tanks who recently signed an open letter denying responsibility of the Chinese communists for unleashing the Wu virus.

In describing their response to the Wu virus, Spalding notes,

"The primary co-signers of the open letter include M. Taylor Fravel, Michael D. Swaine, J. Stapleton Roy, Ezra Vogel, and Susan A. Thornton. Swaine coordinates the U.S.-China Crisis Management Program co-sponsored by the Carnegie Endowment and the China Foundation for International and Strategic Studies (CFISS). He also co-authored Managing Sino-American Crises: Case Studies and Analysis with Zhang Tuosheng, chairman of the CFISS, funded by the People's Liberation Army of China, and mostly staffed by PLA colonels and generals academic committee."

The network of non-profit NGOs obtains funding from the Chinese communists to promote their propaganda. Spalding cites the background of the Chinese $30 million grant to Yale, as an example,

"Susan A. Thornton, former State Department diplomat and (former) acting assistant secretary for East Asian and Pacific Affairs, is similarly subject to the influence of Chinese soft power. Now she is a senior fellow and research scholar at Yale University's Paul Tsai China Center—named for the late Dr. Paul Tsai, after his son Joe Tsai, co-founder and vice-chairman of Alibaba, donated $30 million to the university."

The crony corporate partnership with the CCP permanently damages technological innovation in America, which is one reason why the American Crony Capitalist Corporate Economy permanently damages the entire macro economic structure of the American economy.

American corporate cronyism diverts scarce capital and technological resources into non-productive enterprises, which are based upon political relationships with China, and are not based upon any form of citizen consent of the governed.

American jobs that were previously performed in the intermediate manufacturing supply chains in U. S. metro regions were eliminated after the transition to the Predatory Capitalist State.

For every job lost in the U. S. regional intermediate technology supply chains, an additional 4 jobs were lost in the regional intermediate supply/supply sectors which supported the domestic manufacturing jobs. (Cited in Ian Hathaway, Tech Starts: High-Technology Business Formation and Job Creation in the United States, Kauffman Foundation Research Series, 2013).

In the absence of U. S. manufacturing jobs, the displaced U. S. workers did not have opportunities for upward occupational progress, and were forced to work for fast food chains and motels, or they entered a permanent dependency on government welfare payments.

With the loss of domestic intermediate demand supply chains, the rate of technological innovation in the U. S. was permanently damaged because the supply chains were the pathway of technological knowledge creation and knowledge diffusion that causes technology commercialization and economic growth.

As we described in Chapter 2, Illya Prigogine's work on dissipative structures demonstrates how complex systems can spontaneously organize into stable, higher-order patterns without central control.

Prigogine's theory of emergence in natural systems is the same conclusion reached by Kenneth Arrow, in 1988, for beneficial emergence in complex adaptive economic systems.

As applied to a beneficial constitutional framework, this suggests that when the constitutional rules serve everyone's long-term interests, citizen compliance with the unwritten rule of law becomes voluntary.

The voluntary compliance with the unwritten rule of law is the mechanism that allows a beneficial social order to emerge.

In highly controlled crony corporatist economy, the brain's market decision-making processes become restricted by the existing power structures and crony relationships rather than imagining the best path to attain an individual's future.

In other words, like the example of the Fed bailing out the crony capitalists after the 2008 collapse, the only market choice open to middle and working class citizens is the choice to remain in an exploitative relationship with global crony corporatists.

The opportunity for citizens to opt out of the crony capitalist exploitive relationship is not on the ballot.

Beneficial social outcomes only emerge when the institutional constitutional framework allows for:

1. Individual risk-taking without catastrophic consequences for failure.
2. Sufficient social stability to plan for the future and obtain romised future rewards.
3. Intellectual freedom to imagine different futures that may disrupt existing status quo power relationships.
4. Market reward systems that incentivize value creation rather than rent-seeking or welfare dependence.

Prigogine's theory of emergent order, applied to economic theory, shows how voluntary citizen compliance with the rule of law can replace coercive enforcement and economic exploitation, but only when grounded in moral and cultural values, shared by all citizens, which aim at maximum individual liberty.

The shared moral values and cultural rules are agreed upon, in the pre-constitutional setting, and establish the rules of the game, after the constitution has been ratified..

Just as Adam Smith's invisible hand works through individual self-interest, guided by moral sentiments, a beneficial constitutional system would be guided by moral principles of trust and honesty in economic exchange, so that citizens can trust each other to adhere to promises made, and promises kept.

Chapter 7. The Emergence of American Beneficial Social Order Under Buchanan's Fair Constitutional Rules and Kant's Moral Values.

In Chapter 2, we described how Illya Prigogine's theory of emergent order in nature, applied to beneficial economic theory, describes how voluntary citizen compliance with the rule of law allows for beneficial social order to emerge,.

In Chapter 5, we explained why majority rule democratic voting, as applied in Madison's constitution, cannot solve the problem of eliminating the American Predatory State.

In Madison's system, every proposed "constitutional reform" gets filtered through institutions that are already captured by the Predatory State.

The regulatory agencies are staffed by industry insiders, legislative processes are dominated by crony special interest lobbying, elected representatives go through the revolving door to become lobbyists when they leave Congress, judicial appointments are made in secret collusion with corporate-funded think tanks.

In this chapter, we argue that a new, beneficial economic constitution would be based upon fair constitutional rules and universal moral values that are shared by citizens, agreed upon in the pre-constitutional rule-making period.

We rely upon the framework of James Buchanan for designing fair rules, aimed at drafting a constitution that treats all citizens as equal in civil and natural rights.

We use the philosophy of Immanuel Kant to apply moral principles in the Preamble of the new constitution that would define the improvement of individual welfare as the purpose of the government.

We apply the conclusions of Michael Polanyi that demonstrate how beneficial spontaneous order emerges naturally when people operate under constitutional fair rules without coercive interference.

The moral and ethical flaw in Madison's rules that we address in this chapter is that his amoral rules of civil procedure can be followed perfectly, and lead to unjust legal and unfair economic outcomes.

When Kant's universal moral rules are inserted into the Preamble of the new constitution, the defect in Madison's rules are eliminated.

Kant's moral rules establish the constitutional goal of the sovereignty of the individual that places the protection of individual liberty beyond the reach of political manipulation or economic exploitation by ruling class elites.

In other words, the insertion of Kant's moral values about individual sovereignty in the new Preamble, provides a bright-line test for future justices on the Supreme Court to interpret the intent of the beneficial constitution.

Kant's moral categorical imperative provides exactly what Madison's Preamble was missing. (Groundwork of the Metaphysics of Morals, 1785).

Kant believed that humans possessed an innate morality which could potentially be developed into a moral personality or a moral individual.

In Kant's Critique of Practical Reason, (1788), he describes the latent "moral law within individuals."

The latent moral personality can be actualized, in reality, under certain cultural conditions and moral rules.

Kant goes on to describe that the development of human latent individual morality occurs over a life time, as an individual becomes conscious, or aware, of his own behavior, and how the pursuit of his own behavior affects the welfare of other humans.

Kant connects the latent morality to the human brain's mental cognitive awareness by stating,

"A person is something that is conscious at different times of the numerical identity of its self."

For Kant, the expression of individual morality is an essential ingredient to the functioning of civil laws in a democratic republic, and the development of individual moral personalities is an ongoing function of citizen allegiance to continue to obey the unwritten rule of law.

In other words, the ambient cultural and moral rules of a society determine how the human brain will interpret the moral behavior required of a citizen to live in that civil society.

Morals are "metaphysical" in the sense that the morals are logically derived independent of the physical laws of natural empirical science.

In this sense, Kant's metaphysical moral values fit into Prigogine's framework of natural emergence that are not derived by application of the scientific laws of nature.

Moral behavior, according to Kant, occurs in decision making when the person making the decision sees other humans as ends in themselves, not as a means to attain the decision-maker's own goals.

This moral behavior of citizens is an essential ingredient to the emergence of a future beneficial society in the context of the future American society.

The first principle of Kant's moral philosophy is that a moral value must be universally recognized and voluntarily obeyed by citizens.

In addition to the principle of universality, Kant also defined the principle that citizens must see themselves, and see each other, as moral ends, or moral agents, with equal rights to pursue their own destiny.

Kant generally stated this principle in the negative, meaning that seeing citizens as moral ends meant that other citizens could not use a citizen as a means to attain other citizen's ends.

The emergence of beneficial spontaneous order only occurs under a unique set of fair constitutional rules in the ambient cultural context of Kant's moral values.

Kant's moral imperative is the basis in a free society to generate the emergence of spontaneous social order because of the citizen's free will to share allegiance to obey the Rule of Law.

In the evolutionary context, rational individuals are motivated to enter the constitutional relationship because the brain perceives a long term survival advantage to individual liberty which depends on joint welfare improvement.

The insertion of Kant's moral imperative into the new constitutional Preamble is the difference in social organization based upon the rule of law versus the tyranny of the rule of men.

Madison's constitution is devoid of Kant's moral imperative, and creates the rule of men, in his case very powerful and wealthy men, whose privileged, insulated, status eventually evolved into the Predatory American State.

In his writings, Kant did not define the geographical scope of his universal rule because he believed that such a moral rule would be applied everywhere in the world, when citizens came to believe in the moral rule.

In the application to Buchanan's fair rules, Kant's universal principle applies to citizens, within a defined geographical setting, such as the boundaries of the United States, who are engaged in the pre-constitutional time period of defining the purpose of the new government

Buchanan identifies two important time periods in crafting a new constitution.

In the first period, before a new constitution is ratified and implemented, red citizens have the responsibility to organize and meet each other to define what constitutional rules would be fair and universally applied to all citizens, after the constitution is implemented.

The second period of time is the application and enforcement of the fair rules, which Buchanan calls the rules of the game.

For example, in playing a game of poker, the rules of the game would be established before the players sat down at the table and made their first bet.

The rules of the game would determine the winning hand, after all the bets had been made.

In other words, if the poker players agree to continue to play, after the first round of bets is finished, the players believe that the rules are fair.

Fair constitutional rules are judged as fair, in the post-constitutional time period, because all citizens continue to voluntarily agree to obey the rules, after the constitution has been ratified and implemented.

Buchanan defines this method of agreeing upon fair rules with his test of the veil of uncertainty for citizens in the pre-constitutional time period.

Under the veil of uncertainty, citizens would not know where they would end up in society, and would choose fair rules for everyone, so that wherever they ended up, after the constitution had been implemented, they would agree to voluntarily continue to obey the unwritten rule of law.

Buchanan's framework for creating fair rules is grounded in rational individual self-interest under uncertainty.

Buchanan's pre-constitutional method shows how self-interested individuals might arrive at fair rules through constitutional choice.

Fair rules emerge from rational self-interest when people must choose rules without knowing their future social class position, after the constitution had been ratified.

Buchanan's insight about the two time periods for creating a new constitution is that after ratification of the existing constitutional framework, all citizens are constrained by the rules and incentives that the existing framework creates.

As Buchanan writes, that universal shared morality is only relevant in a society based upon the sovereignty of the individual citizen, which Buchanan describes as "radical subjectivism." (James Buchanan and Viktor Vanberg, The Market As a Creative Process, 1991).

Buchanan identifies two essential written constitutional limits on government that rational citizens would choose, which he calls the protective state and the productive state.

In the theory of beneficial economics, we add two additional functions to Buchanan's limits on a limited government:
:

1. The citizen sovereignty state.
2. The entrepreneurial technological innovation state.

In Buchanan's protective state, the written constitutional rules establish the baseline conditions for secure property rights, and individual privacy protections from the Predatory Capitalist State.

Buchanan's productive state provides for the provisions of public goods that enhance everyone's ability to participate in wealth-creating activities.

In that uncertain pre-constitutional time period, Buchanan concludes that citizens would agree on post-constitutional rules that would limit the power and scope of government over the lives of citizens.

In other words, citizens would rationally choose a fair constitution that creates a level playing field for all citizens by placing written constitutional barriers to the power of the national government.

With a level playing field, citizens can make informed decisions about their future, based on the application of fair and known rules, knowing in advance that all citizens share these same moral values, extending into future time periods.

The pre-constitutional agreement on fair rules means that fair social and economic outcomes of an exchange are determined by the citizens who are playing the game, not by imaginary observers who determine fair outcomes, after the game has been played.

Individual success in playing the game of life, under fair rules, depends on individual initiative and effort, not on an artificial application of imaginary ideas about social justice for collectivist social groups.

The beneficial economic addition of our third function of government is aimed at eliminating the illegitimate authority of corporate predators by establishing citizen sovereignty as the mission of the government, where corporations are not viewed as having the same civil rights as citizens.

Buchanan places the post-constitutional enforcement of fair rules into a market exchange framework that features voluntary agreement of the players to abide by the rules of market exchange.

Playing the game, in this sense, means citizens engaging in exchange, both legal and economic, with other citizens during the game, that causes a beneficial social order to emerge, spontaneously.

We contend, in Chapter 5, that without the required constitutional fair rules and moral values, the operation of the unfettered American economy would result in monopoly capitalism and crony rent-seeking, much like what the American economy and society looked like during the Robber Baron years, from 1875 – 1913.

In that period, an unjust social order emerged, based upon Madison's rules, but that social order would not be called a beneficial social order. (Laurie Thomas Vass, America's Final Revolution: Reconstructing Jefferson's American Dream of An Entrepreneurial Capitalist Society, 2022).

We agree with Buchanan that consent of the citizens occurs during the pre-constitutional period, and in on-going consent to follow the rule of law, after the constitution has been ratified and implemented.

The plausibility of our argument about the emergence of a beneficial social order hinges on our interpretation that the recent evolution of the brain created the capacity to anticipate the behavior of other humans.

The ability of the brain to anticipate the behavior of another human evolved into the brain's ability to anticipate how their behavior would affect the other human, and that ability allowed an individual to see the other human as an end, in and of themselves.

The brain's ability to see other individuals as Kant's moral ends allowed the entrance of rules of social cooperation among humans, which eventually evolved into moral rules about justice, fairness and civil rights.

Stuart A. Kauffman, in the Origins of Order: Self-Organization and Selection in Evolution, (1991), describes how the brain's latent morality arises in the context of market exchange.

Kaufman explains that the presence of morality causes a citizen to feel guilt when the citizen's decisions violate the unwritten rule of law, because the citizen is aware that the decision may have adverse effects on the welfare of other citizens.

Kaufman writes,

"Individual morality acts as a behavior modifier during and after an exchange in both a positive and negative way. In a positive way, morality allows each individual to place greater reliance on the rules of justice being followed. In a negative way, guilt acts as a force against not following the rules."

Guilt arises as a result of a person's self-awareness of a transgression against a cultural moral boundary. The behavior would be considered evil if the individual knew in advance that his decision would harm other people, but decided to inflict the harm, anyway.

In the special interest driven political system of the American Predatory State, there is very little guilt about breaking moral or political rules.

Obedience of citizens to follow the rule of in an individualistic society, meaning the judicial system, the economic system, and the system of political representation, all rest upon a very fragile foundation of faith that other brains are processing mental images of another's welfare.

In our proposed constitutional solution, that element of faith is codified as the framework of a new constitution, as citizens cooperate in creating the rules that they give to themselves.

Citizens obey fair rules because they see that these rules protect and enable the innovative processes that create real economic growth, and they realize that real economic growth improves their own welfare.

Citizen allegiance to obey the rules that they give to themselves depends on continuous future economic growth, in the defined geographical territory of the nation.

As we describe in Chapter 8, (The Imperative of Economic Growth For the Emergence of A Beneficial Social Order), the citizen shared moral value of equal opportunity for financial success is the glue that holds the constitutional republic together, and that glue is called economic growth.

When fair constitutional rules create the economic conditions for genuine financial success and when capital investment in new technologies generate entirely new future markets and pathways for upward mobility, middle and working class citizens experience tangible financial benefits from their voluntary compliance with the rule of law.

In the absence of economic growth, after the 1992 transition to global Predatory Capitalism, the social class divisions in the American economy have become more violent, as middle and lower working class citizens fight each other over the declining economic benefits.

Buchanan's framework for creating fair rules is grounded in rational individual self-interest under uncertainty, and is placed in a market exchange model.

Other writers have also made extensive use of the individual exchange model, and we cite three other authors.

Michael Polanyi integrates Kant’s moral individualism with Buchanan’s market exchange model.

Polanyi develops an individualist exchange model to describe how a beneficial social order emerges in the context of the operation of a free competitive market economy.

In The Logic of Liberty, (1951), Polyani represented the emergence of social order as grounded on individual freedom and spontaneously emerging from mutual adjustment of free market exchange.

Polanyi defines the emergence of spontaneous social order in terms of individuals acting "on their own initiative,"

As a result of individual interaction as the market exchange progresses, Polanyi writes that social order emerges.

He states,

"Individuals intereract with each other on their own initiative subject to laws which uniformly apply to all of them,"

His characterizes this society as "decentralized decision-making in complex systems," to describe how complex systems can emerge from individual actions without central planning.

He stated that social relations become "disembedded" in a market economy when individuals were not free to make their own choices and decisions.

His term disembedded means that individual social relations were not embedded into a ambient culture of trust and honesty.

Social relationships, in the absence of individual social interaction, become subordinated to the powerful interests who control social decisions.

In The Great Transformation, (1944), Polanyi describes a society where common people resist the destructive forces of monopoly capitalism through what he calls the "double movement" - the spontaneous social response to protect human dignity and social bonds.

Polanyi shows that social order emerges from below, through the practical moral judgment of ordinary middle and working class people living their daily lives under fair rules

Where Polanyi differs from Buchanan, and from our interpretation of beneficial social exchange, is in defining the importance of the pre-constitutional period when common citizens agree on fair rules and shared moral values.

Harold Kelley and John Thibaut's work in Interpersonal Relations: A Theory of Interdependence and The Social Psychology of Groups, offers a model of both market and social exchange between individuals that also allows for the emergence of beneficial social order, as a natural outcome of voluntary exchange.

Their model of exchange can easily be adapted to accommodate both the creation of Buchanan's rules and the inclusion of Kant's moral values in crafting a new constitution.

In their model, as the sequence of exchanges occur through time, the society can be visualized as moving towards the emergence of a beneficial social order, as a consequence of multiple mutual beneficial adjustments in behavior, in each individual exchange.

The antecedent conditions of a pro-social exchange, according to Kelley and Thibaut, involve social and psychological values learned in the ambient culture.

These ambient cultural values are products of social learning that involve the acquisition of knowledge and the development of beliefs about how the social structure works.

Peter Blau also adopts a market exchange framework to describe pro-social behavior, and makes a distinction between the function of trust in economic free market exchanges and trust in political exchanges that involve how a current exchange creates future, unknown obligations on both parties to the exchange. (Exchange and Power in Social Life, 1964).

According to Blau, social/political exchanges, in the current time period, involving the value of trust, create an open-ended future joint behavior obligation.

The exact nature of the future discharge of obligation cannot be measured precisely at the moment of the political exchange.

Nor can the future benefits being exchanged be subject to negotiation or bargaining, after the initial exchange of trust occurs.

In other words, modifying the rules of the game, is prohibited during the playing of the game.

Blau writes, that in addition to common cultural values, the discharge of future obligations depend upon a set of social and political institutions that act as the medium through which the future obligations are discharged.

In Blau's model of social exchange, a set of stable institutions must exist over long periods of time, that act as credible vessels through which individuals exchange obligations involving future trust.

The political/legal institutions act as the equivalent of the market exchange mechanism that coordinates voluntary behavior in free market transactions

Friedrich Hayek also develops an individualist exchange model to describe how a beneficial social order emerges in the context of the operation of competitive markets.

In The Constitution of Liberty, (1960), Hayek's model begins with existing cultural and moral rules, and from that initial set of moral values, Hayek explains how beneficial social order emerges.

In contrast to Hayek, Buchanan's model suggests that shared cultural understandings emerge from citizen deliberations in the pre-constitutional time period.

Hayek applies the concept of just laws in The Road to Serfdom (1944), in his critique of Marxism and communist centralized societies.

What we add to Hayek is that the concept of "justice" must be embedded in the Preamble of the constitution, as Kant's moral condition, to allow a beneficial social order to emerge.

In the conclusion of this chapter, we address a gap or weakness in Buchanan's two step constitutional rule making format.

Buchanan did not explain how citizens first come together in a mass social movement to begin the process of crafting new constitutional rules.

We suggest that Buchanan's gap can be fixed with the aid of the very recent technological tool of blockchain algorithms, applied in the metro regional geographical setting.

Blockchain, as a new technological tool, was not available during the time Buchanan was writing about how to create a new constitution. (Constitutional Economics, 1991).

The tool is valuable in two different settings. The tool helps to solve Buchanan's gap in how citizens meet each other to begin the process of defining the purpose of government, in the pre-constitutional period.

Blockchain is also a useful tool that helps technology entrepreneurs raise venture capital, generally in a defined geographical setting that extends about 50 miles from the location of the new venture.

In the application to Buchanan's pre-constitutional rule making, blockchain offers the first rule of fairness of equal citizen opportunity for democratic citizen participation in defining fair rules.

Any citizen who wants to participate in the creation of a new constitution can add and modify their ideas, without external manipulation or coercion by ruling class gatekeepers.

Blockchain is both transparent and verifiable for the authorship of ideas as they are added by citizens to the pre-constitutional rule making.

This feature of blockchain makes it difficult for vested political interests of the Predatory State to insert anonymous rules that would benefit their own social class interests.

In the pre-constitutional period, the application of blockchain would allow citizens to define rules that eliminated coercion or exploitation in the enforcement of the rules of the game in the post-implementation time period.

In the post implementation period of time, blockchain would continue to function as an open democratic forum for citizens to express their opinions on defects in the constitution, and methods for improving the rules of the game.

The decentralized application of blockchain, in distinct metro regions, avoids the defect in Madison's constitution, which created a centralized political power, controlled by powerful elites, who were intent on eliminating the participation of common citizens in the operation of the government.

As we mentioned in the Introduction, the implementation and management of the state-level blockchain algorithm requires that red state citizens apply political pressure to their elected state legislative representatives to create and fund the blockchain framework in their respective states.

Chapter 8. The Imperative of Economic Growth For The Emergence of A Beneficial Social Order.

Illya Prigogine's theory of complex adaptive systems explains how a very small change in a natural environment can yield huge, startling effects. The entire ecological system may reorganize itself in ways that strike observers as bizarre.

We apply Prigogine's complex adaptive system to social and economic systems, and suggest that small changes in the economy, such as a capital investment in a new technology, can have huge, unforeseen effects that change the entire market structure.

At the moment of a change in Prigogine's natural system, it is very hard to predict, in advance, how the system may re-organize into a self-organizing, stable future system, or if the system may disintegrate into a chaotic state of dis-organization. (Ilya Prigogine and Isabelle Stengers, Order Out of Chaos: Man's New Dialogue With Nature, 1984).

Prigogine and Stengers write,

"At this revolutionary moment, or "singular moment" or a "bifurcation point", it is inherently impossible to determine in advance which direction the change will take: whether the system will disintegrate into "chaos" or leap to a new, more differentiated, higher level of "order" or organization, called a "dissipative structure."

Their term "dissipative" means that the natural force, in their case, energy, that is causing the change, dissipates throughout the natural system, and as a consequence of energy dissipating, self-organization and a future stable order may arise spontaneously, out of the initial cause of chaos.

Prigogine makes a distinction between open systems, and closed natural environments, and the force which dissipates throughout the system is a form of energy.

In an open natural system, energy may dissipate, leading to a future, unknown stable order.

In the closed natural system, energy cannot find a pathway to dissipate, and the system may collapse to a future unknown point of chaos.

In our application of Prigogine's theory to economic theory, a regional economy may be viewed as either an open economic system, which dissipates knowledge throughout the regional geography, or a closed economic system, characterized by closed, or controlled, knowledge diffusion.

The element that we add to beneficial economic theory is that the emergence of a beneficial political and economic order only occurs under a specific set of constitutional rules and shared moral and cultural values, of trust and honesty among citizens, within the specific regional geographic boundary.

John Holland, in Hidden Order: How Adaptation Builds Complexity, (1996), explains that social, institutional variables, such as honesty, affect the emergence of future social order.

In Holland's interpretation of hidden order, human adaptations are rule based changes in behavior. Most of the adaptive behavior is based upon adapting to other humans, through a process of learning and mental anticipations.

As we explained in Chapter 3 (How A Person's Brain Naturally Creates Social Order Through Their Everyday Market Choices),, humans anticipate the future just like they anticipate the possible sequences of moves in a game of chess.

In the presence of novelty, the old rules and routines (Popper World 2), may not be adequate for adapting to the novel situation, and humans combine time-tested old rules and routines with new hypothesis to anticipate what may happen next (Popper World 3).

Applying Holland's interpretation of hidden order to the workings of the market provides a contrast to the neoclassical equilibrium interpretation of technology as an external given that does not change.

"From the classical point of view, markets should always clear rapidly," states Holland,

"moving in narrow ranges dictated by changing supply and demand...economic theory is built around agents of perfect rationality – agents that can perfectly foresee the consequences of their actions, including the reactions of other agents."

Holland's interpretation of markets is that they are complex adaptive systems where humans anticipate the future and attempt to make decisions based upon their mental hypothesis about what may happen next.

In our application of the emergence of beneficial social order, new markets emerge when the old rules and old behavior adaptations do not fit the changing structure of relationships that humans have with each other, as a result of the novel circumstances brought about by the introduction of new technology.

Individuals in markets are busy creating their own futures, and the markets that emerge in the future are a result of individual decisions that affect both their own life destiny and change in the economic environment, as their decisions are implemented.

Markets emerge as a result of a growing common perception in the brains of humans in a defined geographical territory about the implications of the novelty.

What happens next, after the appearance of technological innovation depends on the exchange of loyalty, trust, and truth that exists in the ambient cultural environment.

In the presence of uncertainty about the future, and a lack of information about who to trust, the type of market that emerges in a closed economy may lead to chaos, not beneficial social order. Trust allows human imagination in the realm of economic behaviors to be fulfilled over a long period of time, which may eventually lead to the emergence of new markets, if the cultural value of trust is inherited over successive generations.

Trust is a moral and cultural value that is inherited when the social and legal structure is characterized by a certain configuration of civil rules of exchange and laws regarding property and appropriation of profit.

The legal, political and social institutions of the regional economy, as observed in market relationships, provide the framework for observing the communications and interactions between people as well as between organizations and thus feeds the process of technical, organizational and institutional change.

In Prigogine's theory, the process of energy dissipation may lead to the emergence of "self-organization."

In our application of Prigogine's theory to economic theory, the process of knowledge dissipation, in an open, regional economy, leads to a beneficial society of citizen "self-government," where citizens agree on fair rules to share the benefits of economic growth, and trust each other to obey the unwritten rule of law.

Prigogine places his complex adaptive theory into the framework of the evolution of a natural environment.

Prigogine writes,

"Wherever we look, we find evolution, diversification and instabilities… The basic characteristics of complexity are irreversibility and stochasticity. These concepts begin now to diffuse into the fundamental level of description of nature… The remarkable feature is that when we move from equilibrium to far-from equilibrium conditions, we move away from the repetitive and the universal to the specific and the unique. Indeed, the laws of equilibrium are universal. Matter near equilibrium behaves in a "repetitive" way. On the other hand, far from equilibrium there appears a variety of mechanisms corresponding to the possibility of occurrence of various types of dissipative structures (Exploring Complexity, 1987).

We agree with Prigogine's insight that economic evolution is irreversible, which means that a prior equilibrium can never be re-established.

Unlike general equilibrium theory, which assumes markets return to stable states after a disruption, Prigogine's framework suggests that economic evolution creates new market structures that cannot simply revert to previous configurations.

In our application of evolutionary economic theory, the future evolves to what Prigogine calls a "distant non-equilibrium" future state, which we call a distant future attractor point.

The regional economy evolves to a future attractor point, and the force that causes the economy to evolve is technology innovation. In our application, technology innovation is caused by knowledge creation and knowledge diffusion.

In the application of the biological evolutionary metaphor, technological knowledge is the food that gets eaten in the regional economy.

Technology evolves in a regional economy, much like biological evolution in a natural environment.

Technology evolves in products, and technical characteristics of products are inherited.

Political power is also inherited as a result of laws enduring over generations and the units of analysis are humans whose behavior is defined by cultural values.

Given a certain type of prior social and political conditions in political power and cultural values, the economy could be predicted to take a certain type of trajectory.

Given another constellation of political power, the economy would maintain the status quo. In terms of evolutionary logic, the social and political conditions represent the "environment" within which humans adapt or modify their behavior.

In Prigogine, the evolution could possibly result in two future states which he defines as either chaos or order.

In beneficial regional economics, there are 3 possible future states of the economy caused by the dissipation of knowledge:

- economic growth,
- economic decline, and
- nearly neutral economic drift.

In the economic growth phase, in the progression of time, after a radical technological innovation, the evolutionary change caused by radical innovation is irreversible.

The appearance of a new-to-the world radical technology innovation causes large, unanticipated, changes in the future economy, if consumers begin to buy the new product.

In other words, in beneficial economics, technology evolution is primarily a market selection phenomena, not a scientific or engineering break-through.

The market, in beneficial economics, is the mechanism through which consumer choice takes place. The market, itself, does not have a future defined end point, or telos, as it would in equilibrium theory.

In beneficial economics, consumers are "guessing" about how a new product may "fit" into their welfare function.

The consumer guesses are based upon the notion of the "rational pursuit of self interest," as perceived in the brain of the individual making the decision. (Chapter 3).

The consumer's brain is filtering thousands of images, trying to come up with something that looks like the new product. The internal images in the brain are comparing the old product images with the new external images of the product, in order to come up with a strategy of how to respond to the new thing. (Popper World 3).

This guessing activity of consumers about novel events is in contrast to consumer behavior in existing markets, with older versions of the product.

With old products, the consumer brain has developed rules of thumb for making selections, primarily based upon maximizing utility at the lowest cost. (Popper World 2).

With new products, the selection behavior of consumers is not a priced-based activity, it is an insight-imagination, mental-guess-based activity, based upon anticipating what other humans are going to do.

Much of what happens in the theory of technology evolution depends on what the consumer does when she first "sees" the new product.

When she first "sees" the new product, she "imagines" how the new product may "fit" with her expectations of the future.

The regional economic market occupies the same position in beneficial economics, as the natural environment plays in Prigogine's theory of complex adaptive systems.

On the downward movement of economic decline, the loss of a region's knowledge networks is irreversible.

In the application of biological evolution, the loss of a region's knowledge networks is like the loss of the human brain's neural cognitive networks.

As the loss of knowledge networks increases, on the downward trajectory, the regional economy goes through ratchet points, similar to bifurcation points, through which a return to prior economic growth becomes increasingly unlikely.

In the application of Kimura's nearly neutral drift to beneficial economics, at the micro economic level, random evolutionary drift among selectively neutral technology variants causes long periods in the economy where no force is strong enough to move the economy towards an upward future attractor point, or downward through economic ratchet points. (Motoo Kimura, The Neutral Theory of Molecular Evolution, 1983).

In general equilibrium theory, this same idea of nearly neutral drift is called a Nash Equilibrium, where no agent in the regional economy is motivated to change behavior that would cause the economy to move towards a distant future attractor point.

The three possible states of the regional economy are depicted in the following diagrams.

Chapter 8. Diagram 1. Regional Economy Breaking Away From Initial State In Time Period 1..

Diagram 1. Regional Economy Breaking Away From Initial State In Time Period 1 to Distant Future Attractor Point in Time Period 2.

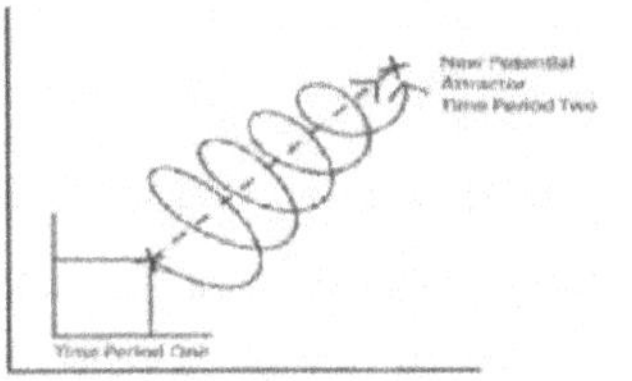

Image credit: Laurie Thomas Vass, Theory of Technology Evolution, 2019.

On the upward spiral of growth, the center points of each oscillation could be determined and connected as a line through those center points.

Even though the amplitude of the oscillations are declining, the center points would be tracing out a logarithmic curve whose rate of change would be approaching zero at some future point in time.

As the economy breaks away from the old equilibrium, each initial increment of growth adds a large amount of transactions to the cycle of growth.

Later increments of growth add to the cycle, but at a diminishing marginal rate.

The hypothesized future attractor point is where the marginal rate of change is close to zero, which represents the economy's next bifurcation point.

The economy reaches its future attractor point through a series of micro bifurcations in economic growth.

At some point in time, given new products and new capital investments in technology, these micro bifurcations lead the economy to the unknown potential attractor point in time period two.

Following Prigogine's insight, the precise location of the future attractor point, in time period 2, is not knowable in time period 1, when the technological innovation first appears.

At some future point in time, after several micro bifurcations, towards time period 2, the economic structure would no longer look the earlier economic structure because the internal supply networks had changed.

The changing industrial structure of the regional economy creates new future intermediate demand markets. The regional economy could never return to the prior state of equilibrium because that prior market structure no longer exists.

The process of breaking away from equilibrium in time period one can also be described as a downward trajectory to a future attractor point of economic decline, characterized as Muller's Ratchet.

Chapter 8. Diagram 2. Regional Economy Breaking Away From Equilibrium in Time Period 1 to Distant Future Attractor Point of Economic Decline in Time Period 2.

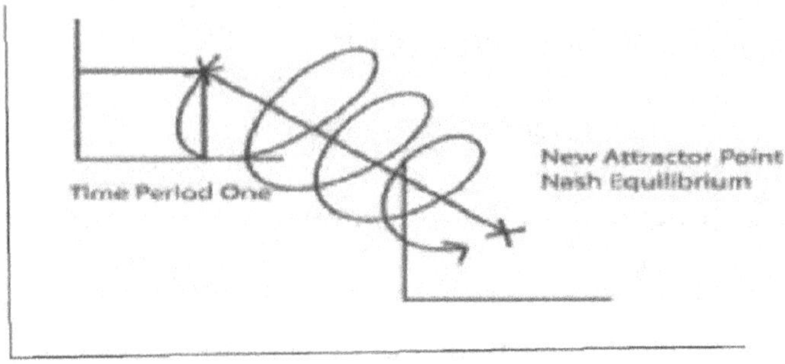

Future Potential Attractor Point of Economic Decline

Image Credit: Laurie Thomas Vass, Theory of Technology Evolution, 2019.

On the downward spiral of economic decline, the amplitudes of each cycle become smaller, representing the idea that the overall economic activity of exchange transactions in the regional economy is diminishing.

Once a regional economy loses the ability to generate new technological knowledge, it loses its neuronal pathways of knowledge creation and diffusion in the intermediate demand supply chains.

If no new knowledge is added, the economy slowly drifts down through micro bifurcation points, called Muller's Ratchet of Economic Decline, through which a return to economic growth is very difficult because technological diversity of the initial economic structure is eroding over time. (H. J. Muller, The Relation of Recombination to Mutational Advance, 1964).

Losing technological knowledge for a regional economy is just like the human brain losing neuronal pathways. Once the brain's neuronal pathways are destroyed, the brain loses its ability to imagine new futures. (Popper World 3).

Once a regional economy loses its ability to create technological knowledge, it loses the ability to generate radical new technological innovation.

As in the case of biological evolution, in regional economics, there are long periods of time where nothing happens. In biological evolution, new genetic diversity acts to stir up the environment, possibly creating new species.

In the application to regional beneficial economics, a regional economy can drift around a hypothetical Nash Equilibrium, in nearly neutral evolutionary drift, for long periods of time, with nothing happening to stir up new technological knowledge.

Diagram 3, below, depicts this state of economic nearly neutral drift as slow oscillations around a Nash Equilibrium.

Chapter 8. Diagram 3. Nearly Neutral Economic Drift of Nash Equilibrium.

Diagram 3. Regional Economy In Nearly Neutral Evolutionary Drift, Slowly Circling A Nash Equilibrium.

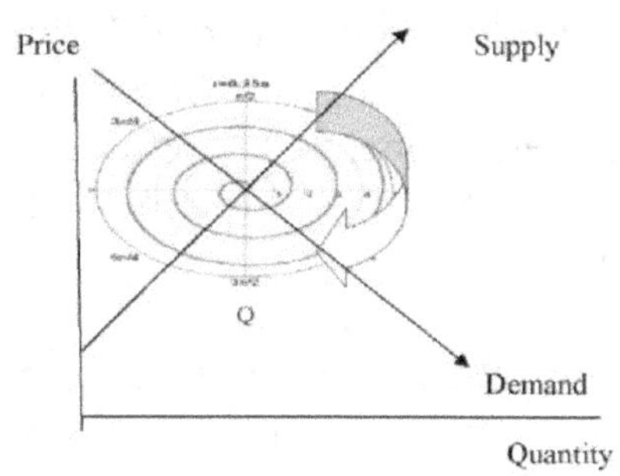

Image Credit: Laurie Thomas Vass, Theory of Technology Evolution, 2019.

The environmental conditions for breaking away from a Nash Equilibrium depends both on the supply of technology genetic diversity, caused by firms seeking new sources of technological food, and environmental chance, in the form of initial technological conditions that allow for inter-species technology cross breeding.

The slowly revolving equilibrium point in Diagram 3 can be described as a relationship between regional production output and technology genetic diversity in time period one.

The initial supply of regional technology knowledge, in time period 1, limits the future rate of economic growth.

Clayton Christensen makes a useful distinction between sustaining innovation, which makes an existing product, in an existing market, more user-friendly, and a radical new-to-the world product. (The Innovator's Dilemma: When New Technologies Cause Great Firms to Fail, 1997).

Creating a new-to-the world technology innovation is a risky endeavor, and requires capital investments in new production facilities and skilled staff.

The risk for the entrepreneur and the venture capitalists contemplating an investment in the new product is that consumers may not buy the new product.

As technology genetic diversity is used up in time period 1, through sustaining innovation, the economy approaches it's theoretical equilibrium attractor point, in time period one. (Clayton Christensen and Michael E Raynor, The Innovator's Solution: Creating and Sustaining Successful Growth, 2003).

In the theory of beneficial economics, the rate of capital investment in Christensen's sustaining innovation is just sufficient to keep the regional economy slowly revolving around the Nash Equilibrium.

From that Nash Equilibrium point in time period one, the regional economy can follow either an upward trajectory of economic growth, to a hypothetical attractor point in time period two, or, in the absence of a new supply of technological knowledge, the economy can follow a downward trajectory of economic decline.

Or, the regional economy may drift around in a nearly neutral state, until new knowledge causes the economy to begin a new trajectory.

So, in addition to the emergence of a possible new future final demand product markets, the future evolution of a regional economy depends on the existence of a capital market, in time period 1, that facilitates capital investments in risky new ventures, that may cause the emergence of entirely new final demand and intermediate demand markets in time period 2.

Income competition and social class conflicts arise in the Nash Equilibrium because the rate of regional economic growth is not great enough to allow ordinary common citizens to attain financial success.

To recall the earlier discussion, in Chapter 5, on crony capitalism and corruption in the American political system, in the absence of economic growth, the existing pie is not growing, which causes political actors and corporations to try to obtain a bigger piece of the existing pie, in a non-beneficial society.

Beneficial economic theory explains how capital investments in radical new technology ventures, in time period 1, causes future regional economic growth

New future markets emerge as a result of a growing common perception in the brains of humans about the implications of novel market event.

"Consumer wants and preferences are created gradually by means of a learning process involving both producers and consumers," states Koen Frenken, (Technological Innovation and Complexity Theory, 2006).

Consumers learn about new products through the business social networks that feed forward, and feedback, information from the final demand market.

Novelty starts in the brains of individuals as they imagine the future, and novelty is actualized when technology is commercialized in the form of capital investments in new ventures.

Diagram 4 describes the chronology of events in a regional economy, leading up to the emergence of a new future regional market.

Chapter 8. Diagram 4. Chronology of Events Leading to A New Future Regional Market.

Appearance of novel radical product from two-parent crossover.	Emergence of small niche market, as consumers select the new product.	Displacement of old product by new radical product. Product market micro bifurcation.	Creation of intermediate demand markets to support production and distribution of product.	Creation of new income flows where none had previously existed.	Profit reinvestment from capital "exit " events into technology trajectory created by new radical product.

Image Credit: Laurie Thomas Vass, Theory of Technology Evolution, 2019.

The reason future market emergence is contingent and difficult to predict, in time period 1, is that the underlying causal factors are human behavior in the presence of novelty.

Predicting the economic future, after the appearance of technological innovation, requires a statistical method of very small steps to judge what consumers are doing, and from each small step into the future, taking a further small step to see what may come next, if buyers continue to buy the newer versions of the new product.

New future markets will generate new sources of income.

The business owners of the new technological ventures perform the essential economic function of keeping dollars flowing in the regional economy by continually buying and selling goods and services to each other and to local consumers.

In some rare cases, the introduction of a radical product far up in the regional intermediate demand value chain induces changes in the regional market, and that change in the value chain leads to the emergence of an entirely new market.

In their research, Choosing Between Similar to What I Have Versus Different From What I Have: An Analysis of Consumers' Choice of a Late Entrant In Place of a Preferred Pioneer. Maneesh Thakkar (Working Paper April 2008), writes that,

"... most research shows that on various grounds, pioneers (the first to introduce the innovation) possess an edge over its late rivals. Many research studies have approached pioneering advantage from the perspective of consumer behavior and some studies have specifically showed how consumer preference formation processes tend to put pioneers in an ever advantageous position. Such research studies observe that consumer preferences for ideal product in market are formed by the pioneer's in that market."

The market acceptance of the radical product innovation by the niche market consumer is the key factor in predicting the emergence of a new future market.

A social cultural configuration of trust and honesty would allow consumers more risk taking on a new product because they trusted the other humans to continue to obey the rule of law, in the distant future.

The process of regional economic growth and the emergence of new future markets can be described by a series of "then if" contingent logical statements:

Diagram 5 describes this series of chronological "if-then" logical statements.

The initial capital investment in a new technology venture is not sufficient to cause the potential new future market to emerge.

Successful radical innovation occurs in regional markets that have multiple diverse networks of citizens who share cognitive maps about innovation. These shared cognitive maps are geographically-bounded.

Chapter 8. Diagram 5. Chronology of If-Then Statements.

Diagram 5. The Series of If-Then Contingent Logical Statements Leading to the Emergence of A New Future Regional Market.

- If exit events in the past create a pool of entrepreneurial profits, then if,
- The entrepreneurial profit is used to fund new ventures that create new products, then if,
- Technological genetic crossover occurs between two products, then if,
- Markets select new products, then if,
- Complementary markets are created, then if,
- New patterns of income distribution are created, then if,
- New technological knowledge is created, then if,
- New technological knowledge is diffused, then if,
- New genetic technological variety is "called forth" from the expanding production possibilities frontier, the new genetic variety has a greater probability of being "inherited" by subsequent generations of products, and the evolution of the market can continue through a macro bifurcation and the emergence of an entirely new market.

In their recent article, "Thinking About Technology: Applying a Cognitive Lens to Technical Change, Sarah Kaplan and Mary Tripsas explain that the regional innovation process requires a type of regional "cognitive" map inside the heads of many different actors. (2008).

"We also show that interactions of producers, users and institutions shape the development of collective frames around the meaning of new technologies."

What they mean by collective cognitive frames is that the citizens in the regional market share some common definitions, or a mental lens, through which they interpret the economic growth of the region.

In most cases, the shared cognitive maps occur within 50 miles of the metro regional boundaries, just about the same distance for both regional private capital markets to function when financing innovation projects, and for the regional envelope of trust among citizens.

In our application to beneficial economic theory, we explain that when citizens in a region share common moral and cultural values about trust and honesty, that region will experience higher rates of economic growth than regions where the citizens do not trust each other.

Longer-term human economic strategies for improving welfare are regionally specific and time-based, not price-based, and depend on the institutional framework of permanent personal relationships in the ambient culture.

Most of the permanent human relationships require the anticipation of who to trust in future exchanges based upon the cultural values of reciprocity and mutuality.

Benjamin Chinitz, in City and Suburb: The Economics of Metropolitan Growth, (1964), explains the importance of how regional institutional structures allows citizens to exchange moral values of trust and share knowledge through tacit, or face-to-face, personal relationships.

Chinitz placed the term "institutional structure" in the context of how humans learn from each other in regional industrial districts.

As we describe in beneficial economic theory, it is not simply the appearance of a radical new technology in the regional economy that causes the emergence of future beneficial economic growth, but the social, cultural, and political factors, including trust, business customs, social ties, and other institutional considerations that inform citizens about the distribution of common benefits associated with economic growth that causes beneficial markets to emerge.

As Edward Feser, of Oregon State University, explained, the future market emerges in cooperative human relationships that occur as "interrelationships between economic actors" within a geographic cluster of firms.

Feser writes,

"Some findings support what many rural people believe to be true: civically engaged religious groups and other identities that bind people together can really matter." (Why Some Rural Places Prosper and Others Do Not, 2009).

Feser distinguishes between industrial production, which he defines in terms of input-output models and a regional cluster of citizens in the surrounding social, civic and political institutions in the region.

For Feser, the regional input-output models describe interindustrial production relationships among firms in the region, and the regional social and political institutional is the framework, through which political and knowledge exchange takes place. (What Regions Do Rather Than Make: A Proposed Set of Knowledge-based Occupation Clusters, 2003).

Rikard Stankiewicz provides an example of what Feser was describing in terms of regional occupation structure. (The Role of the Science and Technology Infrastructure in the Development and Diffusion of Industrial Automation in Sweden, 1995).

Stankiewicz writes,

"Every engineer is embedded in a particular technological tradition characterizing his profession, the company he works for and the team he is a part of- the technological community...The accumulation and transmission of knowledge occurs in, and through, the formation of technological communities, and is strongly affected by their structure and dynamics."

He notes that the individual engineer "bears" knowledge, and works for a firm that is producing the range of product phenotypes within a region's industrial cluster, or as Stankiewicz calls it, the "technological community."

In a closed regional economy, the knowledge that the engineer bears does not flow through the regional social networks, but is contained and controlled by the political values in the region, related to the future distribution of income.

In an open regional economy, tacit, personal knowledge flows freely through the social networks, and the free flow of knowledge allows for the emergence of a future beneficial economy.

In Diagram 6, we combine the insight from Feser, that a type of economic model can describe both production relationships in the regional economy, and also perform an additional function of describing the social political human relationships that take place during market transactions in the regional market.

Chapter 8. Diagram 6. The Dual Flow Of Knowledge and Price Transactions In A Regional Market.

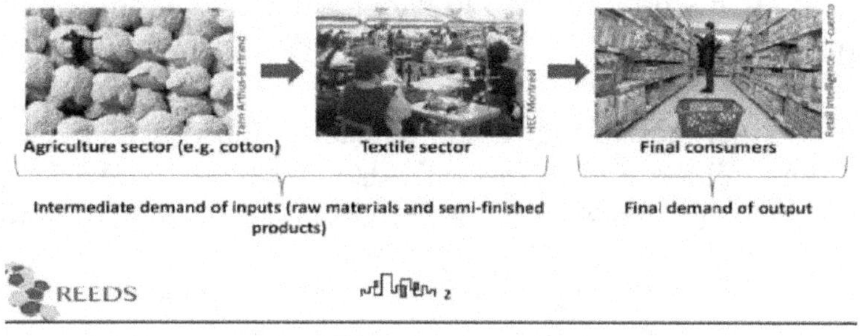

Image Credit: The I O Matrix From Leontief , University of Versailles, No Date.

In the first block of the cotton agricultural section, hundreds of daily personal communications take place between farmers, bankers, fertilizer sales people, transportation providers, and hundreds of other service and support people engaged in getting the cotton out of the field and into the textile manufacturing plant.

Many of this personal communications are face-to-face exchanges, and the communications that are not face-to-face rely on the prior establishment of trust and honesty, in the regional market, to conduct business.

When the bales of cotton finally get to the textile plant, hundreds of people in the manufacturing plant talk to each other about how the cotton gets processed.

Those people inside the textile plant talk to hundreds of other people outside of the plant in personal communications about the colors of dyes to use, the textures of the cotton, and market demand for the semi-finished goods being produced inside the plant.

Those communications are based upon a common mental cognitive map of the people about how business gets done in the region.

Before the finished product of shirts, and pants, and shoes get delivered to the store, hundreds and hundreds of people talk to each other about market conditions, financial conditions global trade conditions, and many other issues, all undergirded by cultural values of trust, honesty and truth.

In addition to direct face-to-face communications, all of the people in all of the blocks, all the way from the fields to the store, see each other at bars, golfing events, churches, professional associations, and civic clubs like the local chamber of commerce.

At every encounter, the people share a common historical heritage and common values about who to trust, who is honest, and who to go have a beer with on Friday afternoon.

In our application of beneficial economics, all of those business and personal relationships involve the transmission of tacit knowledge about how people engage each other in their home communities.

It is only at the point of the final demand, and the finished goods market that codified knowledge, based upon written legal contracts, and written scientific documents, that the personal direct communications in the shared regional cognitive map for conducting business are replaced with the more formal codified written communications, in non-personal knowledge exchange.

The moral values of honesty and trust are still relevant in the more global market, but those values are not based upon the personal direct face-to-face communications that occur in the regional market.

We agree with the insight from Harald Bathelt, related to metro regional production relationships, that a type of production, capital market, moral values and venture capital envelope seems to exist within a 50 mile radius of a metro region, especially metro regions characterized as high technology industry.

Bathelt writes,

"According to the linkage structure identified in the survey, (of 5 different metro regions) a substantial share of key technology firms in each of the five key technology centres are mainly regionally oriented. Furthermore, the regional orientation of sample firms is manifested predominantly through input linkages. For all key technology centres, the percentage of firms having at least 50% regional input linkages appears to be significantly higher than the percentage of firms with at least 50% regional output linkages… The proportion of inputs acquired within a fifty mile radius ranges from a low of 11% for the sample firms based in Atlanta to a high of 40% for the CTT sample firms. In Boston, the Research Triangle and Ottawa, about 25% of the inputs are acquired regionally." (Employment Changes and Input-Output Linkages in Key Technology Industries: A Comparative Analysis, 1990).

The 50 mile envelope, in beneficial economic theory, is the location boundary of shared cognitive mental maps about how business gets done in a metro region.

We modify Wassily Leontief's conventional input output model in order to present a dual analytical model that describes both inter-industry production relationships, based upon price transactions, and the underlying tacit knowledge flows, that occur during either the upward growth trajectory, or the downward economic decline trajectory of the regional economy. (Input-Output Economics, 1966).

Leontief won the Nobel Memorial Prize in Economic Sciences, in 1973, based upon his analysis of how intermediate, semi-finished goods from one industry produce inputs for other industries, eventually leading to the final demand, finished goods market.

In the conventional usage of Leontief's model, a change in the final demand, finished goods market can describe how the intermediate demand for the semi-finished goods changes.

For example, in Diagram 6, above, if consumers in the finished goods cotton industry starting buying more shirts than pants, in period 1, then Leontief's model could describe how that change in final demand effected all the other industries, all the way back to the cotton fields, in time period two.

Towards the end of his life, in 1999, Leontief was working on a refinement to his conventional model to describe what would happen in a regional economy if the capital investments in new ventures changed, in time period 1. (Input-Output Data Base For Analysis of Technological Change, Economic Systems Research, (Vol. 1 #3), 1989).

In other words, rather than describing how a change in final demand affected the production relationships in the existing regional economy, Leontief was describing what would happen in time period 2, if capital investments in new ventures changed in time period 1.

Leontief pointed out that the entire combination of capital, available in the region in time period 1, was called "undistributed surplus."

In his modification of his conventional model, Leontief said that this supply of undistributed surplus, or to use a Marxian term, undistributed profit, plays a double role for the firms in the regional economy.

"On the one hand, Leontief said, "it [profits] represents the values of materials, additional pay rolls, and other cost elements, on which, it usually is spent in the process of new investment."

In conventional neo-classical theory, this supply of profits is called Gross Domestic Product.

According to Leontief, the supply of profits in the region, in time period 1, also represents potential venture capital that could be re-invested in the region for "the productive services of capital and entrepreneurship."

Leontief stated that his new application,

"...describes the structural relationships that governs the successive states of the economic systems from the beginning to the end of a particular stretch of historical time... Past relationships (among firms) suggest the technological trajectory of the region… the past (I-O) relationships suggest the technological trajectory of the region. The trajectory is used for manufacturing engineering estimates on the next period inputs."

Leontief referred to this second round of investment of profit re-investment as "the tapestry of the economy as it was being woven through time."

In the evolutionary economic metaphor, Leontief described how the earlier rounds of investments in capital equipment, in time period 1, become obsolete and less valuable when the subsequent rounds of investments are made. (Studies in the Structure of the American Economy, The Journal of Business of the University of Chicago, 1953).

If the profits from the earlier capital investments are subsequently reinvested in new radical technological ventures, which are subsequently selected by consumers, the regional trajectory will be economic growth.

If those profits are not re-invested in radical new technology, the economic trajectory will be economic decline.

If the profits are invested in sustaining innovation improvements, the economy will slowly rotate around the Nash Equilibrium.

In a modification of Leontief's conventional model, Edward Feser and Edward Bergman, pioneered a modification in Leontief's conventional regional input-output by adding the step of identifying technological affinities in production among different firms in the region.

The additional step of factor analysis allowed for the discovery of underlying technological affinities in manufacturing and production technology that exist between different industrial sectors.

These technological input-output affinities between different firms are not obvious.

For example, Feser and Renski identify 9 high technology sectors in the North Carolina economy that share technological production affinities.

It would not be immediately obvious that the occupational skill sets and production technology in the tobacco industry would share technological affinities with the pharmaceutical industry. (High-Tech Clusters in North Carolina, North Carolina Board of Science and Technology, 2000).

In our application of Leontief's refinement of profit reinvestment, and the Feser/Bergman/Renski modification, we explain that the technological closeness in production, in different industrial sectors, in the same metro region, means a much faster rate of knowledge creation and knowledge diffusion in the region because scientific staff from different firms are engaged in a high rate of face-to-face personal communication.

In our application of tacit knowledge flows, it is not simply because of the similar occupational skill sets, educational backgrounds, or the arrangement of capital equipment on the plant floor, but the increased rate of knowledge creation and diffusion occurs primarily in the non-market social and political institutions within the 50-mile envelope of the shared cognitive map of the region. (Using Feser's Input-Output Model of Technological Affinities To Target Innovation Investments To Regional Industrial Value Chains, SSRN, 2008).

For example, we describe the engineer in the Stankiewicz article, who "bears knowledge, and is embedded in his technological community," as a knowledge "boundary spanner," who meets other engineers from other firms, in daily personal exchanges, in his home community.

In every personal face-to-face- communication, those engineers in the region create and diffuse tacit knowledge based upon their common social and political information networks.

Every statistical entry in Leontief's new capital investment model represents both a price transaction and a tacit knowledge transaction in the regional economy.

For example, in a region with both chemical and pharmaceutical industrial sectors, Leontief's new model would describe what an increase of $10 million in capital investments in the chemical industrial sector, in time period 1, would modify the production output in the pharmaceutical sector, in time period 2.

In the logical chronology of economic growth, tacit knowledge creation and diffusion comes first, and later, when entrepreneurs and venture capitalists imagine new investment opportunities from knowledge diffusion, the capital investments in new ventures may occur.

What happens next in capital investment in the region depends on whether the region has open flows of tacit knowledge, or closed, and politically controlled flows of knowledge.

Any statistical entry in Leontief's model, in time period 1, indicates the existence of a certain level, or an initial factor endowment, of knowledge creation and diffusion.

Over time, if those technological coefficients, in Leontief's model strengthen, the regional economy is creating and diffusing tacit knowledge, which potentially creates capital investment opportunities, in time period 2.

On the other hand, if previous technological coefficients disappear over time, then the region is losing neuronal cognitive ability to generate new knowledge, and the economy is on a downward trajectory of economic decline.

Geoffrey J.D. Hewings, et al., used a variant of the modified Leontief model to describe how the loss of technological coefficients in the Chicago metro regional economy caused regional economic decline, from 1975 to 2011. (The Hollowing Out Process in the Chicago Economy, 1975–2011, The Federal Reserve Bank of Chicago, 1998).

In our application of tacit knowledge creation and diffusion, the hollowing out process they describe means that the regional economy lost its neuronal networks for creating new knowledge.

We describe the chronology of capital market investments as a deal flow pipeline, which incorporates both Leontief's new capital investment model, and the Feser-Bergman technological affinities model to describe how the sequence of capital investment events leads to regional capital growth..

Chapter 8. Diagram 7. The Tacit Knowledge Regional Deal Flow Pipeline.

The Small Business Deal Creation Pipeline™

Deal Mapping To convert knowledge and ideas into small business ventures and new products	*Deal Creation* To prepare new ventures or product ideas to enter the market	*Deal Funding* To find capital to fund commercial ventures	*Deal Exits* To manage the reinvestment of profit from the first generati of ideas into the next generation of innovation

Image Credit: Laurie Thomas Vass, Doing More Deals: Re-Envisioning the Use of Industrial Clusters to Target Regional Innovation Investments, SSRN, 2013

The entire regional tacit knowledge capital investment model can be visualized as taking place within the new internet-based blockchain algorithm, as a regional policy tool to facilitate a higher rate of regional economic growth.

In Diagram 8, the four blocks of the deal creation pipeline are displayed in the vertical axis to describe the chronological passage of time.

The emergence of beneficial economic growth occurs when capital gain profits, in the early time periods are re-invested into new radical technological ventures in time period 2.

Chapter 8. Diagram 8. The Tacit Knowledge Regional Economic Growth Model, Leading to the Emergence of Beneficial Economic Growth.

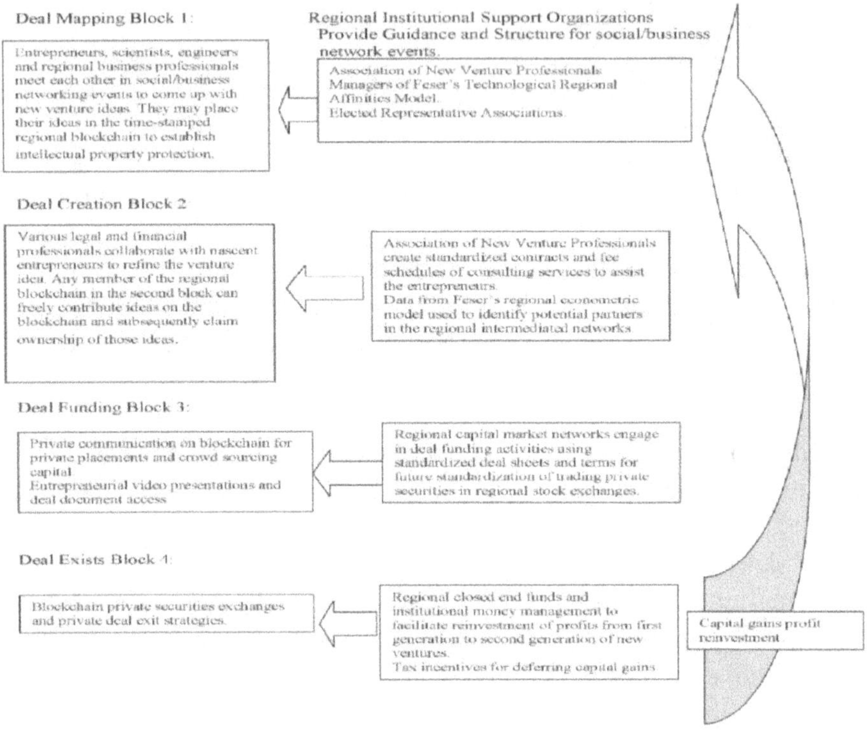

Image Credit: Laurie Thomas Vass, Updating Schumpeter's Gales of Creative Destruction: Exploiting the Vulnerability of New World Order Corporate Globalism With Regional Blockchain Entrepreneurial Economic Growth, 2022),

The contingent logical sequence of capital market events, shown in Diagram 5, illustrates why understanding the dual flows of both capital and knowledge is crucial for understanding the emergence of regional beneficial economic growth.

Wassily Leontief's capital input-output model, combined with the Feser-Bergman model, provides the analytical framework for tracking both dimensions of this contingent economic process.

As is the case with Prigogine's emergence of natural order, the emergence of a beneficial economy is not a certain outcome, and the uncertainty at the beginning of the period could easily lead to different economic outcomes in later periods of time.

Whether the dual progression of capital and knowledge culminates in beneficial growth, economic decline, or neutral drift depends not only on the monetary flows of capital investment that Leontief's input-output analysis reveals, but also on whether knowledge flows through those same pathways to generate the re-investment opportunities for profit from capital gains to be made in the future time periods.

That economic future contingency depends on whether the region has open knowledge flows or closed knowledge flows.

The future contingency also depends on whether the citizens in the region share common cultural and moral values related to the exchange of trust and honesty in the distribution of benefits from economic growth.

The model of beneficial economic growth, described in this Chapter, would probably be a factor in Bathelt's research on the Research Triangle, in North Carolina, where knowledge flows freely and citizens share common values of trust and honesty.

In the Research Triangle, citizens share a common cognitive map about how regional economic growth benefits all social classes.

Bathelt falsely attributes the beneficial economic success in the RTP resulted from being a "planned" economic strategy.

The success of the economic growth in the RTP was not due to being planned strategy, like the economic system of communist China, or the planned economy of the Soviet Union.

The success of the RTP was due to a shared citizen cognitive map that economic growth would benefit all social classes in the RTP metro region.

The shard cognitive map is based upon historical cultural values of trust and honesty that undergird citizen allegiance to obey the rule of law.

Citizen allegiance to obey the rule of law means that when citizens work hard and play by the rules, economic benefits everyone.

That same emergence of a beneficial economic society would probably not emerge in Bathelt's research in the East China region of Shanghai, where knowledge is controlled by political authorities and economic benefits flow to party elites rather than ordinary citizens.

In Chinese communism, individual citizens are used by the communist regime as economic resources to increase the military power of the communist regime.

In China, the shared cognitive map is the ideology of the goodness of communism, imposed on the citizens, as if communism was their own cognitive map that defined the future that their brains were imagining.

The myth of the benefits of global trade with China, in 2001, was based upon the false idea that trade would make the Chinese society more open and democratic, like the U. S. society.

The opposite happened.

After 2001, the U. S. society became more authoritarian and repressive, resembling the ruling class economic structure of the Chinese society, where the top 1% of the American society benefits from trade with China, and thc rest of the population struggles to make a living..

Beneficial economic growth is caused by private capital investment in new technology ventures.

And, the cause of capital investment is increased rates of open knowledge creation and knowledge diffusion, in distinct metro economic regions.

The choice for red state citizens today is crafting a new beneficial economic constitution, or continued downward drift to economic decline and a totalitarian global society, controlled by people who look, and act, just like the leaders in Communist China.

Chapter 9. The Beneficial Economics of Tacit Knowledge Creation and Diffusion In The Metro Regional Ecosystem of Trust.

The concept of regional knowledge, viewed in the context of an economic asset, could be measured directly as a regional stock of knowledge, in a specific period of time. by counting the number of technical workers or scientists employed in the region.

For example, all the scientists, engineers, and skilled technology workers could be counted, at the end of a year, to determine a region's stock of knowledge.

Alternatively, knowledge could be measured as a flow by counting up the number of cases where tacit knowledge had been converted into action in a metro region.

For example, in Chapter 8, we described how a flow of knowledge over different periods of time could be measured by using Leontief's capital matrix by showing how coefficients in his model changed over time, resulting from new capital investments. (Wassily Leontief, Input-Output Data Base For Analysis of Technological Change, 1989).

The addition or subtraction of technical data entries in his model, over time, would describe how regional knowledge was either increasing or decreasing.

We combined Leontief's model with Feser's concept of closeness in production technology between different industrial sectors to describe the concept of how regional boundaries, such as a metro region, could contain a community of citizens who shared tacit knowledge because of the common technological knowledge of the scientists and engineers who lived in the region. (Edward Feser, and Stuart Sweeney, A Test For the Coincident Economic and Spatial Clustering of Business Enterprises, 2002).

In our application of Prigogine's complex adaptive natural systems to beneficial economic systems, spontaneous beneficial social order occurs when individuals and groups, with limited individual knowledge, interact with other individuals, to increase the initial stock of tacit knowledge in the metro region.

In Prigogine's complex adaptive system, energy is the force which dissipates in an open natural system. As the energy dissipates, a new natural order emerges that is completely different than the natural system that existed before.

In beneficial economic theory, tacit knowledge is the force which diffuses in an open regional economy. After the knowledge has been converted to action, the regional economic structure is completely different than the economic structure that existed before.

We agree with Peter M. Allen, in Cities and Regions as Self-Organizing Systems, (1996), that a beneficial economic order will emerge in metro regions based upon the insight that metro regions are self-organizing systems, when left to function in a free society.

Allen writes,

"Which solution will emerge [in a metro region] is determined by fluctuations and is not submitted to deterministic laws. We come to the concepts of 'self organization' of 'dissipative structures' and to 'order through fluctuations'... [metro regions] are socio-economic and socio-cultural systems are composed of individual elements capable of internal adaptation and learning as a result of their experience."

The beneficial social order in metro regions emerges because individual humans are free to determine how best to obtain the future that their brains are imagining.

Allen continues,

"the autonomy of the actors, [individual citizens] and their ability to add and subtract energy [tacit knowledge] to the system according to their own wishes is what makes prediction impossible unless we can find some fixed rules of behaviour, or some fixed 'goal' from which behaviour can be derived."

In our concept of knowledge, as a flow over different periods of time, the force that converts tacit knowledge to action is capital investment in new technology ventures, within the metro regional boundaries.

In our application of the emergence of spontaneous beneficial order, a community of shared tacit knowledge among the citizens who live in the region creates a community of shared trust among citizens.

In other words, shared tacit knowledge comes first, and after tacit knowledge is shared, in personal face-to-face exchange, the citizens develop a sense of trust among themselves about who to trust and who is honest in conducting business.

Pamela Mueller also makes a distinction between a region's initial stock of knowledge, and a region's ability to add to that stock of knowledge through shared tacit knowledge. ("Exploiting Entrepreneurial Opportunities: The Impact of Entrepreneurship on Growth," cited in Zoltan Acs, Innovation and The Growth of Cities, 2002).

Mueller writes,

"...although the [initial] stock of knowledge in a region is an important determinant of local economic growth, it is new firms in general – seen as the exploitation of the opportunities that arise from R&D activities – and not public institutions that are the means by which knowledge contributes to the local economy."

Mueller's research on entrepreneurial investments in new technology ventures suggests that the contribution of public institutions and universities to regional growth pales in comparison with the contribution made by high-tech start-ups.

She noted,

“Starting a firm in order to realize an entrepreneurial opportunity is assumed as a mechanism for knowledge diffusion and for the exploitation of knowledge. Ultimately, however, the firm is started with the purpose of introducing a new good or service.”

Her distinction between a new good or service, and a technological improvement in an existing good, called a sustaining innovation, is important to how the diffusion of tacit knowledge eventually leads to beneficial regional economic growth. (Clayton Christensen and Michael Raynor, The Innovator’s Solution: Creating and Sustaining Successful Growth, 2003).

We agree with Mueller’s insight about new technology ventures, and add a prior step that capital investment in new-to-the world technology products is the cause of spontaneous beneficial order created by regional economic growth.

The future beneficial economic growth does not occur immediately after an initial capital investment in a metro region. The future order emerges slowly, as a result of the human brain’s response to the appearance of something new, or novel, in their regional economic environment.

As the new tacit knowledge diffuses slowly through the community of knowledge workers, new future markets emerge, as citizens begin to realize the opportunity for additional capital investments that service and support the initial new capital investment.

What type of future economic order that emerges from knowledge diffusion in one regional economic environment, given historical social rules or antecedent moral values of trust, would be entirely different than a different region with another set of antecedent social or cultural traditions.

The emergence of beneficial social order is contingent upon whether the flow of tacit knowledge occurs in an open, trust community, where knowledge flows freely, or in a closed, controlled society, where the flow of knowledge is controlled by social and political elites.

In his book, The Tacit Dimension, (1967), Michael Polanyi described the contingent nature of tacit knowledge flows as arising in conditions of uncertainty, when a new situation occurs.

Polanyi views tacit knowledge as an individual personal attribute, in the brains of humans.

He used the example of an apprentice, being taught a skilled trade by a master craft worker. Even when the student cannot analyze and account in detail for the instructions from the master, the tacit knowledge transfer occurs because the student trusts the master in his instructions.

Polanyi wrote,

"While tacit knowledge can be possessed by itself, explicit knowledge [codified] must rely on being tacitly understood and applied. Hence all knowledge is either tacit or rooted in tacit knowledge. A wholly explicit [codified] knowledge is unthinkable."

Citing Polanyi, Wioleta Kucharska, et al., writes that tacit knowledge sharing is the result of the human brain's free will to imagine a new future.

Kucharska writes,

"Tacit knowledge sharing is an act of commitment which cannot be formalized because it is the result of a free will. [Tacit] knowledge sharing, unlike data sharing and information sharing, [codified] is characterized by strong contextuality, a fact emphasized by Polanyi (1966). Young and Milton (2011) claimed that "knowledge is situational and what works in one situation may not work in another" (Trust, Tacit Knowledge Sharing, Project Performance and Their Managerial Implications, SSRN, 2017).

Polanyi writes that tacit knowledge is "embedded" into the social business networks that exist within a community. Citizens in a metro may not be cognizant of all the tacit knowledge that they, or the region, possess, until the recognition that tacit knowledge exists, confirmed in face-to-face communication exchange

In Chapter 3, we described this awareness of tacit knowledge in the human brain's evolution of free will, which Popper describes as World 3 insight-imagination.

In other words, after a capital investment in new technology is made in a region, citizens begin to imagine how that investment may create future investment opportunities, for themselves.

Friedrich Hayek extends the concept of human free will to imagine the future by placing the diffusion of knowledge into the political framework of constitutional citizen liberty. (The Use of Knowledge in Society, The American Economic Review, 1945).

The social problem that Hayek addresses is that a single individual can never grasp all of the tacit knowledge that is available in a given metro region. An individual citizen begins to grasp the existence of tacit knowledge through social interaction with other humans.

Hayek writes,

"the dispersed bits of incomplete and frequently contradictory knowledge which all the separate individuals possess. The economic problem of society is thus not merely a problem of how to allocate "given" resources-if "given" is taken to mean given to a single mind which deliberately solves the problem set by these "data."... knowledge which ought to be used but which is initially dispersed among many different individuals, or in conveying to the individuals such additional knowledge as they need in order to enable them to fit their plans in with those of others."

The solution to the problem of diffusing knowledge, according to Hayek, is a constitutional system which allows for the greatest freedom and liberty for citizens to access all the potential knowledge available to them.

Hayek writes,

"Since no one has sufficient knowledge to pick and choose such individuals, freedom must be given to all…individual freedom is essential to the long-term growth of civilisation and the advance of humanity at large. The progress of civilisation depends on man's freedom to experiment with new ways of doing things." (The Constitution of Liberty, 1978).

In Chapter 7, (The Emergence of American Beneficial Social Order Under Buchanan's Fair Constitutional Rules and Kant's Moral Values), we extended Hayek's insight about constitutional liberty to include Buchanan's fair rules and Kant's moral values, as the prior necessary conditions for the emergence of spontaneous beneficial economic order.

In our application of Prigogine's emergence in natural systems, the conversion of tacit knowledge into action is "socially-embedded" in the community of knowledge-bearing citizens who live in the metro region.

Potential entrepreneurs, or scientists, live in a regional community which helps them interpret the meaning of the new tacit knowledge, and thus its applicability to an entrepreneurial capital investment opportunity, when they first see a new product or new production process. (Etienne Wenger, Communities of Practice: Learning, Meaning, and Identity, 1999).

The idea that knowledge is socially embedded in a community of practice means that the regional environment contains a social structure of organizations, like civic clubs or professional associations, which allow an individual to work with other individuals in converting knowledge to action.

In our application of converting knowledge to capital investments, the number and type of firms in the region described by Feser's model of technological closeness provides the institutional and geographical context of tacit knowledge creation and diffusion. (Laurie Thomas Vass, Using Feser's Input-Output Model of Technological Affinities to Target Innovation Investments to Regional Industrial Value Chains, SSRN, 2008).

The individuals in the regional firms communicate with individuals in other firms, with other technological associates and attend professional association meetings.

During these meetings, the citizens become aware of potential investment opportunities, and some of them may convert the tacit knowledge to action in the form of a new capital investment.

Adam Smith (1776), described this same process of converting knowledge to action in the early American entrepreneurial community of farmers.

"The colonists carryout a knowledge of agriculture and of other useful arts....Every colonist gets more land than he can possibly cultivate... He is eager, therefore, to collect labourers from all quarters, and to reward them with the most liberal wages. But those liberal wages, joined to the plenty and cheapness of the land, soon make those labourers leave him, in order to become landlords themselves, and to reward, with equal liberality, other labourers, who soon leave them for the same reason ...." (The Wealth of Nations, 1776).

The American colonists who initially worked on the farms of other landowners learned the farming techniques, and soon left the farm to create their own farm.

As Smith's insight about the early American farming community indicates, the flow of regional tacit knowledge in free markets emerged from the individual brains making decisions based on local information, combined with a free society that allowed farmers to convert tacit knowledge to action.

In beneficial economic systems, beneficial order emerges from countless individual interactions without central government direction.

The emergence of beneficial social order is contingent upon whether the flow of tacit knowledge occurs in an open, trust community, where knowledge flows freely, or in a closed, controlled society, where the flow of knowledge is controlled by social and government elites.

In our application of a beneficial economic order, the free flow of tacit knowledge among citizens in a metro regional economy creates a "trust ecosystem" where an individual's reputation of integrity and honesty have economic value.

The metro regional community of trust is an economic institutional infrastructure that emerges from knowledge sharing.

Without the infrastructure of trust, tacit knowledge diffusion remains isolated in individual minds, and is not converted into action, because no citizen trusts any other citizen not to exploit the value of the tacit knowledge.

The transformation of a metro region's tacit knowledge into beneficial economic growth hinges on a critical intermediate step of capital investment in new technology ventures.

However, it is not simply a capital investment in what Clayton Christensen calls a sustaining technological innovation that causes the emergence of a future beneficial economy.

As we described in Chapter 8, capital investments in sustaining technological innovation allows the regional economy to slowly rotate around a Nash Equilibrium,

The transformation of a metro region's tacit knowledge into beneficial economic growth hinges on a critical intermediate step of capital investment in technology ventures that create new-to-the-world products or services, or what Christensen calls radical innovation.

This type of capital investment in radical innovation operates at the highest risk threshold of trust because it requires wealthy citizens to commit capital to ventures that create entirely new products and services, rather than incremental improvements to the existing economic structure.

Following Christensen's distinction between sustaining innovation and radical innovation, this high level of risk requires a wealthy citizen to have confidence in an entrepreneur's ability to navigate the uncertainty inherent in radical innovation, where traditional market price signals may not exist. (Clayton Christensen, The Innovator's Dilemma: When New Technologies Cause Great Firms To Fail, 1997).

When wealthy knowledge-bearing citizens, who live in the region's community of trust, develop confidence in an entrepreneur's capacity to execute sound capital investments in new-to-the-world technology ventures, the investors become willing to invest capital in ventures that fundamentally disrupt the existing status quo markets.

The emergence of this specialized high-risk trust becomes the decisive factor determining whether a metro region's initial stock of tacit knowledge assets translate into breakthrough economic growth or causes the regional economy to remain in the Nash Equilibrium.

Trust allows human imagination in the realm of economic behaviors to be fulfilled over a long period of time, which may eventually lead to the emergence of new markets, if the cultural value of trust is inherited over successive generations.

Trust is one of Kant's a moral and cultural values that is inherited, over generations, when the social and legal structure is characterized by fair civil rules of exchange and laws regarding appropriation of future profit.

Within any distinct region, the mental map and perceptions about the region's future tend to be shared by both firms and consumers. (Fiorenza Belussi, Are Industrial Districts Formed by Networks Without Technologies?: The Diffusion of Internet Applications in Three Italian Clusters, 2005).

Moedas and Grenier et al., in their research on knowledge networks in regional industrial clusters, found that,

"Trust is usually one important characteristic of a regional cluster."

They wrote that,

"Proximity and trust facilitate, rather than prevent or being viewed as opposed to, both competition and cooperation among their [cluster firm] members (Porter, 1998) which are dual strategic and relational modes of acting within clusters strongly useful for firm and technology development." (Céline Abecassis-Moedas and Corinne Grenier, Un modèle étendu de la structuration entre et organisation au sein des districts industriels, 2007).

Part of the common mental regional map about the future has the effect of reducing the risk associated with creating new firms and radical new products.

Another part of the dynamic market behavior within the region is a negative force that opposes free flow of tacit knowledge that potentially could be converted to action.

Existing firms in the regional industrial cluster have a vested financial interest in creating common perceptions that continue the status quo into the future because their capital investments in current technology are so difficult to alter if they must compete with radical new technology.

Those type of existing firms favor capital investments in existing, or sustaining innovations, which do not disrupt their status quo flow distribution of income and wealth

What happens in a regional trust ecosystem, after a capital investment, is that many different humans see the phenomena and use their individual different mental images to interpret the meaning of the innovation.

This slow emergence of a common mental perception among different humans means that the regional geographic market is providing the cognitive validation of the individual shared mental maps, and that shared understanding is the force that allows tacit knowledge to be converted to action.

In the absence of regional trust among citizens who live in the region, shared tacit knowledge does not occur.

When shared tacit knowledge does not occur, the regional rates of economic growth decline because of a lower rates of capital investment.

In their research on the link between trust and regional economic growth, Knack and Zak conclude,

"The simple correlation between national rates of investment (gross investment/GDP) and trust is strongly negative; when trust is low, investment lags. The same negative correlation holds for GDP growth and trust. This can be understood in terms of „transactions cost economics." Trust facilitates transactions by reducing the number of contingencies that must be considered when doing a [venture capital] deal."

They describe a type of economic development trap that occurs in regional economies that are not characterized by trust.

"Our analysis also shows that if trust is sufficiently low (below 30% for the average country, then the investment rate will be so low that income will stagnate or even decline. Economists call this a "poverty trap", and we show that the primary reason for a poverty trap is ineffective legal structures that result in low levels of generalized trust, and therefore little investment." (Stephen Knack and Paul J. Zak, Interpersonal Trust, and Economic Development. 2003).

In Chapter 3, we used the model of how Proctor & Gamble manages the conversion of tacit knowledge to the creation of new products, and suggest that this same corporate management model would be effective to convert regional tacit knowledge to capital investments in the regional ecosystem of trust.

In our model of beneficial economics, the concept of democratic citizen self-government includes citizen self-management of the regional asset of tacit knowledge, as if the asset of regional trust was like an asset in a private corporation, such as Proctor & Gamble.

Citizen self-management of regional tacit knowledge resources entails the same management tasks as those in Proctor & Gamble.

The citizens in a metro region would nurture a culture of knowledge sharing, promote communities of technological practice, recruit and retain skilled technology workers, and create social and administrative institutions to manage the intellectual and social capital business networks in the region.

In her internet power point presentation of how Proctor & Gamble converts tacit knowledge to new products, Karen A. Kreutz begins with the idea that breakthrough innovation starts with a new idea or thought of one person. (Knowledge Creation for Breakthrough Innovation, 2013).

She then suggests that the next step in tacit knowledge management is for that one person to share the idea with 2 more people, who may be sitting together at a table, or in a meeting.

The next step is for those people to share the idea with 4 or more people who may have a similar professional education or scientific background.

She notes that the sharing of tacit knowledge is a very fragile process.

She writes,

"Breakthrough innovation requires tacit knowledge exchange. The sharing of tacit knowledge is an "extremely fragile process. The speed of tacit knowledge exchange depends on the degree to which the environment is collaborative."

Her use of the term "collaborative," has the same meaning in beneficial economics as an ecosystem of trust.

In her description, the term "collaborative culture" is linked to her use of the term "community of practice," within the corporation.

In other words, within the Proctor & Gamble corporate staffing structure, employees share a community of technological or scientific practice, and when that community of practice occurs in a trusting, collaborative environment, tacit knowledge may be exchanged.

She explains the difference between tacit knowledge and "explicit" knowledge, which we describe as "codified" knowledge.

She writes,

"Explicit knowledge: can be transferred through language (speech, writing and graphics). It is codified, structured, accessible to people other than the creator of that knowledge. Tacit knowledge lies beneath the surface of conscious thought and is derived from a lifetime of experience, practice, perception and learning, It is content specific, personal, hard to formalize and stored semi-consciously and exist in peoples' heads."

Kreutz uses the following power point diagram to explain the difference between tacit knowledge and codified knowledge.

Within her corporation, “breakthrough innovation”, which we describe as radical product innovation, occurs when the corporate environment is characterized as a collaborative community of practice, as she describes in the diagram below.

While the power point presentation of tacit knowledge management inside of Proctor & Gamble uses complex terms and ideas, the basic concept is simple to understand, and simple to transfer to a regional metro economy.

Chapter 9. Diagram 1. The Creation of Knowledge: from Kreutz.

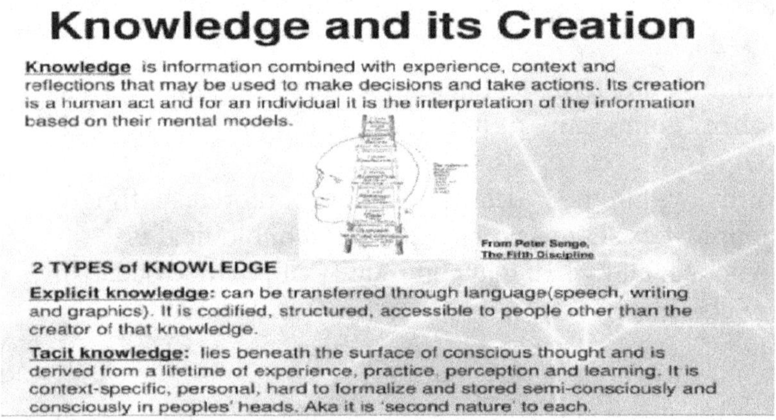

Image credit: Karen A. Kreutz, Internet Power Point Presentation, 2013.

When the citizens in a regional metro economy see themselves as a regional business enterprise whose mission is high rates of economic growth, then the process of tacit knowledge exchange begins when citizens meet each other to discuss new ideas and technology ventures for the regional economy.

Chapter 9. Diagram 2. Organizational Management of Tacit Knowledge Creation Within Proctor & Gamble.

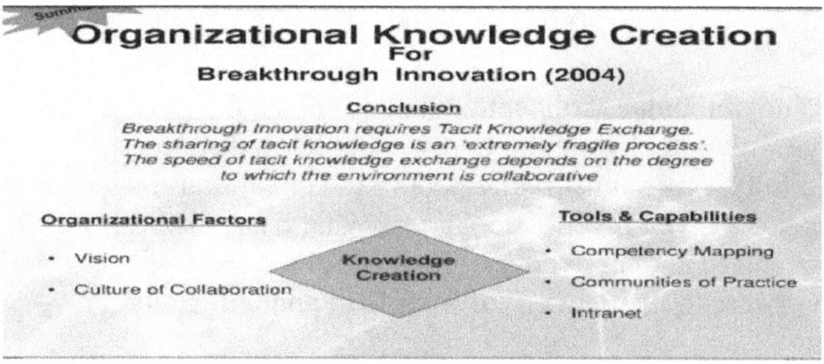

Image credit: Karen A. Kreutz, Internet Power Point Presentation, 2013.

This same type of regional tacit knowledge management system was successfully implemented in the Research Triangle Park, N. C. in 1984. (Laurie Thomas Vass, Industrial Recruitment and the Path of North Carolina's Economic Development to the Year 2000: A Public Discussion Paper for North Carolina's Project 2000 - Advocating the Creation of the NC Council for Entrepreneurial Development (CED), SSRN, 1983).

As the CED states on its website,

"CED acts as the connective center for all of this to happen. Through high-touch support, education, access to capital, and crucial connections, we bring entrepreneurs together with the optimal resources needed to turn a new company into a success story."

In our economic theory of beneficial economics and the emergence of beneficial social order, we explain that it is not sufficient for a region to simply promote the industrial recruitment of co-located firms, who may share similar technology of production.

As the case of the Canadian biotech industrial cluster indicates, the culture of trust and collaboration is a required prerequisite for tacit knowledge to create a beneficial order. (Barak S. Aharonson et al., "Inventive and Uninventive Clusters: The Case of Canadian Biotechnology, SSRN, 2008).

They write,

"Thus, it is not enough to collocate with and match the R&D effort of inventive firms; to capture the benefits of external sources of knowledge fully a firm must participate in the collaboration network… For a given inventive location, what makes the difference between inventive and uninventive firms is not the level of R&D effort; it is access to the network of inter firm and university collaboration."

We describe a more comprehensive theory to explain the logical sequence of events required to promote the emergence of beneficial regional economic growth.

Chapter 9. Diagram 3. Theoretical Chronology of Regional Tacit Knowledge.

Logical Progression of Thought and Time Chronology of Analysis

Knowledge Units of Analysis	Basic Rules/ Algorithms	Antecedent Conditions	Existing Environment	Future Environment
Entrepreneurs Scientists Engineers who "bear" technical knowledge	Contagion Clusters Tacit Knowledge Property rights Rates of taxation	Rate of new venture creation. Status Quo Form of government. Rate of investments Historical stock of knowledge	Open or closed society, diversity, Rules, of civil procedure Traditions Educational Attainment Knowledge flows or leaks.	New knowledge. Status Quo. Decline Market bifurcation

Image Credit. Laurie Thomas Vass, Theory of Technology Evolution, 2019).

In our explanation of tacit knowledge creation and diffusion, a metro region begins with an initial stock of knowledge workers.

In time period 1, there are social rules and algorithms which describe how this initial stock of knowledge may lead to the creation of new tacit knowledge.

The events and conditions in the prior time periods affect the rate of economic growth and knowledge diffusion in time period 1.

The future economy could emerge as being on either a growth trajectory, or a declining economic trajectory.

At some future time, the economy in time period 1, could bifurcate into a new trajectory of a growth economy, or bifurcate into a declining regional economy.

Or, given a status quo rate of capital investment in sustaining technology, the economy may slowly rotate around a Nash Equilibrium, sometimes for decades at a time.

We use a series of statements to further explain our economic theory of regional knowledge creation and diffusion.

What Is Beneficial Regional Technological Change?

Beneficial technical change causes new income flows to be created where none had existed before. Part of the new income is a result of increased productivity, meaning that output increases with reduced inputs in the regional production units.

Part of the new income is in the form of profits related to new goods produced by new production units.

Another part of the income is in the form of wages and salaries paid to people who work in the new firms that are producing the new products.

There is nothing about the relationship between future new incomes and new consumer preferences resulting from technical change that is preordained or automatic, in the same way that there is nothing preordained about how biological evolution of species may occur in a distinct environment, such as the Galapagos Islands.

In the region experiencing economic growth caused by technical change, capital investments made by firms to create new products, in the current period, create new inter-industry relationships, and new market relationships that did not exist before.

How Does Technological Change Create New Future Markets?

Technical change in products causes relationships between economic, social and political agents within the region to change. One of the possible outcomes associated with technical change, over time, is that more wealth and greater per capita incomes are created in the region.

The new wealth results from the creation of new future markets, when consumers shift their buying preferences from old products to new products.

There is nothing preordained or certain that this desirable outcome of more wealth or greater income will occur.

There are social, political and economic forces that favor technical change, and there are other forces that inhibit change.

Regional economic growth is a contingent outcome of the configuration of political power that supports or opposes technical change.

What promotes regional tacit knowledge creation?

Knowledge creation is one of the most important variables in understanding the direction of the technology in the economy. Understanding where knowledge is created, and then watching how new knowledge diffuses in a local economy, provides the basis to understand the direction of technology.

Richard Nelson describes how the regional community of practice combines with the diffusion of tacit knowledge because of the way technology workers learn their trades. ("Technical Change As Cultural Evolution," in Ross, Thomson, (Ed.), Learning and Technical Change, 1993).

Nelson describes three types of technological learning: learning by doing, learning by using, and inter-industry learning.

In our application of beneficial economic theory, learning about technology generally occurs as a result of social processes characterized by all three types of learning.

Tacit knowledge sharing results when suppliers, vendors, and customers share knowledge about technology. Each case of learning occurs within a regional network of social-business relationships, some of which occur on the floor of the production unit working with machines.

What happens in the process of learning is that mid-level managers, supervisors, technicians, scientists, engineers, technicians inside the production unit talk with each other every day about how things work, and they also talk about binding constraints and problems that they face.

Nelson writes,

"Insofar as the pace of learning depends on the accumulation of experience, it is influenced by the pace at which engineers and businessmen come into contact with new methods of production and with the capital goods in which they are embodied. Thus, the pace of technical advance may depend on the portion of production activities that involves constructing and installing new capital equipment and related structures, as well as on the growth rate of the cumulative gross stocks [of regional knowledge] that constitute the setting for learning by doing, and learning by using capital embodied technologies."

Sarah J. Marsh and Gregory N. Stock, in their article, Creating Dynamic Capability: The Role of Intertemporal Integration, Knowledge Retention, and Interpretation, describe how difficult it is for any single corporation to acquire external knowledge, that originates outside the company, or even to understand and codify prior internal corporate knowledge. (2006).

"Uncertainty about the ability for technological knowledge to be transformed to meet market demands, lack of complementary technologies, the lack of developed markets for a given technical feature, and other types of uncertainty add significant challenges to organizations as they develop products for future markets," they state.

As we described in the management model of innovation at Proctor & Gamble, tacit knowledge creation begins when knowledge workers meet with each other to discuss common issues, and the uncertainty they face in understanding the direction of technology

As Nathan Rosenberg and Stephen Kline have pointed out,

"...most innovation is done with the available knowledge already in the heads of the people in the organizations doing the work." (An Overview of Innovation, 1986).

If the people doing the work have connections to other parts of the regional economy, especially parts of the economy outside the routine patterns of communication, (Popper World 2), within their company, then contingently, knowledge may be converted to innovations.

How Do New, Small Technology Ventures In a Metro Region Create and Diffuse Technological Knowledge?

As Marsh and Stock point out, "Suppliers, customers, consultants, and the results of benchmarking and reverse engineering all provide sources of external knowledge that may be utilized in the new product development process, as do patent applications, scientific and trade publications, and conferences."

Someone, or some entity, in the region must organize this set of knowledge resources in a way that creates and diffuses technological knowledge so that entrepreneurs in the region can take advantage of new market opportunities.

For example, in the case of the North Carolina Council for Entrepreneurial Development, a group of securities attorneys and prominent business leaders decided to promote regional entrepreneurial economics as a supplemental strategy to the recruitment of large global corporations.

The Role of the Entrepreneur Who Perceives The Future Opportunity.

Pier Saviotti describes why the supply of entrepreneurs in a distinct economic region is so important to the process of technical change.

"The knowledge of engineers, scientists, managers, technicians, etc., involved in the implementation of the technology becomes specialized around the process, technical and service characteristics used (in the region)." (Pier Paolo Saviotti, Technological Evolution, Variety, and The Economy, 1996).

Saviotti describes where and how the entrepreneurs obtain their ideas for new ventures.

In an existing social-business network, skilled individuals, working in a production unit, share some specialized knowledge about a process.

Within this network, potential entrepreneurs meet with each other and discuss the feasibility of starting a new venture, based upon their technical knowledge and their understanding of the potential market for the products produced.

The entrepreneur provides an ingredient to the process of technical change that is absent in the framework of the existing old production unit, which is based upon codified knowledge.

Peter Temin makes this same point in describing the difference between potential entrepreneurs and mid-level managers.

Temin describes the role of entrepreneurs as the agents of economic change.

He states that,

"...entrepreneurs are the agents of change, ...(they) see new opportunities, invent new machines, discover new markets, ...(they) perform a different function from that of the manager, who works within a known technology, organization, and market."

(Entrepreneurs and Managers," in Higonnet, P., Landes, D. Rosovsky, H., (Eds.), Favorites of Fortune, 1991).

The entrepreneur is the agent that links the unknown future of consumer preferences to technological possibilities, the result of which is economic growth.

In making the distinction between unknown costs and risks of the future, and the known costs and risks in the existing old production unit, Temin hits upon the single greatest economic contribution that entrepreneurs make to the evolution of technical change.

Entrepreneurs perform the economic function of creating the future markets by imagining how that market will work. They provide the guesses of prices and profits, and how technological change in production units will interact with, as yet unseen, consumer preferences.

In contrast, the existing firm does not create a future market, it adjusts itself to the prices and profits of the status quo market.

The Importance of Citizen Regional Allegiance and Loyalty to Their Metro Community.

Technological knowledge is not distributed uniformly across different regions.

Saviotti notes that innovative firms,

"...tend to cluster in those (areas) that were already innovating countries...this specificity can not be explained by factor endowments, but is more likely to be caused by specific institutional configurations, and by the cumulative, local and specific character of the knowledge that the institutions possess." (1996).

Some regions have clusters of technological innovating firms and supportive social networks and some do not.

The accumulation of technological knowledge and the pace of technical change are contingent outcomes of the social and political institutional structure of a region.

For technological progress to occur, according to Joel Mokyr,

"...it must be born into a socially sympathetic environment." (The Lever of Riches: Technological Creativity and Economic Progress, 1990).

Whether the region has a sympathetic environment for technical change explains much about why economic growth occurs in some regions and not in others.

As Udo Staber points out,

"Mutual trust, social expectations, and the force of tradition and history, may be powerful mechanisms for blunting opportunistic motives and preventing the breakdown of cooperative relations." (Business Networks: Prospects For Development, 1996).

The stronger the regional citizen allegiance and loyalty, the better the small firms can resist the cultural and political forces in the region which oppose technological change.

Part of the dynamic market behavior within the region is that existing large corporation in the region have a vested financial interest in creating common perceptions that continue the status quo into the future because their capital investments in current technology are so difficult to alter if they must compete with radical new technology.

In our model of citizen self-management of the regional asset of tacit knowledge, citizens have the obligation to defend their financial future from the political forces that are committed to the staus quo distribution of income and political power. (Laurie Thomas Vass, Exploiting Knowledge: The Importance of Regional Allegiance and Territorial Loyalty In Implementing A Regional Small Business Innovation System, SSRN, 2009).

From the regional economic growth perspective, the shared value of trust among citizens reduces the risk of innovation for a single individual entrepreneur and, in certain specific geographical settings, the entrepreneurial risk is socialized, or collectivized, across the entire inter-industrial production cluster.

In other words, the historical circumstances related to trust in the region is an explanatory variable for reducing risk of new venture creation, because the risk of a single investment are socialized to the entire regional environment, and thus the environmental conditions are favorable for the creation of more new ventures.

The same inter-industrial institutional framework that diffuses tacit knowledge and information in a regional environment serves as the institutional arrangement through which the regional eco system of trust is created.

The Role of Regional Sources of Venture Capital In Technological Change.

In his historical review of technology, Robert McAdams noted that historians share a widely-held belief about the origins of venture capital in the eighteenth century that fueled the industrial revolution.

McAdams wrote,

"...all of the sources are in agreement that considerable increases in disposable wealth came into the hands of a substantial elite during the later part of the eighteenth century. Perhaps it is not so much their diversified and growing desires as consumers that quickened the pace of technological advance (during that era) but rather the increasing supply of potential venture capital for which this elite was beginning more aggressively to seek new avenues for profitable investment." (Paths of Fire: An Anthropologists Inquiry Into Western Technology, 1996).

McAdams noted that the elites in the eighteenth century were looking for new ventures to invest their wealth.

If a new pool of regional venture capital is created, in a capital gain exit event many years after the initial capital investment and if that supply of potential new disposable wealth is then re-invested into subsequent new products, equipment and machinery, then the conditions for self-sustaining regional economic growth for future periods will have been established.

The pool of capital that becomes available for reinvestment does not depend on cash flow from old production units, nor is it related to the conventional loans made by commercial bankers.

The potential pool of capital is created by profits on exit events made by the first round of venture capital investments.

The reinvestment decision depends on what the wealthy citizens in the region decide to do with the disposable wealth that is created by the forces of technical change.

If the regional economy is characterized as an eco system of trust, where citizens share common mental maps of the future of the region, and if profits from the first round of technology investments are subsequently re-invested in radical innovation, then a future beneficial social order may emerge.

Successful radical innovation occurs in regional eco systems that have multiple diverse tacit knowledge networks of citizens who share cognitive maps about their community.

These shared cognitive maps are geographically-bounded.

In most cases, the shared mental maps occur within 50 miles of the metro regional boundaries, just about the same distance that regional private capital markets function when financing innovation projects. (Laurie Thomas Vass, The Regional Market Dynamics of Radical Innovation, SSRN, 2008).

The overlap between regional technological innovation and regional capital markets is not happenstance.

Regionally dynamic open flows of tacit knowledge networks create the environment for radical innovation, because open flows of tacit knowledge create the conditions of trust for wealthy citizens to fund new ultra risky technology ventures.

From the perspective of a metro region being a self-organizing adaptive system, a distant future market becomes the present market based upon consumer selection of the newer, better products.

A regional economy characterized by Feser's close technological correlation coefficients and which have a history of social/business relationships based on trust would be expected to generate a higher rate of risky new venture creation, and thus have an evolutionary advantage in regional economic growth over regions which did not possess these characteristics.

Archibugi and Michie use the term "path-dependent" to describe how the economic past could be related to a future economic growth trap, the same term used by Stephen Knack and Paul J. Zak to describe what happens if the level of trust in the region is too low to generate capital investment. (Daniele Archibugi and Jonathan Michie, Technology, Globalisation and Economic Performance, 1997).

Existing firms, and existing commercial bankers who may have loaned money to those existing firms, have a motivation to control the direction of technology in order to maintain their incomes.

The social and political resistance to technological innovation contains the most ironic outcome associated with the application of Prigogine's emergence of natural order to the emergence of beneficial social order.

By manipulating the free flow of tacit knowledge, the status quo forces who oppose technological change can maintain the short term stable attractor point of a Nash Equilibrium.

However, as existing products become more standardized in their technological features and more uniform in their production process, their marginal profit is headed to zero, and as the profit heads to zero, the political manipulation of the rules becomes more pronounced as income competition regarding maintenance of the status quo intensifies.

Without the flow of new tacit knowledge, existing regional firms experience a decline in the available diversity of technology. All new tacit knowledge may jeopardize the status quo distribution of income.

The political manipulation of the rules has the effect of eroding "the ecosystem of trust" and, without the regional asset of trust, the expected future returns on new investments made today become less certain.

With less certain future returns from investments made today, the more rational behavior is to intensify the manipulation of rules to obtain more of the static income in the current period.

As the region loses its ability to create new ventures, the political inbred elites, who are fighting over the shreds of legacy income, seek political alliances with multi-national corporations, who act as gateways to the global final demand market for finished goods.

Regional tax incentives and other inducements are used by the regional political elites to attract external sources of economic growth as a substitute for the previously internallygenerated new venture growth.

The appearance of new knowledge at this stage would potentially upset the status quo distribution of legacy income, if the knowledge were to result in new investments in new products.

For that reason, the politically inbred elites must gain political control over the sources of venture capital and commercial banking functions to maintain control over the direction of technology.

The rule of law, and the role of trust gives way to the rule by the elites and secret dealings over the use of public resources to benefit private individuals.

The effects of political inbreeding are to destroy the functions and operational capacity of free markets, which, in a regional economy, perform the socially valuable role of creating and diffusing knowledge.

The ironic economic outcome, in the United States, is the emergence of monopoly corporate capitalism, in a society where wealth and incomes are concentrated in the top 1% of the ruling social class.

Chapter 10. Self Managed Regional Securities Markets Where Citizens Manage Their Own Regional Economic Growth

In Chapter 8, on the imperative of regional economic growth for the emergence of a beneficial economy, we described why economic growth is caused by private capital investment in new technology ventures.

In Chapter 9, we explained that the cause of capital investment is increased rates of tacit knowledge creation and diffusion in distinct metro economic regions.

We ended Chapter 9 by making a distinction between economic growth rates caused by private capital investments in sustaining innovation, and the more beneficial economic growth caused by radical, or new-to-the world capital investments in regional technology ventures.

We explained that tacit knowledge exchange in personal face-to-face communication creates an geographic envelope of trust, which we called a regional trust ecosystem.

As George Homans points out, capital is not just money used for investment.

"Capital may take the form of a moral code, especially a code supporting trust and confidence between men; a well-founded belief that they will not always let you down in favor of their private short-term gain." (George, C Homans, Social Behavior: Its Elementary Forms, 1974).

Contemporary economists call this type of capital "social capital," whose effects usually extend about 50 miles from the center of a metro regional economy.

Mark Granovetter has called this effect the "moral economy."

In his concept, the moral economy is the

"...degree to which a group's operations presuppose a moral community in which trustworthy behavior can be expected, normative standards understood, and opportunism foregone." (The Economic Sociology of Firms and Entrepreneurs, 2000).

We use the U. S. Census Bureau research on metro regional commuting patterns to make our claim that the regional envelope of trust extends about 50 miles from the metro boundaries of metro regions. (Melanie A. Rapino, and Alison K. Fields, Mega Commuters in the U.S. Time and Distance in Defining the Long Commute using the American Community Survey, 2013).

They found that,

- 95% of all U. S. commuters commute 50 miles or less.
- 40.7% of all commuters (28 million) were employed in knowledge work occupations of management, business science, and arts occupations.
- 15.8% of all commuters earn $80,000 or more. (11million workers)
- The mean distance of commute in miles was 18.8, which means that about 45% of all commuters commute between 19 miles to 50 miles in their commute to work.
- They found that 90% of the 64 million commuters who commute to work live in the same metro region where they work.

The logical flow of our argument about the emergence of beneficial social order begins with our application of Prigogine's theory of complex adaptive order in natural systems.

The application of Prigogine's theory to beneficial economics is that the regional eco system of trust is a metaphor of Prigogine's natural environment.

The logic of our 50-mile claim is that knowledge workers who are commuting to the metro region meet other knowledge workers, who live in the region, every day, and exchange tacit knowledge.

The beneficial economic chain of logic is:

- Regional economic commuting patterns →
- tacit knowledge exchange →
- trust ecosystems →
- capital investment decisions →
- self-managed regional securities markets.

The exchange of tacit knowledge in a metro region creates a regional moral culture of trust among knowledge workers on who to trust for doing business.

The regional ecosystem of trust encloses the geographic boundaries of regional capital investments in new technology ventures.

As we explained in Chapter 9, the capital investment in a radical new technology venture operates at the highest threshold of risk because conventional market price signals are not available to guide decisions by regional wealthy citizens.

At that high level of risk, trust replaces standard capital market decision-making, based upon price and supply and demand relationships in existing markets of products and production technology.

Cultural values of personal integrity, honesty and trust are geographically specific, and each region must be treated differently from a capital market investment analysis perspective.

The moral value of trust extends into the distant future because both the entrepreneur and the wealthy investor must extend trust many years into the future, in order to appropriate their profits from an investment made in the current period of time.

As we explained in Chapter 7 (The Emergence of American Beneficial Social Order Under Buchanan's Fair Constitutional Rules and Kant's Moral Values), given a certain type of prior social and political conditions in political power and cultural values, the regional economy could be predicted to take a certain type of trajectory.

Given another constellation of political power and trust ecosystem,, the regional economy would maintain the status quo, or slip into a downward economic trajectory.

Laura Bottazzi et al., in The Importance of Trust for Investment: Evidence from Venture Capital, cite the relationship between trust and economic growth.

They write,

"We define trust as a subjective belief about the likelihood that a potential trading partner will act honestly…Personalized trust, instead, concerns the evolving relationship between two specific agents

In our application of the concept of trust in the emergence of beneficial social order, tacit knowledge exchange among knowledge workers within the envelope of trust occurs first, in the creation and diffusion of knowledge creates trust between citizens.

The subsequent capital investment in a risky technology venture comes after trust has been established, both between the wealthy citizens and entrepreneur, and more widely, in the regional moral economy, described by Granovetter.

Bottazzi et al., make the same distinction about personal trust and general regional trust within the moral economy that we use in our application of trust to beneficial economics.

They write,

"Personalized trust is a set of beliefs that one person has about the behavior of another specific person. It is based on a repeated interaction between the two individuals and can thus be thought of as an informed belief. Generalized trust, by contrast, is a set of beliefs about the behavior of a random member of an identifiable group of individuals."

In their application of the moral value of trust in capital investment decisions, they make a connection between trust and the concept of the rule of law, which in their terms, means the legal enforceability of venture capital contracts.

They write,

"Given the costs of contracting, two parties will only find it worthwhile to write a sophisticated contract if they can trust that each party will abide by it. With low trust the contracting parties prefer to avoid the cost of writing a sophisticated contract, and the risk of remaining entangled in uncertain litigation; therefore they use a simpler contract."

Adherence to the standards of behavior in the moral economy is equivalent to the allegiance to obey the rule of law, not in the strict judicial application of contract law, but in the civil norms and values that guide everyday market behavior.

In our application of Illya Prigogine's emergence of stable order, in natural systems, the emergence of beneficial social order occurs in a regional eco system of trust, where citizens obey the rule of law in order to attain the future that their brains are imagining.

The establishment of the 50 mile envelope of trust is a prerequisite condition for the decision of wealthy citizens to take a risk on capital investment in a technological startup venture because of the close proximity of the investor and the entrepreneur.

Recent research by Xuan Tian, conducted at the Kelley School of Business, Indiana University (2009), suggests that most private companies raised capital within 25 miles of the company.

While Tian's research was more focused on the legal structure of the terms and conditions of capital investment, his findings are relevant to the issue of geographical trust of wealthy investors.

What he found was that local investors tended to have greater loyalty and allegiance, with closer geographical proximity and that the legal structure of the offering tended to be "company-friendly," the closer the company was located to the investor.

Tian's evidence is contrary to the conclusion reached in Hellmann and Puri, (2002), cited by Bottazzi, that wealthy investors did not know the entrepreneur before making the investment decision.

They write,

"A venture capitalist and an entrepreneur typically do not know each other before contracting. After investing, they work closely together. At the beginning of their relationship, the (generalized) trust between a potential venture capitalist investor and an entrepreneur is exogenous. Once their relationship has developed, trust becomes personalized and endogenous to the numerous decisions and interactions made along the way." (Battazzi, citing Thomas Hellmann, and Puri Manju, "Venture Capital and the Professionalization of Start-ups: Empirical Evidence).

A more realistic interpretation of the dynamics of a regional capital investment is that the wealthy investor knows the potential entrepreneur, and so do the entire regional business social networks of lawyers, accountants, bankers, and suppliers, who service and support the capital investment.

In marketing research conducted by Pierre Desrochers, he noted that,

"...geographic concentration of economic activity is explained, among other factors by the importance of geography in the transmission of tacit knowledge... there is thus much evidence pointing toward the importance of geographical proximity for communication between people sharing a "common cognitive ground," it seems obvious that its importance is even greater for people possessing diverse backgrounds." (Proximity and the Transmission of Tacit Knowledge, (2001),

"Yet the essence of innovation," states Desrochers,

"is the combination of previously unrelated knowledge and the collaboration of individuals possessing previously unrelated types of knowledge."

As explained by Desrochers,

"the collaboration occurs as a result of close geographical proximity by allowing certain individuals better opportunities to tap into tacit knowledge than individuals located elsewhere."

Ola Bengtsson and S. Abraham Ravid surveyed 1800 private firms that raised capital, They found that VCs prefer to invest in companies that are located close to where the VC lives. (The Geography of Venture Capital Contracts, SSRN, 2009).

About 32% of all companies raised their capital from investors located within 10 miles of the lead VC, and 42% of companies were located no more than 50 miles from the lead VC.

"Our results confirm that differences in contract design that refer to regional culture and customs," they state.

The data in the U. S Census Bureau commuting patterns, cited above in Rapino and Fields, define the entire geographic boundary of all citizens who exchange tacit knowledge with other citizens, which creates the trust environment for those citizens to invest in their own economic futures.

Garrett Nelson and Alasdair Rae applied statistical analysis to this same data set of commuters to derive their map of U. S. metro regions. (An Economic Geography of the United States: From Commutes to Megaregions, 2016).

They described their data methodology as,

"For this purpose, the Census Tract was deemed the most appropriate spatial unit, since it has an average population of just over 4,000 and Census Tracts are geographically large enough to contain major numbers of employees, unlike smaller Census units such as Blocks or Block Groups. Data on journeys to work are reported for just over 74,000 Census Tracts in the United States and are available from two different sources: the American Community Survey (ACS) commuting and workplace data and the Longitudinal Employer-Household Dynamics Origin-Destination Employment Statistics (LODES)."

Their map extends the analysis of Rapino and Fields by describing distinct large metro regions, where knowledge workers engage each other every day in knowledge creation and diffusion.

We reproduce their map below, and rely on their map to explain that their commuting regions are the same geographic regions that define the boundaries of trust that enable regional capital investments in high-risk technology ventures.

As they caution, the computed communities are subject to interpretive analysis, but are valuable to the description of how regional trust ecosystems describe the geographic boundaries of capital investments in technology ventures.

Their map describes a decentralized U. S. economic geography of distinct regions, each of which has its own history and moral culture.

Chapter 10. Diagram 1. U. S. Metro Regions Based upon Commuting Patterns, by Garrett Nelson and Alasdair Rae.

Fig 11. Computed communities subject to interpretive analysis.
https://doi.org/10.1371/journal.pone.0166083.g011

We apply the concept of political and economic decentralization as an important component of crafting a better beneficial economic constitution to overcome the current defect in the current centralized, global corporate predatory capitalist economic structure.

We agree with James Buchanan and Viktor Vanberg that the market is a self-organizing creative system that functions best in a decentralized structure that creates and diffuses knowledge.

They write,

"Only a decentralized market structure of economic interaction can exploit fully the knowledge of localized circumstances required to allow a definition of the ultimate valuation that is placed on resource use. Only the market can allow persons the effective liberty to discover the particular localized eccentricities that give form to value. This extension of the neoclassical emphasis on incentive structures is important and relevant." (The Market As A Creative Process, 1991).

Our emphasis on political and economic decentralization leads to our conclusion about the necessity of self-managed regional securities markets in each of the economic regions identified by Nelson and Rae.

There are about 8 million individual investors, in about 5 million U. S. households, with incomes that would qualify as a potential Reg D accredited investor under the Reg D Rule 506c rules for a direct capital investment in a technology venture. (U. S. Securities and Exchange Commission, General Solicitation: Rule 506(c)).

More importantly for a regional economic development strategy, clusters of very wealthy investors live in distinct geographical locations, primarily in the 350 U. S. metro regions with over 150,000 population. (Eliminating the Prohibition on General Solicitation and General Advertising in Certain Offerings, FACT SHEET, SEC Open Meeting, July 10, 2013).

That population of 8 million potential accredited investors in all metro regions has an existing affinity interest in promoting local economic development in their home communities.

According to the data in the SEC report on solicitation, in 2012, about 234,000 accredited investors made either a direct investment in a single venture, or invested through a pooled investment, combined with other investors.

As the SEC report states,

"In 2012, approximately 153,000 investors participated in offerings by operating companies, while approximately 81,000 investors invested in offerings by pooled investment funds."

The 81,000 investors who made Reg D investments in pooled funds, primarily invested in venture capital limited partnerships, and the VCs then turned around and invested in private deals, primarily in high risk technology ventures.

More than two thirds of all Reg D private offerings in 2012 had 10 or fewer investors, and less than 5% of all offerings had more than 30 investors.

In other words, 95 percent of Reg D offerings in 2012 involved less than 30 investors per deal and involved very small amounts of capital, invested in very small companies, with very few non-accredited investors.

Most of the small Reg D deals between 2009 and 2012 involved equity, and almost 1/3 of all offerings during that period involved the issuance of bonds, not stock or equity interests.

As the SEC noted,

"Between 2009 and 2012, approximately 66% of Regulation D offerings were of equity securities, and almost two-thirds of these were by issuers other than pooled investment funds."

The terms and language used to describe the difference between the 153,000 investors who made direct investments, and the 81,000 investors who made investments through pooled accounts is "Lone Wolf" investors and "angels."

Lone Wolfs are wealthy investors who make direct capital investments in regional new ventures, usually with one or two other wealthy investors.

Angels are wealthy investors who primarily invest through the venture capital pooled trusts.

In the application to creating metro regional securities markets, both types of investors would be targets for making capital investments in new technology ventures.

As the investors do currently, the future regional securities market would offer both direct corporate private offerings issued directly by the venture, to the Lone Wolfs, and create pooled funds, which function just like current mutual funds, regulated by the self regulatory organizations (SRO), in the regional securities markets.

We agree with part of the regional economic development policy advice provided by Henry Chen et al., in Buy Local? The Geography of Successful and Unsuccessful Venture Capital Expansion, 2009).

They write,

"Therefore, if local governments outside the nation's three VC centers seek to attract VC branch offices, one strategy they might consider is providing support to VC-backed businesses in their communities. The study concludes that "anything that policymakers do that contributes to an increase in the number of successful venture-backed investments in a region will also increase the probability of a venture branch office opening in that region."

"Providing support" to new technology ventures is important, but we disagree with them about the importance of trying to attract other outside venture capital firms to the region.

The support that technology ventures need to be successful is a full, comprehensive regional securities market, not simply one small part of the securities market of venture capital.

As we explain below, if the economic goal of the regional self-managed securities market is economic growth, then the venture capital business model is the wrong management model to replicate.

The Regional Securities Market Self Management Model

In the model of self-management of the regional securities market, beneficial economic order emerges when the regional securities market provides a pathway for capital gains from exit events to be continuously re-invested in the region.

Our model of regional securities market self-management begins with a description of the entire sequence of events in managing the capital market deal flow that precedes a capital investment in a new technology venture.

The responsibility to manage the deal flow pipeline is the social business networks of lawyers, CPAs, commercial real estate brokers, product developers, bankers and service and support professionals in the region who have a financial interest in getting more deals done.

Their management tasks are described in Diagram 2, below.

Our emphasis is not on the initial capital investment in a deal.

The more important management tasks are managing the initial regional tacit knowledge networks and targeting the re-investments of capital gains from exit events into future high technology industrial clusters in the region.

Chapter 10. Diagram 2. Managing the Regional Securities Market Deal Flow Pipeline.

The Small Business Deal Creation Pipeline™

Deal Mapping To convert knowledge and ideas into small business ventures and new products	*Deal Creation* To prepare new ventures or product ideas to enter the market	*Deal Funding* To find capital to fund commercial ventures	*Deal Exits* To manage the reinvestment of profit from the first generati of ideas into the next generation of innovation

Image credit: Laurie Thomas Vass, How Economic Developers Can Manage the Regional Deal Flow Pipeline, SSRN, 2013.

Assumption of the responsibility of citizens to manage the deal flow pipeline in the social/business networks entails a mental cognitive insight that re-imagines the metro regional economy, as if the regional economy was an economic growth enterprise.

This cognitive insight by citizens means that citizens would adopt the moral values of regional allegiance and territorial loyalty, that places the prosperity of citizens first, as the main political priority. (Laurie Thomas Vass, The Importance of Regional Allegiance and Territorial Loyalty For Elected Representatives In Implementing Economic Development and Job Creation Policies,SSRN, 2023).

In other words, goals like production efficiency, globalism, or the ideology of crony corporate capitalism, prevalent in existing non-profit groups like the Chamber of Commerce, would be replaced by the management goal of citizen regional well-being and future regional prosperity.

Diagram 3, below describes the list of regional professionals who have a current financial interest in promoting economic growth and who also share tacit knowledge with each other in their daily business/social networks.

Chapter 10. Diagram 3. List of Regional Professional Deal Flow Managers.

Professional economic development associations and trade groups, like economic development partnerships and chambers of commerce	Promotes the financial interests of member firms and the economic growth prospects of regions. Coordinates resources within regions to facilitate technology innovation and capital market transactions
Registered Investment Advisors	Acts as a fiduciary to the private company in providing advice, and conducts third party verification of the potential investor's credentials.
Marketing and sales professionals	Coordinates the marketing of the company's offering with other marketing and sales efforts of the company during the period of the CrowdFunding project.
Product design and prototype firms	Assists the company in product re-design for existing products or helps prototype new products.
Media and public relations firms	Prepares and distributes news stories and press releases for company and helps the company develop a market message.
Business life insurance agents	Assists the owners in creating a business buy-sell agreement
Business property and casualty agents	Assists the owners with issues involving product liability, owner liability and professional errors and omissions related to offering securities.
Employee benefit firms	Provides guidance and advice related to how additional capital may affect existing employee benefit arrangements, including non-qualified deferred compensation related to employee stock options on new capital.
Commercial real estate brokers and development firms	Provides real estate leasing guidance and brokerage for new facilities for firms. Assists firms within an industrial cluster to locate close to each other.
Business buy/sell brokers and investment bankers	Assists companies in finding new partners and new sources of supply.
CPAs and tax advisors to firms	Prepares statements related to an offering, including the statements for companies that fall into categories that require audited statements to raise capital.
Securities lawyers	Creates offering documents and legal agreements for a private offering. Provides advice and counsel to owners to meet rules. Answers questions about the offering for investor inquiries.
Professional Association Event Managers	Conducts business networking events for companies to present their message to interested parties to the transaction.
Trade Show Event Managers	Conducts events for companies within a trade group or trade association.
Capital Market and VC Event Managers	Conducts events for investors interested in learning more about a company.
Mobile Application Firms	Places company offering promotions on mobile devices
Mobile Device Firms	Provides mobile devices for company.
Software and Coding Firms	Creates software that makes company promotional material available on mobile devices.
Website and eCommerce Developers	Assists the company in website development related to investor relations. Coordinates company website with outside websites to direct viewers to due diligence websites.
Social Network Marketing Firms	Assists the company in website optimization and social networking linkages on outside sites like LinkedIn.
Angel Matching Websites	Provides internet websites that aggregate potential investors who want to have a flow of information about companies that are raising capital

Image credit. Laurie Thomas Vass. The Crowd Funding Business Bonanza for Lawyers, Accountants and Consultants, SSRN, 2013).

All of these professional workers would be potential managers of the regional deal flow pipeline in their metro region. Some of the professional workers would be involved in the management of the early parts of the deal flow pipeline, and some of the professionals would manage the later stages of the deal flow process.

The management objective of citizens in the business/social network of professional advisors is to increase the rate of regional economic growth by increasing the rate of capital market investments in radical new technology ventures.

In the flow of events surrounding innovation, the capital market funding events usually occur after the mental deal mapping and deal creation events.

In other words, the chronology of events in innovation involves idea generation, venture creation, and then venture funding.

Regional Securities Market Institutional and Administration Framework

All of the events in the deal flow pipeline need to be managed and coordinated by private sector citizens who have a moral and financial interest in the prosperity of citizens who live in the region.

In other words, the management responsibilities of the regional securities market are not the responsibility of local governments or government employees.

Citizens who benefit financially from regional economic growth have the greatest incentive to participate in the management of the regional deal flow pipeline.

In regional self-management of the deal flow pipeline, citizens have at their disposal a number of tools and methods to use. These tools and methods require the involvement of a wide range of citizens, in the business-social networks, at each step of the deal flow pipeline.

Diagram 4 describes how these methods and tools can be used at each step of managing the regional deal flow pipeline.

We mentioned some of these tools in Chapter 6, and re-state the importance of Leontief's model of analyzing the economic effect of capital investments, and Feser's model of identifying industrial sectors that have hidden, or non-obvious, technological affinities.

Chapter 10. Diagram 4. The Regional Citizen Self-Management Tools and Methods For Managing the Regional Securities Market.

Deal Mapping Tools:	Deal Creation Tools:	Deal Funding Tools:	Deal Exit Tools:
The Feser Technological Affinities Model to find latent or hidden innovation investment opportunities in the region's technology value chains. The Regional Knowledge Creation and Diffusion Social Network Analysis Mapping Tool to see latent or hidden knowledge flows in the region. The Regional Innovation Competitive Assessment Social Network Mapping Tool to see which existing business and social networks would potentially support innovation in the region.	The New Business Sales and Marketing Social Network Mapping Tool to see how potential investments may create new regional value chain relationships. The Regional Product Development Assessment of Engineering Consulting Firms. The Regional/Global Supply Chain Network Mapping Tool to describe relationships between small regional firms and MNCs that would provide the marketing portal to the global markets.	The Private Capital Market Assessment Social Network Analysis Tool to see all the private market transactions required to fund both new ventures commercializing radical innovations, and existing small manufacturing firms involved in sustaining innovations.	The Investment Banking Resource Assessment Social Network Analysis Tool to see regional resources that can offer M&A services. The Political Elite Influence Analysis Tool to see which political elites would support tax credit policies for reinvestment of capital gains into the next generation of innovation investments.

Image credit: Laurie Thomas Vass, Exploiting Knowledge: The Importance of Regional Allegiance and Territorial Loyalty In Implementing A Regional Small Business Innovation System, SSRN, 2009.

Feser used a version of his model to identify nine high technology industrial clusters, and we identify those nine sectors as the primary targets for capital re-investments in radical new technology ventures in each region. (Laurie Thomas Vass, Searching for Investments in the Nine High Technology Clusters, SSRN, 2008).

One of the tools that we mention in Diagram 4 is social network analysis of the existing business political and financial networks in the region, because as we mention above, some citizens in the region support technology innovation, and some citizens oppose technology innovation.

We cited Mokyr, who wrote that technology innovation must be born into a sympathetic environment, and we identify social networks who have a vested financial interest in maintaining the status quo distribution of income and wealth as not being sympathetic to the emergence of an entirely new regional economic structure.

In Diagram 5, we place the components of the deal pipeline into the social/business networks for regional administration to begin to describe how the different professionals coordinate the management and administration of the regional securities market model.

For example, in the first block of the deal flow pipeline, lawyers, CPAs, and product development professionals manage and administer the deal creation events and meetings of the process, like the Council for Entrepreneurial Development, in North Carolina manages the quarterly meetings of citizens interested in creating deals.

Chapter 10. Diagram 5. Regional Administration and Management of the Deal Flow Pipeline.

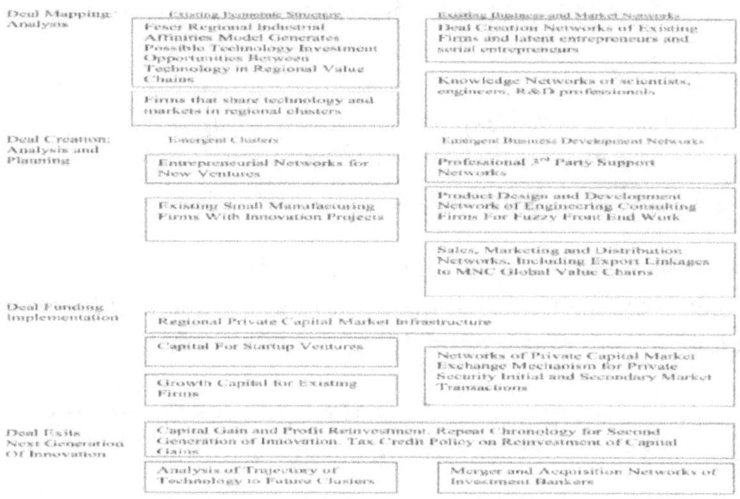

Image credit. Laurie Thomas Vass, The Regional Capital Market Institutional Support Structure For Regional New Venture Creation, SSRN. 2024).

As potential deal ideas gain traction, those deals are handed off to another component of professional advisors in the deal creation pipeline.

Eventually, some deal ideas may reach the initial funding stage, which is where the professionals in the regional securities market work to fund the new venture, throughout its life.

And, as we argue above, the cognitive realization by advisors to obtain an increased financial reward from regional economic growth, requires those professional firms to adopt a common mental map of the regional securities market, as if the regional market was its own business entity. (Laurie Thomas Vass, The Crowd Funding Business Bonanza for Lawyers, Accountants and Consultants:. SSRN, 2015).

We emphasize the critically important management function of the regional supply of securities law firms, who prepare the initial offering documents and insure compliance with securities markets regulation. (Laurie Thomas Vass, The Case for Increasing the Supply of Private Placement Securities Lawyers in North Carolina: The Law of Supply and Demand for Securities Lawyers, SSRN, 2015).

Based upon our professional experience in providing advice to technology ventures, we estimate that the total hours of legal work involved in a Reg D private placement is about 65 hours.

In other words, at the status quo legal fee of $350 per hour, a technology new venture firm that needed to raise initial capital would be facing a legal bill of about $20,000.

In North Carolina, there are only about 100 lawyers who practice securities law, and most of them live in either Charlotte or Raleigh.

The limited supply of lawyers, combined with the increased rate of capital investment in regional technology firms implies that the legal costs for a Reg D offering, in the future strategy, would increase to about $45,000, simply because there are not enough securities attorneys in North Carolina to provide capital market legal services.

We estimate that the costs for legal services of a more complex Reg A offering by a sophisticated securities attorney would be about $100,000.

The network of securities lawyers in each region can perform essential management tasks for decreasing the cost of raising capital, when they cooperate and collaborate with other regional professional advisors in creating uniform and standardized offering documents.

The goal of legal collaboration is the creation of documents with common terms and conditions that can be used throughout the venture's life of raising capital.

As we described above, in Diagram 5 (Managing the Regional Securities Market Deal Flow Pipeline), the collaboration of securities lawyers in deal funding, would allow for the creation of regionally unique securities that would take a new venture all the way through the life cycle of capital to the end stage of deal exits.

The uniform and standardized legal documents prepared by regional securities professionals include:

- Standardized and uniform terms and conditions of regional private placement memorandums.
- Standardized and uniform terms and conditions for each different type of investment contract, including the convertible preferred equity, and convertible preferred debt offerings.
- Uniform favorable terms and conditions for both investors and entrepreneurs at the initial and exit stage of the venture.
- Uniform and standardized financial reporting documents to describe the financial condition of the venture, over time.
- Uniform and standardized offering documents, and regional mutual fund registration for new regional innovation mutual funds.

In the bottom portion of Diagram 5, we describe a second type of social/business network, composed of all commercial banking and investment banking professionals in the regional economy that work with ventures to raise capital throughout the life cycle of the new venture, ending in either a deal exit or the on-going operation of the firm.

The regional securities market institutional infrastructure will contain the following components:

1. FINRA Broker Dealers, whose sales staff conduct buying and selling of both private and public securities.
2. FDIC commercial bankers, who extend loans and credit, when the small company has sufficient collateral. In the case of Reg D 506c, the capital obtained through the offering will act as collateral for the commercial banks to extend credit.
3. Registered investment advisors, who provide professional guidance to CEOs on how to issue the securities and qualify the securities for trading in the secondary market.
4. Institutional merger and acquisition bankers, who act as market intermediaries for combining companies into larger entities.
5. Asset-based lenders and commercial finance companies who provide inventory financing and factoring.
6. Pooled investment funds and private equity funds that raise larger amounts of capital, and use the capital much like venture capitalists do when they raise a large VC fund.
7. Venture capital firms and angel capital partnerships.
8. Back-office stock custodians and transfer agents who handle the administration of issuing securities, and subsequently trading both private and public securities.

In other words, the regional securities exchange management infrastructure in each region consists of any firm that makes money and has a vested financial interest in the operation of the initial offering of securities and the on-going sale and exchange of both private and public securities in the regional stock exchange.

This same set of firms also performs the double-duty of regional self regulation of the regional security markets, as described below.

Capital market firms in the region would join the regional Self Regulatory Organization, just like brokers and dealers currently join the Financial Industry Regulatory Agency, (FINRA).

The administration and management of the deal flow pipeline requires a certain type of institutional capital market framework in each region. (Laurie Thomas Vass, The Regional Capital Market Institutional Support Structure For Regional New Venture Creation, SSRN,).

The institutional framework is a full service small capital exchange market that involves the issuance of initial capital, generally equity, and also secondary market transactions of both small units of debt and equity for both existing small manufacturing firms and new technology startups.

In our conception of the self managed regional securities market, the local social business networks of firms in the regional securities markets become the equivalent of the institutional networks on Wall Street, and become the members of each regional self regulatory agency.

The New Investment Securities Issued and Exchanged In the Regional Securities Markets.

Currently, an investor has the option to invest directly in a new venture, commonly known as the 153,000 "Lone Wolfs," or to invest through a venture capital pooled fund, commonly known as "Angels."

The idea behind the self managed regional securities markets is to replicate this existing framework, with the added features of regionally specific investment vehicles.

This regional securities model has the appearance of being similar to the Toronto Stock Exchange, and the Toronto Venture Exchange, for small companies.

New ventures in Toronto usually raise private capital on the junior exchange, and then “graduate” to the senior exchange when they go public.

The terms and conditions for the company in the early rounds of capital must be compatible with future rounds, all the way to the exit event, in the regional public securities market.

This means that a logical sequence of terms and conditions must flow through all of the eventual rounds of capital raising, in regionally-specific securities, that are crafted by regional securities firms, located in the region.

The priority for collaboration among regional securities lawyers is the creation of securities documents that are fair, for both the investors and the new ventures, from the beginning seed stage, and continue to be fair for future investors, throughout the life of the company.

Common terms and conditions in securities documents would lead to greater liquidity in the private capital marketplace because less time and expense would be involved in determining how one security’s rights and features differed from another security.

The workhorse of direct corporate private offerings is preferred stock, with its feature of being issued with conversion rights into common stock at some point in the future.

As the name suggests, convertible preferred stock can also convert into common stock at either the holder's option or at the option of the company. This important feature allows the potential investor to participate in a buy-out or an initial public offering, if the venture goes public.

Usually, there is some form of coerced or mandatory conversion feature for all investors if the company becomes involved in an Initial Public Offering (IPO), or company buy-out, where all the private stock is converted to publicly-traded stock.

Creating common terms and conditions for regionally-specific preferred stock is the main goal for collaboration among regional securities firms.

We used the example of how a hypothetical regional capital market growth fund in Atlanta could "bootstrap" capital from one generation of innovation to the next. (Laurie Thomas Vass, "Bootstrapping Capital for Regional Innovation Economic Growth: New Regional Securities Markets," SSRN, 2008).

The hypothetical regional mutual fund does not exist, but replicates the existing angel pooled venture capital funds in its function of combining many small venture deals into a much larger, professionally managed fund that targets investments in each metro region.

The creation, drafting, and mutual fund registration would be the responsibility of the network of regional securities law firms.

Bootstrapping innovation means that profits from an earlier exit event are used to support subsequent regional capital market investment events.

The professional advisors in the region who are members of the regional capital market exchange would function to package the small ticket items of individual companies into much larger investment packages, and then to sell those bundles to syndicates of angel investors, or other financial intermediary firms.

In our example of Atlanta, the Atlanta Capital Growth Fund could buy the 506c shares issued by an Atlanta company, and the fund could assist the company by preparing standardized and uniform securities templates that the company would use to issue its securities.

There is nothing that legally prohibits a private company from selling its shares both to the Fund and directly to any accredited Lone Wolf investor outside of the Fund.

The Atlanta Capital Growth Fund can package all the smaller ventures, and sell fund securities, under 506c, to investors who would like to invest in a portfolio of Atlanta companies, rather that investing in a single company.

Under the most recent Federal changes in securities laws, both the Atlanta Capital Growth Fund, and each private Atlanta company can now engage in public promotion to sell their private securities.

The Atlanta Fund would be legally organized and taxed as a pass-through entity under the Internal Revenue Code. As long as the Fund meets certain income, investment diversity, and distribution requirements, the Fund, as a corporate entity, would pay little or no corporate income tax.

The most important function of the regional mutual growth fund is to provide a pathway for profits from the exit events to be re-invested in the regional innovation economy, in a type of Bayesian economic success model.

The regional capital markets, based upon internet technologies, provide the mechanism for this bootstrapping of capital from one generation of innovation to the next.

The hypothetical Atlanta Growth Fund would be able to issue different forms of securities to potential investors and offer investors the option of choosing how their investment in the fund would be allocated to the different internal securities. (Laurie Thomas Vass, Exploring the Idea of the Atlanta Capital Growth Fund: Equity Crowdfunding as One Component of the New Atlanta Private Securities Exchange, SSRN, 2015).

The shares inside the fund include

• Preferred and convertible preferred stock.
• Convertible Debt.
• A Loan agreement and related security agreement.
• Revenue participation securities.

The proposed hypothetical Fund would have a small three person staff, and an outside registered investment advisor:

• A regional managing director.
• A regional fund administrator.
• A regional economist.

The staff of the Fund would perform three important functions as a precursor activity to making investments in regional new ventures and existing operational companies:

- The staff would manage and administer the flow of investment capital into regional ventures.
- The staff would conduct social network analysis to guess at latent social and economic relationships between firms in the Atlanta technology clusters who may have an interest in cross breeding technology. Social network analysis [SNA] is the mapping and measuring of relationships and flows between people, groups, organizations, computers, URLs, and other connected information/knowledge entities.
- The staff would manage the Feser econometric model of the region and use the results of the model to conduct Bayesian statistical analysis to guess at how capital investments in the nine high technology industrial clusters would affect the future trajectory of economic growth in the metro region.

The entire chronology of functions for bootstrapping capital into a regional economic growth innovation strategy is described below in Diagram 6. Diagram 6 mentions the use of the blockchain algorithm as a regional administrative and management tool for the operation of a self-managed regional securities market.

Chapter 10. Diagram 6. The Chronology of Bootstrapping Regional Capital Market Investments.

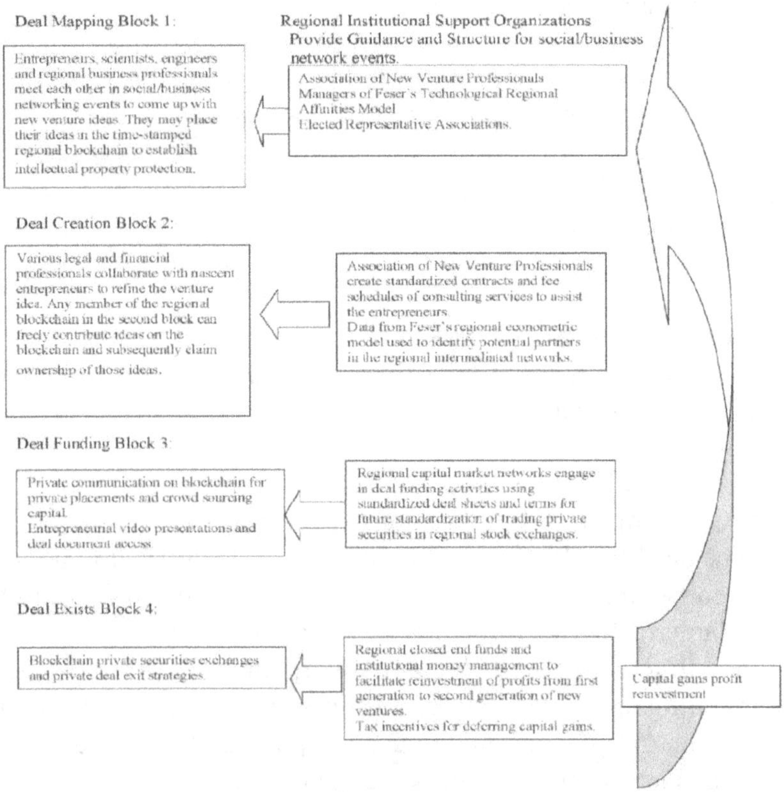

Image credit: Laurie Thomas Vass, Why Exits Matter for Future Innovation Investments, SSRN, 2008.

Regional Securities Market Self Regulation

The securities issued by individual firms would be seen within the context of a vibrant, full-service regional securities market whose goal was the continuing commercial viability of the regional firms.

In an ideal regional private capital market, the new securities would allow for subsequent investments, as capital gains were reinvested back into the regional economy.

In other words, rather than viewing the new securities from the perspective of a single company attempting to attract business angels or venture capitalists, the success of the new securities would be viewed from the contribution they make to the self-renewing and self-sustaining economic growth of regions.

All securities transactions within the regional metro boundaries of the regional capital market are subject to the antifraud provisions of the 1933 Securities Act and the myriad of other federal securities laws.

From the very first moment of deal mapping events, all the way through to the exit events, the new venture firm and all sales and marketing citizens in the self-managed securities market are liable for false or misleading statements, whether oral or written.

Just about anything of value exchanged between an investor and a company can be defined as a security, and almost any form of communication between a potential investor and the company can easily be interpreted as an offer.

As defined in various Federal securities laws, a "security" means any note, stock, treasury stock, security future, security-based swap, bond, debenture, evidence of indebtedness, certificate of interest or participation in any profit-sharing agreement, collateral-trust certificate, preorganization certificate or subscription, transferable share, investment contract, voting-trust certificate, certificate of deposit for a security, fractional undivided interest in oil, gas, or other mineral rights, any put, call, straddle, option, or privilege on any security, certificate of deposit, or group or index of securities (including any interest therein or based on the value thereof), or any put, call, straddle, option, or privilege entered into on a national securities exchange relating to foreign currency, or, in general, any interest or instrument commonly known as a "security", or any certificate of interest or participation in, temporary or interim certificate for, receipt for, guarantee of, or warrant or right to subscribe to or purchase, any of the foregoing.

The term “offer to sell”, “offer for sale”, or “offer” includes every attempt or offer to dispose of, or solicitation of an offer to buy, a security or interest in a security, for value.

The law states that it is unlawful, in connection with the offer, sale, or purchase of a security, to employ a device, scheme, or artifice to defraud; to make an untrue statement of material fact; to omit to state a material fact; or to engage in an act, practice, or course of business that operates as a fraud or deceit upon another person.

The most important legal document to avoid fraud and corruption is prepared by regional securities firms, in advance of the start of the formal offering period is called the private placement memo (PPM).

The PPM serves as an important tool for reducing the risk for the new venture and all of the sales and marketing professionals in the region of making a fraudulent statement. \

The PPM document usually begins with a detailed list of all the many risks and pitfalls an investor would endure by making an investment in the company.

Generally, the PPM follows a standardized format or template, which we propose be uniform for all securities offering conducted in the metro region.

The major parts of the PPM are:

- Summary of the offering.
- The risks and suitability of the offering.
- The use of capital from the offering.
- The legal structure of the company, its history, and its certificate of existence.

- The capitalization of the company and information about current stock and bond holders of the company.
- A description of the company management, company products, business plan, organizational chart, and historical financial data.
- The subscription process.

Each self managed regional securities market would create a self regulatory organization, (SRO), comprised of all capital market firms, based upon the existing regulatory model of the Financial Industry Regulatory Authority, (FINRA) which regulates national capital markets.

The regional FINRAs would consist of all capital market firms in the region that make money and have a vested financial interest in the operation of offering of securities and the on-going sale and exchange of both private and public securities the regional stock exchange.

Capital market firms in the region would join the regional Self Regulatory Organization, just like brokers and dealers, currently join FINRA and be subject to the rules and regulations imposed by the regional SROs.

The Regional Blockchain Investment Networks for Profit Reinvestments

We have mentioned above, in Diagram 6 (The Chronology of Bootstrapping Regional Capital Market Investments), that one of the administrative and management tools of the self-managed regional securities market is a new computer program called "blockchain." (Laurie Thomas Vass, Updating Schumpeter's Gales of Creative Destruction: Exploiting the Vulnerability of New World Order Corporate Globalism With Regional Blockchain Entrepreneurial Economic Growth, 2022).

In our application of the blockchain tool, each company that is raising capital has its own company website, which acts as the main landing pad for many other internet websites and networking groups in the deal mapping and deal creation part of the deal creation pipeline.

Once outside users land on the company website, the new web blockchain technology allows the company to manage communications with outside users with private pass-word protected portals.

The entire process of regional technological innovation can be visualized and facilitated by using Christensen's concept of blockchain as a tool to promote economic growth.

Christensen writes,

"Blockchain is a public, decentralized, distributed digital ledger that is used to record electronic transactions. In a blockchain-based economy, the market-creating innovation [new venture investment] and the institution governing it [social-business networks] are fundamentally intertwined." (Clayton Christensen, et al., How Market-Creating Innovation Drives Economic Growth and Development: Blockchain for Global Development, 2019).

Each "block" in a blockchain contains specific information that cannot be altered, due to the distributed nature of the technology.

For example, at the very top of the deal creation pipeline, blockchain would help resolve intellectual property rights over the genesis of innovation ideas by permanently stamping the contribution of an individual entrepreneur.

As described, below, in Diagram 7, the process of regional new venture creation, using blockchain computer technology, is intended to be an on-going process of profit reinvestment that creates self-sustaining, self-renewing regional economic growth, all the way from deal mapping to deal exits, and the re-investment of capital gain profits back into the regional economy.

The blockchain technology has the potential to reduce uncertainty around ownership of new venture ideas and intellectual property rights and other property claims by providing verified records, and thereby strengthening private capital market institutions

This decentralized blockchain internet architecture is intended to insure that capital investment decisions remain embedded in local trust relationships that are aimed at regional economic growth and regional prosperity of the citizens who live in the region.

Chapter 10. Diagram 7. Regional Securities Market Blockchain Deal Creation Internet Application.

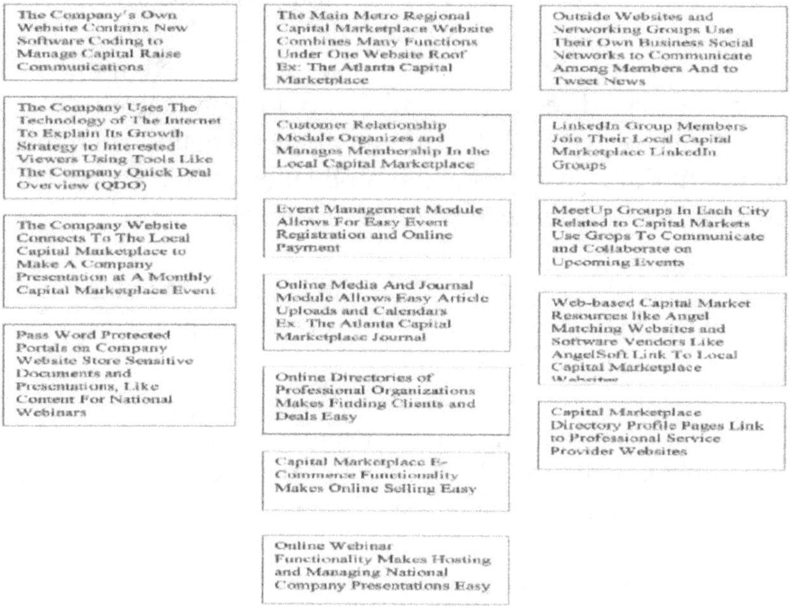

Image Credit: Laurie Thomas Vass, Updating Schumpeter's Gales of Creative Destruction: Exploiting the Vulnerability of New World Order Corporate Globalism With Regional Blockchain Entrepreneurial Economic Growth, 2022.

Crafting a better economic constitution requires a conscious, cognitive, moral commitment from citizens to trust each other in the constitutional discharge of citizen duties to protect each other's freedoms.

The geographic boundaries of the regional trust eco system are a necessary condition for citizen democratic participation in self-managing the regional economy.

The moral values of trust and individual integrity requires citizens to emphasize long-term regional prosperity for all citizens over short-term personal gain.

The moral values of trust and integrity allow citizens to take risks in making capital investments in new technology ventures.

The economic theory of beneficial economics explained in the regional self-managed securities market provides an important alternative to the conventional wisdom of general equilibrium theory. General Equilibrium Theory is about production efficiency, and a return to equilibrium after an economic disturbance.

Production efficiency, according to the theory, leads to maximum output at minimum cost, which results in economic growth, regardless of human consequences

Beneficial economics is about human happiness and shared prosperity aligned with how the human brain makes decisions, which leads to the emergence of a beneficial stable order.

In our use of complex adaptive theory we say

"Let the system find its most beneficial future state."

In other words, beneficial economic theory constrains the emergence of future order to welfare outcomes that enhance human well-being.

Human well-being is enhanced when the human brain is free to obtain the future that the human brain is imagining.

The citizen self managed regional securities markets described in this chapter are aligned with how decisions in the human brain lead to beneficial outcomes.

The beneficial future order emerges because of the on-going human social interactions during the time humans are exchanging tacit knowledge, as the new future markets are being created.

The human social interactions lead to beneficial future economic growth that results from capital investment decisions in radical new technology ventures.

As an example of the distinction between general equilibrium theory and the moral values of beneficial economic theory, we cite the work of the Sante Fe Institute in New Mexico, which also uses a version of Prigogine's complex adaptive theory to explain emergence..

In their use of complex adaptive theory, the macro economy finds the future social order through the efficient use of resources. They claim that the emergent order of the efficient economic system will lead to the lowest cost of production, even if the future entails human misery.

General Equilibrium Theory and the Santa Fe Institute's application of complex adaptive theory are both amoral.

They both ignore human nature, and how the human brain makes decisions, at Popper World 3, which is why they both lead to the emergence of a predatory economic systems that make humans miserable despite being 'efficient.' (Chapter 2. How A Person's Brain Naturally Creates Social Order Through Their Everyday Market Choices),

In this chapter, we described how a regional self managed securities system is based upon how:

- Humans who live in distinct economic regions form trust relationship in tacit face-to-face knowledge exchange.
- Humans actually make capital investment decisions based upon widely shared moral values.
- Humans actually attain the prosperity that their brains are imagining.

The better economic constitution that citizens create may be seen as the "enabling infrastructure of rules" that facilitate the emergence of a beneficial economic future.

In our application of Buchanan's fair constitutional rules and Kant's moral values, we make a moral distinction about the use of capital gains and profits in the emergence of a beneficial social order.

We believe that unequal wealth and income distribution are morally justified in a society where the profits are re-invested to create economic growth that benefits the citizens who live in the region. (Diagram 6. The Chronology of Bootstrapping Regional Capital Market Investments).

The reinvestment of profits from capital gain exits in new ventures creates the condition for the emergence of a beneficial stable social order as citizens in the region continue to interact with each other as new future markets are created.

When profits and unequal wealth are used to maintain the social class status quo, and to manipulate the political system, in order to lock citizens into a static economic system, the profits become morally repugnant because the deployment of profits by the ruling class prohibits the emergence of a beneficial social order.

For example, we view the Fed's manipulation of interest rates and money supply as morally repugnant because their actions cause a business cycle of economic depressions about every 10 years.

Since 1913, the Fed's actions have prohibited the American society from the emergence of a future beneficial order that would occur under the conditions of allowing a natural complex adaptive economic system to function without government interference.

As we described in Chapter 5, (The American Economic Transition to Predatory State Capitalism), that future globalist crony state capitalist system would be replaced by a decentralized state sovereignty constitution, crafted by citizens who realize that the U. S. government has failed the citizens. (Laurie Thomas Vass, Rebuilding the Broken American Economy One City at a Time, SSRN, 2008).

Bibliography of Books and Monographs

Adams, John. Thoughts on Government.

Allen, Peter M. Cities and Regions as Self-Organizing Systems (1996)

Anderson, Philip W., Kenneth J. Arrow, David Pines. The economy as an evolving complex system : the proceedings of the evolutionary paths of the global workshop, held September 1987, in Santa Fe, New Mexico (1988)

Archibugi, Daniele and Jonathan Michie. Technology, Globalisation and Economic Performance (1997)

Arrow, Kenneth. Social Choice and Individual Values (1951, 1963)

Arthur, W. Bryan. Complexity Economics: Why Does Economics Need This Different Approach? (2019)

Baran, Paul and Paul Sweezy. Monopoly Capital: An Essay on the American Economic and Social Order (1966)

Beard, Charles. An Economic Interpretation of The Constitution of The United States (1962)

Blau, Peter. Exchange and Power in Social Life (1964)

Böckenförde, Markus et al. Rule of Law: A Practical Guide to Constitution Building (2011)

Bordo, Michael and William Roberds. A Return to Jekyll Island. The Origins, History, and Future of the Federal Reserve (2013)

Bouton, Terry. Taming Democracy: "The People," the Founders, and the Troubled Ending of the American Revolution (2009)

Brenner, Robert. The Boom and the Bubble: The U. S. in the World Economy (2002)

Buchanan, James. The Limits of Liberty (1975)

Buchanan, James. Constitutional Economics (1991)

Buchanan, James and Gordon Tullock. The Calculus of Consent (1999)

Buchanan, James and Viktor Vanberg. The Market As A Creative Process (1991)

Calvin, William. The Cerebral Symphony (1990)

Chinitz, Benjamin. City and Suburb: The Economics of Metropolitan Growth (1964)

Christensen, Clayton. The Innovator's Dilemma: When New Technologies Cause Great Firms to Fail (1997)

Christensen, Clayton and Michael E Raynor. The Innovator's Solution: Creating and Sustaining Successful Growth (2003)
Codevilla, Angelo. "America's Ruling Class And the Perils of Revolution" (2010)
Cook, Richard C. "The Dark Forces in Control of the Anglo-American-Zionist Empire Are the Source of the World Crisis" (2025)
Dennett, Daniel C. Consciousness Explained (1992)
DeTocqueville, Alexis. Democracy in America (1836)
Domhoff, William. Who Rules America? (1967)
Eagleman, David. The Brain: The Story of You (2015)
Eccles, John. Evolution of the Brain (1991)
Eccles, John. Evolution of the Brain: Creation of the Self (1989)
Eccles, John and Karl Popper. The Self and Its Brain (1977, 1985)
Farrand, Max. The Records of the Federal Convention of 1787 (1911)
Feldman, Noah. The Broken Constitution: Lincoln, Slavery, and the Refounding of America (2021)
Fishkin, Joseph. The Anti-oligarchy Constitution : Reconstructing the Economic Foundations of American Democracy (2022)
Foner, Eric. The Second Founding: How the Civil War and Reconstruction Remade the Constitution (2019)
Galbraith, James K. The Predator State (2008)
Gazzaniga, Michael. Nature's Mind (1994)
Hayek, Friedrich. The Road to Serfdom (1944)
Hayek, Friedrich. The Constitution of Liberty (1960, 1978)
Hayek, Friedrich. Law, Legislation and Liberty (3 volumes 1973 – 1979)
Hill, Stuart. Democratic Values and Technological Choice (1992)
Holland, John. Hidden Order: How Adaptation Builds Complexity (1996)
Holland, John. Emergence: From Chaos to Order (1998)
Homans, George C. Social Behavior: Its Elementary Forms (1974)
Horwitz, Robert. The Moral Foundations of the American Republic (1986)
Jefferson, Thomas. Various letters and writings
Jensen, Merrill. The Articles of Confederation
Jerison, Harry. Intelligence and Evolutionary Biology (1988)

Kaminsky, John and Richard Leffler, eds. Federalists and Antifederalists: The Debate Over the Ratification of the Constitution (1998)
Kant, Immanuel. Groundwork of the Metaphysics of Morals (1785)
Kant, Immanuel. Critique of Practical Reason (1788)
Kauffman, Stuart. At Home In The Universe (1995)
Kauffman, Stuart. The Origins of Order: Self-Organization and Selection in Evolution (1991)
Kelley, Harold and John Thibaut. Interpersonal Relations: A Theory of Interdependence
Kelley, Harold and John Thibaut. The Social Psychology of Groups (1959)
Kimura, Motoo. The Neutral Theory of Molecular Evolution (1983)
Klarman, Michael. The Framers Coup (2016)
Leakey, Richard and Roger Lewin. Origins Reconsidered: In Search of What Makes Us Human (1992)
Leontief, Wassily. Input-Output Economics (1966)
Lewin, Roger. The Origins of Modern Humans (1984)
Livingston, James. Origins of the Federal Reserve System, Money, Class, and Corporate Capitalism, 1890-1913 (1986)
Mackie, J. L. Ethics: Inventing Right and Wrong (1991)
MacPherson, C.B. The Political Theory of Possessive Individualism (1964)
Madison, James. Federalist Papers (various numbers cited)
McDonald, Forrest. A Constitutional History of the United States (1982)
Meyers, Marvin. The Mind of the Founder: Sources of the Political Thought of James Madison (1981)
Mokyr, Joel. The Lever of Riches: Technological Creativity and Economic Progress (1990, 1992)
Munger, Michael and Mario Villarreal-Diaz. The Road to Crony Capitalism (2019)
Nelson, Garrett and Alasdair Rae. "An Economic Geography of the United States: From Commutes to Megaregions" (2016)
Nelson, Richard. "Technical Change As Cultural Evolution," in Ross, Thomson, (Ed.), Learning and Technical Change (1993)
Ottaway, Marina. Corporatism Goes Global (2001)
Paine, Thomas. Letters To the Citizens of the United States (1805)

Parisot, James. Capitalism and the Creation of the U.S. Constitution (2023)
Penfield, Wilder. The Mystery of the Mind: A Critical Study of Consciousness and the Human Brain (2015)
Peterson, Merrill. The Jefferson Image in the American Mind (1999)
Polanyi, Karl. The Great Transformation (1944)
Polanyi, Michael. The Growth of Thought in Society (1941)
Polanyi, Michael. The Logic of Liberty (1951)
Polanyi, Michael. The Tacit Dimension (1967)
Popper, Karl. Various works (1981, 1989)
Posner, Richard A. An Economic Approach to the Law of Evidence (1999)
Prigogine, Ilya. "Exploring Complexity" European Journal of Operational Research (1987)
Prigogine, Ilya and Isabelle Stengers. Order Out of Chaos: Man's New Dialogue With Nature (1984)
Rapino, Melanie A. and Alison K. Fields. "Mega Commuters in the U.S. Time and Distance in Defining the Long Commute using the American Community Survey" (2013)
Rosenberg, Nathan and Stephen Kline. "An Overview of Innovation" (1986)
Schumpeter, Joseph. The Theory of Economic Development (1934, originally 1911)
Searle, John. Intentionality: An Essay in the Philosophy of Mind (1983)
Searle, John. Minds, Brains, and Science (1984)
Selgin, George, William D. Lastrapes, and Lawrence H. White. "Has the Fed Been a Failure?" SSRN (2012, 2013)
Siemers, David J. The Antifederalists: Men of Great Faith and Forbearance
Slonim, Shlomo. Framers' Construction/Beardian Deconstruction: Essays on the Constitutional Design of 1787 (2001)
Sloan, Douglas. Insight-Imagination: The Emancipation of Thought and the Modern World (1983)
Smith, Adam. The Wealth of Nations (1776)
Staber, Udo. "Business Networks: Prospects For Development" (1996)

Stylman, Josh. "The Technocratic Blueprint" The Brownstone Institute (2025)
Stylman, Josh. "America, LLC: The Corporate Takeover We Were Never Taught" (2024)
Sweezy, Paul M. and Harry Magdoff. The Dynamics of U. S. Capitalism (1972)
Taylor, John. "Systemic Risk and the Role of Government" (2009)
Temin, Peter. "Entrepreneurs and Managers," in Higonnet, P., Landes, D. Rosovsky, H., (Eds.), Favorites of Fortune (1991)
Tuck, Richard. Natural Rights Theories: Their Origin and Development (1981)
Vass, Laurie Thomas. Multiple works (various years, 2008-2025)
Veblen, Thorstein. The Theory of the Leisure Class (1899)
Warnock, Mary. Imagining (1978)
Wenger, Etienne. Communities of Practice: Learning, Meaning, and Identity (1999)
White, Richard. The Republic for Which It Stands: The United States during Reconstruction and the Gilded Age, 1865-1896 (2017)
Wilentz, Sean. The Rise of American Democracy: Jefferson to Lincoln (2006)
Winkler, Adam. "Corporations Are People' Is Built on an Incredible 19th-Century Lie" The Atlantic (2018)
Wood, Gordon. The Creation of the American Republic
Woodward, C. Vann. The Burden of Southern History (2008)
Zuckert, Michael. The Natural Rights Republic (1997)
Zywicki, Todd. "Senators and Special Interests : A Public Choice Analysis of the Seventeenth Amendment" (1994)
Zywicki, Todd. "Rent-seeking, Crony Capitalism, and the Crony Constitution" (2015)

www.ingramcontent.com/pod-product-compliance
Lightning Source LLC
LaVergne TN
LVHW052227200926
848481LV00001B/230